New Public Management

New public management is a topical phrase to describe how management techniques from the private sector are now being applied to public services. This book provides a completely up-to-date overview of the main theoretical models of public sector management, and examines the key changes that have occurred as more and more public services are contracted out to private organisations, and as the public sector itself grapples with 'internal markets'. Drawing on economics, organisational theory and politics, Jan-Erik Lane presents new public management from an analytical perspective. This book uses game theory and empirical studies in order to assess the pros and cons of new public management.

Jan-Erik Lane is Professor of Political Science at the University of Geneva, and adjunct professor at the Norwegian School of Management. His previous publications include *New Institutional Politics*, *The Public Sector* and *Constitutions and Political Theory*.

New Public Management

Jan-Erik Lane

London and New York

First published 2000
by Routledge
11 New Fetter Lane, London EC4P 4EE

Simultaneously published in the USA and Canada
by Routledge
29 West 35th Street, New York, NY 10001

Routledge is an imprint of the Taylor & Francis Group

Typeset in Baskerville by Taylor & Francis Books Ltd
Printed and bound in Great Britain by
Biddles Ltd, Guildford and King's Lynn

British Library Cataloguing in Publication Data
A catalogue record for this book is available from the British Library

Library of Congress Cataloging in Publication Data
Lane, Jan-Erik.
    New Public Management / Jan-Erik Lane.
    Includes bibliographical references and index.
    1. Public administration. 2. Contracting out. I. Title.
    JF1351 .L365 2000
    351–dc21   99-059926

ISBN 0–415–23186–8 (hbk)
ISBN 0–415–23187–6 (pbk)

This book I dedicate to Jonathan Boston and John Halligan, because it is the result of my many conversations with them.

Contents

Illustrations

Figures

Tables

Preface

I decided in 1998 to go to New Zealand and Australia to find out what new public management (NPM) consists of. I am grateful for the many discussions with scholars connected with Victoria University and the University of Canberra learning much from, for example, John Martin and Bob Gregory. I have used three already published articles, one in *Public Management*, 1999, vol. 1 and one in *Public Administration*, 2000, as well as one in the *Swiss Political Science Review*, 1999, vol. 5. I am also very grateful to Christophe Perignon (of the Economics Department at the University of Geneva) who drew the figures in the text.

Geneva, April 2000
Jan-Erik Lane

Introduction
The challenge of 2000

The aim of this volume is to assess where we stand in the disciplines of public administration and public management against the background of recent public sector developments, at the end of the twentieth century. Focusing upon the theory of new public management (NPM) and relating it to other established approaches, I attempt to formulate a synthesis of NPM that is appropriate to the public sector of today. The purpose is twofold.

First, the main theoretical models that have dominated these disciplines in the twentieth century will be explored, stating which they are and how they have been evaluated. It is true that NPM draws upon the contributions of scholars from political science, economics and organisational theory (Hood, 1991; Walsh, 1995; Flynn, 1997). Instead of underlining the confrontation between different approaches, theories and concepts, I will explore the possibility of a reunion towards one theory of public sector management.

Second, the lively debate between various approaches to the study of the public sector reflects the ongoing developments in the public sector in the advanced countries combining democracy and the market economy. A number of major recent reforms have altered the public sector profoundly changing public resource allocation, income redistribution and public regulation. Yet, the continued relevance of the public sector is the second theme in this book.

The public and the private

This book is about the public sector and its management. It looks upon society as divided into two distinct sectors, the private sector and the public sector. Although there are so-called quangos, or third sector organisations, the separation between the public and the private is well institutionalised in most countries of the world. The public sector comprises the behaviour of organisations that belong to what is alternatively referred to as 'state' or 'government', but the concept 'public sector' is broader than these two well-known concepts. Into the public sector enters all kinds of government activities at various levels, all kinds of public finance as well as public regulation in general.

What is outside of the public sector enters the private sector, or civil society. Here we have the households and private business – what we will call the 'market economy'. In many countries the size of these two sectors is about the same. However, in some countries the market sector is substantially larger – *the welfare societies* – while in others the public sector is somewhat bigger than the private sector – *the welfare states*. Yet, in very few countries does virtually only one sector exist.

Hong Kong used to be the most extreme case of a civil society with a small public sector, but it no longer exists as a semi-independent unit. Switzerland had been identified as a welfare society in Western Europe, but the OECD has recently changed its way of measuring public expenditures in this country, forcing us to classify it as a welfare state, as with almost all other Western European countries. Almost all command economies have been dismantled. Consequently, we are left with a variety of mixtures of the public and the private in most countries. How, then, is the public sector to be managed?

Modelling the public sector

The public sector can only be understood by means of a knowledge about the basic models used to discuss, describe and explain its various features. These models constitute the core of what is today public management or public administration and they come from all the social sciences. They make data about the public sector intelligible and they lend themselves to predictions about future developments in the public sector. Describing the public sector in terms of a set of models allows us to answer normative questions about better ways of structuring the public sector, or public sector reforms.

The argument in this book is that not only is there a new model of public sector management (NPM) but also that this model of public sector management will be more and more accepted in the countries of the world, whatever civilisation they adhere to. Thus, it predicts the convergence in styles of public sector management around the world despite all cultural and religious differences that set countries apart.

Public sector management is closely connected both with public policy, policy-making and policy implementation that is, as well as with public administration. Yet, these concepts do not overlap, and there are differences in real life between the typical modes of action in public management, i.e. between policy-making and administration. It is impossible to make a sharp separation between managerial action, policies and administration in the public sector. Public sector management embraces objectives and decision-making, as in policy-making, but it also takes into account how institutions constrain the employment of resources, as in administration. The effort in a theory of public sector management is to integrate all three entities: goals, means and rules, modelling the daily running of the public sector.

New public management

Public sector management in the twenty-first century will only to a limited extent be a continuation of the way the public sector has been managed in the twentieth century. Extensive changes have occurred both in real life public institutions as well as in the theory of public management in the second half of the twentieth century, which have made the standard governance approach outdated. The twenty-first century will extend these changes in both theory and practice.

New public management (NPM) is the theory of the most recent paradigm change in how the public sector is to be governed. Initiated in the United Kingdom, it spread to first and foremost the United States, Australia and especially New Zealand, and then further on to Scandinavia and Continental Europe. NPM is part of the managerial revolution that has gone around the world, affecting all countries, although to considerably different degrees. The theory of new public management contains the insights from game theory and from the disciplines of law and economics.

NPM does not replace older frameworks but adds a new approach to public sector governance, i.e. contractualism. The theory of public sector management needs to integrate the positive contribution in NPM, while at the same time stating clearly the limits of NPM. Before presenting NPM as well as the lessons from the use of NPM, we must, however, first clarify the approaches which NPM challenges.

Towards reunion

New public management is the most visible sign of the rapid changes in perspectives upon how government should run the public sector. But it is only one of several 'scientific revolutions' that have occurred in the twentieth century concerning the proper governance mechanisms in the public sector. Public sector governance theory started with public administration and moved to the public policy framework over the management approach. Stating schematically how these three frameworks differ in Part I, I take the position that many of the positive contributions of these three frameworks can indeed be integrated together with NPM into a general theory of public sector governance.

The theoretical background of NPM is to be found in the strong criticism of a large public sector, to be found in the public choice school as well as in Chicago School Economics, both attacking since the mid-1960s prevailing notions about public sector governance. The radical nature of NPM may have served well the politics of the new right or neo-conservatism in the 1980s and the resurgence of neo-liberalism in a globalised world economy in the 1990s. However, without the heavy artillery of Nobel Prize winning economists and the public choice scholars, governments would have been less convinced that they were 'right' from a theoretical point of view in their search for an alternative governance model – see Part II.

Part III will analyse the main ideas in NPM in order to state their usefulness and limitations. NPM is first and foremost contractualism, but it cannot replace the other major approaches to public sector governance. Thus, the theory of public sector governance includes more than NPM, as several elements of public policy and public administration cannot be substituted by contractualism.

Public sector governance

A theory about public sector management would have to start from the following distinction between basic tasks in the public sector: (1) allocation, or the provision of goods and services; (2) income maintenance, or the handling of transfers; (3) regulation or the creation and monitoring of economic rules primarily for the private sector but increasingly also commonly for the public sectors.

Public governance theory is a set of theories about how government can get things done. Thus, it is not primarily a framework for the analysis of how government makes decisions in political arenas, because it theorises how government arranges for the provision of services in a society.

In traditional public governance, government takes on several roles in order to allocate a number of goods and services to its population. Modern public governance separates these roles from each other, based upon a much more refined analysis of how government can fulfil a variety of roles in the economy.

In traditional governance, government would take on the following tasks that are relevant for the provision of goods and services: (1) Inhouse production by means of bureaux and public enterprises; (2) Budget financing by means of taxes and charges; (3) Public regulation by means of bureaux.

Public sector reform in the 1980s and the 1990s has changed all this by the introduction of a number of distinctions between the various roles of government: purchaser, provider, contractor, regulator and umpire.

Providing society with a number of goods and services involves different tasks, which need not be handled by one actor, i.e. government. Thus, modern governance includes several alternatives for the public provision of goods and services as well as regulation depending upon how the following tasks are handled:

1   financing, or the payment for the services could be done by government or by the user;
2   production, or the supply of services could be done *inhouse* or *outhouse*, i.e. government could use a bureau or an enterprise of its own or it may buy the service from a private operator;
3   arrangement, or the method of acquiring the services from an operator, public or private, where the critical distinction is competition or not. The methods of competition include: tendering/bidding, tournaments and auctions, whereas traditional governance used budgetary appropriations and administrative law for inhouse provision and licences for outhouse production. In addition we have:
4   ownership, or who has property rights to the organisation which supplies the goods and services. Whereas tradition governance favoured the employment

of organisations that were closely linked to the state, modern governance displays a preference for the use of *the joint-stock company*, whether it is government who owns the stock or it is a private operator. Finally, we have:

5   regulation, or whether government has set up a regulatory regime which covers the provision of goods and services.

The implication is that government could play three different roles at the same time: purchaser, service provider and umpire. How is this to be done? In fact, modern governance tends to display several combinations of all the various possibilities in financing, production, arrangement, ownership and regulation.

Government does not act directly in public governance, whatever the forms that the public provision of goods and services as well as regulation may take. Government relies upon agents, who handle public sector management for it. Thus, there arises for very basic transaction cost reasons principal–agent relationships in the public sector. In modern public management, government is the principal and the bureau chiefs or the chief executive officers (CEOs), the agents. An elementary understanding of principal–agent theory is essential for the understanding of modern governance (Ricketts, 1987).

Government and its managers may employ inhouse or outhouse production to arrive at a service supply. It may use taxation or user fees to pay for the services. And the supply of the services may be forthcoming by means of competition or authority. Finally, there may be government regulation in place which restricts the degrees of freedom of government, resulting in a situation where government as the regulator regulates itself as the service provider.

In modern governance, government and its CEOs act on the demand side of the public household, facing a number of suppliers or as we will call them 'players' in the economy, looking for government contracts. The modern regulatory scheme requires that all players be treated in an equal manner, entailing that the players with the lowest cost should receive the contract, all other things being equal, e.g. service quality.

Modern public governance, thus, involves four major parties: (1) government; (2) the CEOs and (3) the players in the economy, besides (4) the citizens and the population. The interaction between these four sets takes place within a heavily institutionalised environment. The new institutional setting includes rules about the levelling of the playing field, about how to conduct tendering/bidding, and how to arrange tournaments and auctions, given a basic public law framework, contained primarily in constitutional law but also in administrative law to some extent.

In order to understand modern governance, we need to theorise how the government as principal interacts with its agents, the CEOs as purchasers and as the regulators, as well as how these agents relate to the players in the economy, whether they be public or private ones. NPM offers such an approach to the understanding of modern governance, focusing upon contracting and its logic.

Is new public management no more than fad and fashion?

During the 1990s, many governments have embarked upon some kind of public sector reform. The concept of public sector reform is by now quite multi-dimensional covering a variety of phenomena which do not necessarily hang together. Some countries have tried one or two of these kinds of reforms whereas other countries have embraced all of them: decentralisation, privatisation, incorporation, deregulation and reregulation, the introduction of executive agencies, internal markets or the use of the purchaser–provider split, as well as tendering/bidding schemes (Ferlie *et al.*, 1996).

If there is one label that is used to refer to all kinds of public sector reform, then it would be 'new public management' (Hood, 1991, 1995). Common to all the public sector reform efforts is the attempt to employ new governance mechanisms in the public sector that go beyond the traditional institutions of governance such as the bureau and the public enterprise and that employ or imitate market institutions of governance (Walsh, 1995). The Reinventing Government framework in the US has several notions in common with NPM (Kettl, 1994, 1997), but it lacks the focus upon contracting.

NPM as managerialism focusing upon contract making and enforcement seems to take government once and for all out of the Weberian framework of bureaucracy (Considine and Painter, 1997). Does NPM rest upon a credible theory about public governance or is NPM merely a fad and fashion? Let us examine briefly a few arguments against NPM.

Five contra arguments

It is argued that NPM is running out of steam and that it will prove to have been merely a fashion. Alternatively, it is argued that NPM was in reality never something new and that is was merely a rhetoric with hidden contradictory practices. It was simply a mixture of ideas, which never really hang together. When deconstructed, the NPM rhetoric has a distinct right-wing tone. It merely overemphasises economic efficiency and neglects other criteria – quality, equity – with which public sector activities can be evaluated.

Each of these arguments against NPM as being just a fad or fashion can be rebutted. The advent of NPM is a sign of an ongoing revolution in governance, both theoretically and practically (Pollitt, 1993; Barzelay, 2000).

We examine the following arguments against the NPM claiming that it is: (1) simply right-wing ideology; (2) nothing new but simply old contracting out; (3) a special manipulative discourse; (4) an incoherent mixture of popular ideas; and (5) a mere extension of micro-economic theory from the private sector to the public sector.

A defence of NPM would consist of insisting upon the following points:

1   Ideological neutrality of NPM. NPM has been applied by both conservative or neo-liberal governments and social democratic ones. It is true that NPM has been combined with a strong ambition to roll back the public sector, but it is also the case that it has been used in order to strengthen the welfare state and make it more efficient. NPM does not advocate that the private sector take over the allocation of services from the public sector, but that the public provision of services be managed differently.

2   NPM is contracting, not only *contracting out*. Government has always employed contracting out as a tool for arranging certain rather simple services such as catering or cleaning. NPM not only vastly extends the application of contracting out, using this tool in new areas such as many kinds of infrastructure as well as education and health care and on a much larger scale. But NPM also deals with *contracting in*, i.e. NPM is a practical theory about how government can improve upon its operations through competitive contracting whether the provision is inhouse or outhouse.

3   NPM concerns real phenomena. Symbolically, NPM employs new and technical words that originate and also seem to apply well outside of the public sector. Can one really speak of government and its employees as 'principals' and 'agents' except in a figurative meaning? Can governments be said to arrange 'tournaments' and 'auctions'? Do professional groups in the public sector 'shirk'? Is public policy or administrative law the content of private law 'contracts'? Not denying that NPM employs a new language, I wish to underline that public sector reform under NPM has effected real and sometimes dramatic changes in several countries. It is more than symbolism. At the same time one needs to discuss, criticise and penetrate its special terms.

4   NPM is more original than merely a *mélange* of public choice theory with private management. If NPM was merely an odd mixture of the public choice approach and old private sector management theory, then NPM would indeed be contradictory. The public choice school advocates decentralisation in various forms (political, market, vouchers, user fees), whereas old private sector management advocated centralisation. However, NPM is not simply a prolongation of public choice theory, which really prefers a Manchester Liberal State. And NPM has a management theory that is more advanced than old Taylorism.

5   NPM is not micro-economics applied to the public sector. NPM is much more than a repetition of the cost/benefit approach, which is strict application of standard micro-economics to the public sector (Mishan, 1981). Actually, NPM is much more linked with entirely new ideas in economic theory which deviate considerably from the neo-classical framework. In particular, the economic theory of asymmetric information has played a role in the emergence of several of the core ideas which constitute NPM. But it should be emphasised that NPM has developed through learning from the real experiments and reforms within the public sector. It was never just an application of private sector ideas.

To sum up: NPM amounts to a new theory about governance in the public sector. I do not claim that this theory is complete in any sense or that it is final. I see several problems that need to be resolved, if indeed they can be. NPM is basically a practical theory in the Kantian sense of an opposition between theoretical and practical knowledge from an epistemological point of view.

NPM is a more or less coherent theory about how government may deliver services. Government need not apply this approach, as it may employ the bureaucratic framework of Max Weber or the policy network framework that is frequently used (Rhodes, 1998). NPM does not describe what goes on in public sector reform, but it recommends a new approach, if government wishes to increase efficiency in service delivery.

Weber's old question but a new answer

In his well-known article on domination or authority, Weber starts out by making the assumption that government always and everywhere involves that one small group of people rule another large group of people – the rulers and the ruled as it were (Weber, 1978). Another assumption that he made was that this relationship between political leaders and the population is based upon authority or domination involving the unilateral communication of commands from the first group to the second group. From these two assumptions he arrives at his question: How is political domination concretely achieved, meaning when is it accepted by those ruled?

Governing a country involves getting the job done whatever the tasks of government may be. And the political elite cannot do it by itself. Political leaders employ others to get the job done. Weber calls these people the 'servants' of the political leaders. It is a basic fact of all societies that political domination is based upon the employment of a mechanism involving servants. Weber's theory of bureaucracy amounts to the claim that one special type of mechanism – the legal-rational structuring of the servants into formal organisations, i.e. bureaux – is the most effective means of ruling a country.

When political domination is based upon the legal-rational type of authority, then legitimacy is forthcoming. Legitimacy is the reciprocity of domination making it stable. Weberian theory resulted in a preference for two institutional mechanisms that have played a predominant role in the twentieth century, recognising that various countries have somewhat different rules that guide the structuring of these institutions: (1) the bureau and (2) the public enterprise. NPM entails a rejection of the Weberian theory that government is best served by bureaucratic organisation.

The traditional public enterprise hardly exists any more, at least not in the OECD world of countries. Deregulation in combination with globalisation has made this mechanism obsolete. However, the bureau has also come under pressure, as many governments have sought to reform or replace this institutional mechanism with other instruments for service delivery. NPM suggests that one searches for these new instruments among the mechanisms employed in the private sector focusing upon the management of contracts, how they are awarded, monitored and policed.

Exchange and contracts

Governments typically take on three kinds of task: the allocation of goods and services, income maintenance and the regulation of markets and the private sector. How is the job to be done in relation to these tasks? Political leaders cannot do everything themselves for simple transaction cost reasons. Thus, they tend to concentrate upon the making of broad political decisions.

NPM is highly relevant for the allocative tasks. It is a matter of debate whether its methods can be extended into the delivery of income maintenance programmes – the so-called workfare state (Gutmann, 1998). Making the distribution of transfer payments conditional upon the discretion and arbitration of managers goes against the prevailing conception of these programmes as harbouring rights and entitlements. Yet, allocative reforms made along the lines suggested by NPM have clear implications for regulatory reform. Actually, regulatory reforms may trigger changes in the modes of allocation of public services. NPM does go together with deregulation of both the private and the public sectors.

In a deregulated world there is little place for licences, entry barriers and monopolies. The production of goods and services is handled by the *players* in the economy, whether they be public or private. In order to arrange a public provision of services governments will contract with the players on the basis of competition resulting in contracts stating what is to be delivered: price and quantity. NPM suggests that one substitutes competitive contracting for the traditional tools of public administration. But who is to do the contracting?

For transaction costs reasons, politicians cannot handle all the various forms of contracts that NPM requires. Government needs experts who negotiate, settle and execute the myriad of contracts that are forthcoming under the new institutional mechanism replacing the traditional tools of public administration. NPM proposes that government employs a special group of managers – chief executive officers, who handle the contracting state. Thus, we arrive at the model in Table 0.1.

Table 0.1 NPM – the basic framework

Principals	Agents	Tendering/bidding	Players
(a) government	(a) executive agencies	(1) tournaments	(i) entrepreneurs
(b) state	(b) purchasing agencies		(ii) corporations, private or public
(c) ministries		(2) auctions	(iii) organisations, private, public or third sector
	(c) regulators	level the playing field	third party access

According to NPM, government hires managers who contract with players in a deregulated economy where competition is naturally forthcoming. All the relationships are governed by means of competitive rules, from the hiring of CEOs by government, whether as purchasers or as regulators, to the contracts between CEOs and the players in the economy. The key question is, of course, whether such a framework can be made to operate effectively and without contradictions. It may well be the case that the framework laid out in Table 0.1 is more suitable for some parts of the public sector than others, such as the business sector more than the soft sector.

Merely putting up the NPM framework as in Table 0.1 says nothing about the problems involved in running a contracting state and achieving efficient outcomes. Model building upon paper may amount to little more than idyllic picture drawing, hiding the real difficulties. Yet, one may employ the model set out above for the identification of a few critical difficulties under an NPM regime.

Government will enter into a complex set of contractual relationships. How is this set of contracts to be understood? There will evidently be contractual interaction involving different kinds of contracts of varying duration and complexity (Milgrom and Roberts, 1992). Some of the main problems are discussed below.

What is a contract under NPM?

Under an NPM regime, government manages the public sector by means of a set of contracts (Alford and O'Neill, 1994; Considine and Painter, 1997). Thus, government will have to expand its capacity to conclude and monitor contracts considerably, if NPM is to be a success. Governing by means of contracts may involve using widely different forms of contracts, only one of which is the typical private law contract that is an agreement which is strictly enforceable in court.

It should be pointed out that governing by means of private law contracts is different from government by means of public law instruments such as budgeting and legislation. In principle, government will enter two types of contracts. First, it will contract as a principal with its agents, the CEOs of its departments, boards and enterprises. Second, it will in the last resort be responsible for the contracts that these CEOs make with the players in the economy about the provision of goods and services.

Contracts in an NPM regime consist of a variety of agreements that guide the provision of public services, only some of which are private law contracts. Thus, there may be intentional contracts, or statements of mutual intent, which outline hopes more than binding commitments. Implicit contracts may state promises which are conditional upon the evolution of the course of events without being strictly enforceable.

A basic distinction is that between the employment contract and the performance contract, where only the first type of contract is a strict private law contract. The performance contract would complement the employment contract by stating what the agent is expected to do for the principal, i.e. the government. It could run into hundreds of pages due to the difficulty of specifying all the relevant contingencies and what they require. The performance contract could contain many public law elements, restricting the activities of the agent.

The idea behind the construction of contracts in an NPM regime is that failure of the agent to comply with the agreements in the performance contract would present the principal with the right to act on the basis of the employment contract, including the possibility of firing the agent. However, there is much incertitude about the link between the performance contract and the employment contract, as the agent may always dispute whether there has occurred a break of the terms of agreement in the first type of contract. Sometimes there occurs a kind of contractual degeneration in NPM under which anything that looks like an agreement is called a 'contract'. Thus, any kind of interaction between the principal and the agents in public service provision is described as contractual, whether or not real or private law contracts exist or not.

In other governance regimes like bureaucracy or policy networks, one may also characterise the relationships between the actors as contractual by describing the terms of interaction as implicit contracts. However, if governments are to employ NPM, then the contracts should as far as possible be made explicit and be formulated in such a manner that they come close to private law contracts, i.e. agreements enforceable in ordinary courts.

How long can a contract be?

When contracts are to be used on a massive scale, replacing to a considerable extent other forms of coordination such as planning, budgeting and administrative law, then there is the risk that contracts will become so large that they are rendered unwieldy. How can a performance contract be signed that covers all relevant contingencies and includes all essential elements of public law?

NPM favours in principle short-term contracting, whereas in traditional public administration there is a preference for long-term contracting. The preference for short-term contracts ahead of long-term contracts is to be applied right through all the relationships depicted in Table 0.1, not only in the various tournaments and auctions envisaged but also in the agency interaction between governments and its departments – executive agencies, purchasing boards and regulatory bodies.

But what is a short time period when it comes to government contracts? If the basic purpose is to allow for competition, then one must simply ask: How often should rounds of competition be organised? After two years, or five to ten years? The evidence about the implementation of NPM indicates that one often starts out from an ambition to have competitive rounds as often as possible, but that one soon encounters problems with short time spans, described as increasing transaction costs.

When contracting is employed on a large scale in the provision of public services, then one may well arrive at competition in supply. But there is bound to arise considerable instability, especially among the service providers. Within the service providers, professional groups tend to dominate and they usually prefer long-term engagements to short-term contracts, even if the latter prove to be more lucrative. Thus, the introduction of NPM often encounters widespread resistance from well-organised professional groups.

In addition, it may not be in the best interest of government to employ contracts with a very short length of time. To stabilise the supply of public services, government using the NPM sooner or later begins to commit itself for a longer time period simply to be sure that services will really be forthcoming. Thus, contracts may start running for five years or longer.

Or governments will supplement short-term contracts with long-term promises involving a mutual understanding to the effect that the service providers know that they will not be cut off. Sometimes the running of NPM regimes thus results in a large variety of agreements, of which only some are truly private law contracts.

Selecting agents

There is a risk that government uses proper tendering/bidding procedures only in relation to the provider of services and not in their own agency relationships. The CEOs of executive agencies, purchasing boards or regulatory boards must be selected by means of tournaments of some kind and they cannot be given long-term contracts, if the spirit of NPM is not to be violated. However, the principles of NPM can be applied with various degrees of consistency.

For transaction cost reasons, government cannot do all the contracting as well as monitor and guarantee contractual validity. It needs to do two things:

1   Government must distinguish between alternative roles that it assumes in a contracting governance regime: purchasing, providing, regulation and arbitration.
2   Government will employ agents to act in these different roles, whose behaviour will very much affect outcomes. Not only must government instruct these agents in a consistent manner. But it must also select them picking the 'good' ones and rejecting the 'bad' ones. How?

How thick can a contract be?

Governing by means of private law contracts that are to be tested in ordinary courts raises the difficult question of whether such contracts can be written so that they become complete or almost complete. In the literature called *Law and Economics* it is considered as an axiom that contracts cannot be complete unless it concerns trivial matters (Milgrom and Roberts, 1992). If contracts in the private sector tend not to be complete, then how can public sector contracts be complete, and as these refer to the public domain they seldom concern trivial matters?

In traditional public governance, a host of instruments were used for steering the work of public officials – budget documents, administrative law, instructions, internal procedures and customs. The contract under NPM has to have all the relevant information about what is to be done, i.e. the expectations about the work load that is to be forthcoming as well as the compensation that has been agreed upon. Can the contract also contain policy and administrative law?

When public services are contracted or when the requirements upon the CEOs are laid down in private law contracts, then there are two possibilities. Either the set of contracts governing the public sector simply recognise the existing public law framework, or take this body of rules as given. Or this set of contracts more or less replace administrative law and internal regulations, containing also possibly policy decisions and deliberations.

Since public law contains among other things the basic rights of citizens, it is impossible that private law contracting could entirely replace public law. However, it is conceivable that contracts could be made in such a manner that they contain detailed policy and administrative stipulations. Whether the contracts will be complete even when they start running over 100 or 200 pages is not certain. There is always the risk that the inevitable incompleteness stimulates reneging in combination with opportunistic behaviour resulting in contractual failure.

When policy and citizen rights are entered into contracts, then their publicness may be at risk or may become restricted. Governing by means of contracts may involve opening up such contracts to the public, especially to journalists and the mass media. Even when government manages the public sector by means of private law contracts, their activities remain in the public domain.

Are there limits to the use of NPM?

If NPM offers a new tool for managing the public sector, then we must ask if it is appropriate in relation to all forms of public services. The public sector consists of very different things, the provision of which may call upon the use of alternative governance mechanisms. Government may employ bureaucracy, policy networks or contracting regimes to provide its citizens with goods, services, rules and money.

NPM seems worth trying in relation to *the business sector*, in relation to several government departments and agencies as well as in relation to regulatory boards. When NPM is transferred into the income maintenance programmes – *the workfare state* – then doubts may be raised about whether the pros really outweigh the cons. The use of any governance mechanism is always a question of advantages against disadvantages.

The employment of management techniques in social security must provoke a debate about the legal nature of so-called entitlements. If citizens have lawful claims to income compensation when adversity hits them, then why would they accept that the support in social security becomes conditional upon the arbitrariness of CEOs? Surprisingly, however, where workfare state programmes have been introduced, little resistance has been forthcoming, which means that social security can also be approached in terms of contractual conceptions about mutual obligations.

But can NPM be applied to *the soft sector* where organisations characterised by strong collegiality in professional groups stand against government? Professionals with their distinctive ethos are not only responsible for the provision of services but they are also watching over the implementation of universal values transcending the concerns of government. The use of NPM in relation to the judicial branch of government as well as in relation to higher education institutions seems somehow irrelevant. Organisations dedicated to the pursuit of truth or following the precepts of justice may well use managers to handle a number of tasks. However, their chief mode of operation involves another governance mechanism, namely collegiality and bureaucracy.

There may exist goods and services in the public sector where neither NPM nor bureaucracy offers the best governance mechanism. In for instance the caring sector, trust between government and professional groups plays a major role. And trust cannot be manufactured and put into short-term contracts. On the other hand, bureaucracy also appears to be a governance model that is unsuitable for health care, as the efficient handling of the caring sector is more dependent upon personal initiative than the observation of rules.

When short-term contracting appears unsuitable, then trust expressed in the form of long-term contracts appears attractive for both government and the professional organisations. Perhaps one may look upon the policy network model as a governance mechanism which may handle such loose forms of contracting?

The future relevance of NPM

I am strongly inclined to answer the main question posed at the beginning of this chapter in the negative. NPM offers an alternative governance mechanism which government may find it attractive to employ, but not indiscriminately. If private law contracting is such a powerful institution for getting things done in the private sector, then perhaps government should start using it also in relation to public sector tasks, i.e. using it where it results in more advantages than disadvantages.

NPM is basically about focusing upon efficiency. When it is a question about the employment of inputs in order to produce outputs, then efficiency is a most relevant consideration to take into account. Thus, the possibility of using NPM should be considered, although there is no guarantee that it is the best governance mechanism.

We need to discuss the pros and cons of NPM as well as state the limits of its applicability. Before we start to examine the new contractualism in the public sector, we will provide a background for the emergence of NPM by examining the theories which NPM challenges.

One could argue that NPM received attention as the ideological rationalisation of the strong right-wing forces that happened to come into positions of power in several Western countries around 1980. Yet, such an argument would be open to the objection that it puts the cart before the horse. Perhaps the new right scored a couple of electoral successes because they had a new theory that appealed to citizens. Why would the electorate reject promises about increased efficiency, or the possibility of total production being larger, all other things equal?

The success of NPM became total when social democratic governments confessed a keen interest in putting its main principles into practice. It is not correct to argue today that NPM is a right-wing ideology, as its political appeal is much broader. NPM is not burdened by right-wing notions, typical of conservative or nationalist ideologies.

Plan of the book

The contents of the volume are as follows. First we examine in Part I where we stand. Chapter 1 discusses the basic approaches: the classical approach, the management approach, as well as the policy approach in order to pinpoint their differences in terms of fundamental models of the public sector. Chapter 2 attempts an overview of the major recent changes in the public sector programmes using public finance statistics, in public resource allocation as well as in income redistribution.

Part II deals with from where we are coming. Thus, Chapters 3, 4, 5 and 6 examine the criticism of the governance mechanisms traditionally employed in the public sector: the bureau, the public enterprise, transfer payments schemes and traditional public regulation.

Part III suggests the major theme towards which we are heading in connection with the emergence of new public management. Thus, Chapter 7 pins down the major change from a long-term contracting perspective to a short-term perspective, whereas Chapter 8 outlines generally the pros and cons of contractualism. Chapter 9 deals with the different roles of government in a contracting governance regime. Chapter 10 looks at agency contracting, i.e. the relationships between government and its CEOs. Finally, Chapter 11 raises the question of the risks of organisational failure in an NPM regime.

I have deliberately tried to keep the exposition of the main models of the public sector as short as possible. Thereby I could not do justice to the entire debate for and against various interpretations of public governance. The chief aim has been to clarify the chief features of various approaches to public governance. Similarly, I have kept the exposition of NPM short, pinning down its major advantages as well as pointing out where major difficulties could arise.

Part I

Where we stand

The theory of public sector management covers in principle all the three branches of government: resource allocation, income distribution and public regulation, although it has been most developed in relation to the first and the last type of government activity. The application of management principles in social security has just begun and its effects are contested – the workfare state.

In Chapter 1, I argue that any theory of public sector management must take a stand in relation to a set of difficult theoretical problems that have emerged from the confrontation between three basic approaches in this century. These basic frameworks for the analysis of governance in the public sector include: (1) public administration, (2) management and (3) public policy and implementation. New public management (NPM) cannot bypass the lessons learned in the debate between adherents of these three very different approaches to the public sector and the role of government.

Chapter 2 shows that the size of the public sector in the countries of the world remains so large today that it warrants the continued search for and development of a theory of public sector management. Despite a decade of privatisations, governments remain active in the provision of public services, in the transfer of social security benefits as well as in public regulation (Rosen, 1988; Musgrave and Musgrave, 1989; Castles, 1998).

1 Basic approaches in the twentieth century

Introduction

A number of scholars contributed to the emergence of a science of the public sector in the early decades of the twentieth century. One may perhaps say that the key figure was Max Weber, formulating the theory of the bureau as the chief institutional mechanism in the public sector, but he was certainly not the only major theoretician. One may wish to mention a name like Fayol and especially the early Americans, for instance Wilson, Taylor and Gulick (Fry, 1989; Raadschelders, 1998).

Yet, Weber achieved a dominant position in the classical school – called 'public administration', partly because of the strong evolution of administrative law as the bulk of public law followed his ideas about public governance. However, between 1940 and 1960 there occurred a kind of Kuhnian paradigm shift, the management approach and the policy approach replacing the classical approach.

What we can do here is only to identify the basic ideas of the classical approach. A number of interpretations have been made of the classical authors, which we cannot survey here. What has to be done here is to underline what is common in the models of the classical approach while not paying attention to the differences among them, however important these may be. Consequently, we will not make a critique of the classical authors or point out the contradictions between them or even state the nuances among them.

The classical framework, called 'public administration', at least at times made claims to the effect that it constituted a new discipline within the social sciences or political science. It focused upon the construction of legal mechanisms for the operation of large-scale public programmes, which would work effectively when its rules were followed. If the rules were transparent and the public sector employees followed these rules, then efficiency would be achieved. Thus, public programmes could be administered, almost like a machine could be instructed to obey commands and operate accordingly. The classical framework delivered two major institutional mechanisms in terms of which public administration could be carried out: the bureau and the public enterprise, which we will look at in Chapters 3 and 4.

What we wish to do is to state their basic commitments in terms of a few models of the public sector that they adhered to or held valid. The same method of exposition is followed in relation to the scholars who broke new ground in the 1940s, 1950s and 1960s, suggesting that public administration be replaced by management or by public policy.

It should be pointed out that many of the ideas of public administration are far from outdated. Some of them have been implemented by the states who practise the Rule of Law to the extent that one tends not even to remember that public administration advocated them with great fervour. Other ideas were completely rejected by the new frameworks forthcoming after the Second World War, but they have reappeared again in new public management. Yet, there is truth to the characterisation by Christopher Hood that public administration has lost an empire and has not found yet a new role (Hood, 1990). Which were the key models in public administration?

Key models in public administration

A number of important contributions to public administration were made from the publication of Woodrow Wilson's key article in 1884 up until the appearance of a few major syntheses in the 1930s. The classical approach dominated the modelling of the public sector up until the publication of *The Functions of the Executive* by Chester Barnard in 1938, which initiates the movement away from the classical approach using conceptions from organisational theory. In the 1960s it received another major challenge, this time from the policy approach, which culminates with two books by Aaron Wildavsky, namely *Implementation* from 1973 (with J. Pressman) and *Speaking Truth to Power: The Art and Craft of Policy Analysis* from 1979.

Perhaps the role of Weber in bringing forth the classic framework has been overemphasised, as he neither initiated the framework nor stated a comprehensive formulation of its principles. One finds important contributions to the classical framework from authors such as Willoughby, Goodnow, Parker Follet, White, Unwick and Morstein Marx (Fry, 1989). Yet, Weber's model of bureaucracy was stated in such a forcefully simple manner that it became easily accessible not only for research but also for practitioners. Weber outlined a pure model of bureaucracy as the optimal manner of organising the public sector. It consisted of a short list of features which seemed to form a compact whole (Weber, 1978: 217–223).

The advantage of pinpointing the core models of the classical framework is that it forces us to concentrate upon a few basic ideas, and assess their validity today. These key models constituted not only the core of the emerging discipline of public administration, but they also played a major practical role when designing the legal framework for the public sector early in this century along lines suggested by adherents of the public law instrument (Loughlin, 1992). The disadvantage is that one neglects the complexity of the classical approach, which was far more rich and comprehensive than what is stated below (Hill, 1992).

Positions or tasks

The classical framework models the public sector as essentially different from the private sector. There is a set of differences between the two sectors, which must be institutionalised. The public sector is basically a set of positions or roles which operate in an optimal manner when these are distinguished from the persons that hold or occupy these positions. Thus, one aspect of the core model of the classical framework is:

(CM1)　Positions are to be distinguished from persons.

The public sector is a structure of positions, which operate effectively when they are kept separate from the private motives of the persons who occupy these positions, Thus, the classical framework deals with how this separation is to be institutionalised as well as with how these positions are to be structured.

The classical framework delivers a set of principles or rules that follow up upon (CM1), which all have the purpose of safeguarding this separation between position and person. These principles can be seen as the implications of adhering to (CM1). Here, we find the rules about recruitment:

(R1)　　All positions must be recruited by means of transparent criteria of performance, connected with the position in question.

(R2)　　Persons must be promoted in accordance with transparent criteria of achievement, connected with the position in question.

(R3)　　Persons must be removed from their positions when their performance does not satisfy the requirements of the position.

(R1)–(R3) can only be realised by means of an institutional framework, safeguarded in the final resort by the employment of the judicial machinery. There principles deal with both how positions are to be filled and how persons are to be separated from their positions. Thus, they give substance to the basic model (CM1), i.e. that positions and persons must be completely distinguished.

Yet, what is even more important to (CM1) is the clear separation between the resources of the position and the income and wealth of the individual who occupies the position in question. Thus, we have certain rules to control resources, remuneration and patronage:

(I1)　　Each office holder is to be remunerated according to a contract, which pays the individual a fix monthly sum of money.

(I2)　　The resources connected with the position belong to that office and cannot be appropriated by the office holder for his/her own purposes.

(I3)　　In order to prevent the occurrence of various forms of corruption, the money paid to the office holder must be enough to allow a decent standard of living including a pension.

The rules (I1)–(I3) call for the institutionalisation of budgetary systems which allow for this transparent call for separating the resources of the public sector from the income and wealth of the persons working in that sector. Again, one can view (I1)–(I3) as giving meaning to (CM1), now from the financial point of view.

If indeed (R1)–(R3) as well as (I1)–(I3) enhance (CM1) or institutionalise the separation between positions and individuals, then the remaining rules clarify how the positions are to be organised, given the assumption that positions should dominate over individuals.

In the classical framework the emphasis is upon centralisation and the division of labour. It was understood that positions needed to be organised in a hierarchical manner, based upon minute division of labour. Thus, we have the following rules:

(H1)   Positions are to be organised according to super-subordination, where the spans of control become ever larger the higher up in the hierarchy one ascends.

(H2)   Positions may be organised according to the line-staff principle, where a high division of labour is to be achieved in the line sections.

The rules about recruitment, income and hierarchy substantiate the model about the separation between position and person, which distinction has given rise to much debate concerning both its feasibility and desirability.

Rules

Now, the emphasis upon a clear demarcation between task and person led the classical approach to place rules at the core of the public sector. Thus, public law in general and administrative law in particular is regarded as a powerful governance mechanism in all kinds of public sector activities. Rules play such a prominent role in public administration that we may wish to identify the following model as another core belief:

(CM2)   Public sector governance is or should be rule orientated.

One finds among the classics many variations on these two basic themes, (CM1) and (CM2), all of which we cannot cover in this book, as we are looking for the common core in their writings. This common core is more important than the individual variations of the core, if one wants to take a stand in relation to the classical framework. By 'importance' we refer not only to academic impulse but also to practical weight. In fact, all countries orientated towards the rule of law implemented these principles more or less in their legal systems.

In addition, one may interpret (H1) and (H2) as a clear preference for a top-down approach to the organisation of the public sector. Thus, we have here a third basic model in the classical approach, namely:

(CM3) Top-down structures are conducive to efficiency in the public sector.

In order to take a stand for or against (CM3), one needs to define and measure efficiency in public sector activities. Actually, the concept of efficiency is one of the fundamental concerns for all theories about the public sector. At the same time one may acknowledge that it has proved easier to arrive at a common understanding of its meaning than the concept of equity, which is also crucial for public sector governance.

Facts and values

Means–end efficiency was no doubt what the classics searched for. Thus, although the question about ends is a perfectly relevant one to raise in relation to the public sector activities, the answer provided by the classical framework focused upon the distinction between facts and values, between technology and democracy, or between instrumental ends and final ends. There were a few fundamental distinctions that had to be made, according to the classical framework. Thus, we have:

(CM4) Ends ≠ means, facts ≠ values, technology ≠ democracy.

To the classics, these distinctions were parallel, or identical. They constituted a core body of epistemological commitments that were essential to the approach. Basically, it was argued that public administration could handle one but not the other. Thus, means, facts and technology were endogeneous to the approach whereas ends, values and democracy were exogeneous. If one underlines efficiency, then one is bound to ask questions about ultimate ends: What is the purpose of administrative efficiency? Which ends does it serve? Can a science of public administration deliver the ends of the public sector activities?

The separations offered in (CM4) would, it was believed, solve a number of questions in public administration – pure or applied – by means of a series of dichotomies which all coincided, at least so it was argued. (CM4) soon became an issue of much debate between the classics and their critics. If ends, values and democracy can be distinguished from means, facts and technology in the manner stated by public administration, then what motivated civil servants to try their best in office? Similarly, if one starts from (CM1), or the sharp distinction between tasks and individuals, then one would want to know what motivates persons to act effectively in their various roles.

The problem of motivation

If one underlines efficiency, then one is bound to ask questions about ultimate ends: what is the purpose of administrative efficiency? Which ends does it serve? Can a science of public administration deliver the ends of the public sector activities?

The separations offered in (CM4) would, it was believed, solve a number of questions in public administration – pure or applied – by means of a series of dichotomies which all coincided, at least so it was argued. (CM4) soon became an issue of much debate between the classics and their critics. If ends, values and democracy can be distinguished from means, facts and technology in the manner stated by public administration, then what motivated civil servants to try their best in office? Similarly, if one starts from (CM1), or the sharp distinction between tasks and individuals, then one would want to know what motivates persons to act effectively in their various roles.

In the Weber interpretation another basic idea was added to the classical approach, which is perhaps more typical of Weber than the other classical theorists: the assumption about a call to perform well in public positions. This motivational assumption is also based upon a radical separation between the public and the private, as the latter would accept self-interests whereas the former would require altruism. The problem of motivation was never adequately addressed in the classical framework, nor adequately answered. Yet, we may formulate a final basic model as:

(CM5) Public sector motivation is radically different from private sector motivation.

The model (CM5) is the most risky of all the basic ideas in public administration. Whereas the other models – (CM1)–(CM4) – caused a huge debate about how public organisations really work, stimulating the contributions from different disciplines such as sociology, psychology and political science, the motivational model (CM5) became as easy prey for the public choice school in the 1960s and 1970s, starting from the main economic assumption (self-interest) and applying it consistently to all behaviour in the public sector.

Summing up

The classical framework delivered two basic mechanisms for the conduct of the public sector, the bureau and the public enterprise. The bureau was designed to handle non-economic activities ranging from military matters, police, the judiciary to education and health, whereas the public enterprise was the mechanism recommended for economic activities in so far as the public sector would take care of such activities, i.e. they could not be entrusted to the market – the market failure argument. The main orientation of the classical framework was towards public resource allocation, but it could harbour also regulation and redistribution.

The classical framework laid the basis for the public sector in the twentieth century by the identification of these two basic institutions, but the critical question was whether it provided an adequate analysis of its actual mode of functioning, or whether it had really formulated a model for how they could be made to work effectively. These questions about real life organisations and efficiency surfaced in the critique launched against the classical framework, starting in the late 1940s.

One basic difficulty in the classical framework was entailed in its emphasis upon effectiveness or efficiency. One may argue that the solution given to this problem was inadequate, or even erroneous, but one cannot claim that the classical theorists did not know or recognise the difficulty.

Twilight of public administration

If the classical framework was so successful in having an impact upon the evolution of public law in the twentieth century creating vast bulks of administrative law, then why did the approach begin to disintegrate already a few years after the synthesis had been most vigorously formulated in the 1930s? The answer must be sought in the distinction between rules and behaviour, between legal norms and reality.

Waldo's critique

A number of scholars pointed out early on that the classical framework was more prescriptive than descriptive, more normative than theoretical. The key question for scientific research was not how the public sector should operate, but how in fact it operated. What the classical framework conceived of as scientific generalisations, other scholars regarded as mere proverbs or recommendations that were self-evident or mere half-truths (Dahl, 1947).

Organisational studies emerged during the interwar years as a major new discipline in the social sciences, drawing upon contributions from different disciplines. Organisational sociology and psychology early abandoned the normative focus of Taylor and Fayol, moving towards minute analysis of how organisations really operate, disclosing the immensely important informal side of organisations, as, for example, in the studies by Elton Mayo in the 1930s.

Thus, the classical framework began to come under fire in the 1940s and 1950s, which resulted in its demise. Negatively, two of the basic models in the classical framework – (CM1) and (CM2) – were questioned early. In the 1960s and 1970s, the criticism moved to (CM3), which subsequently was also rejected. Positively, the concept of management and the policy framework were launched in order to model public sector activities more adequately, in particular to provide a better understanding of the conditions for efficiency as well as the place of values and motivation in the public sector.

The twilight of the entire classical approach – public administration – was very much stated explicitly in one book, *The Administrative State*, published in 1948 by Dwight Waldo. Let us pin down the main arguments in this tour de force, which concerned especially one of the basic classical models, namely (CM4).

Waldo's book is a head-on attack on the epistemology inherent in the classical framework. It starts from the position that the entire classical approach is based upon basic philosophical assumptions which are not spelt out explicitly and which cannot stand up to a critical assessment. Waldo takes on the fundamental model (CM4) of the classical approach and he argues that it cannot be considered valid. Waldo completely rejects (CM4): 'as a description of the facts or a scheme of reform, any simple division of government into politics-and-administration is inadequate' (Waldo, 1984: 121).

The attempt at a distinction between politics and administration has been one of the recurrent themes in the criticism of public administration. The argument from its critics has always been that it is impossible to make the separation contained in the model (CM4). It should come as a great surprise to these critics, of whom Waldo is only one of many, that NPM has committed itself to this distinction or these distinctions (CM4).

Waldo was especially concerned about the normative aspects in the classical approach. The search for so-called principles of public administration was to Waldo basically a normative enterprise, delivering behaviour maxims about how to accomplish good or effective administration in terms of governance, budgeting and personnel management. This normative ingredient in the classical approach collided, according to Waldo, with the model (CM4), i.e. with the idea of separating facts and values. If public administration is basically a set of practical principles, then why insist upon (CM4)?

Moreover, Waldo claimed that several of the concepts employed in the classical approach were not only normative ones but also muddled ones, as for instance its notion of efficiency. To Waldo the notion of efficiency lacks a proper foundation within the classical approach: 'as one's frame of mind widens and disagreement about ends becomes important, "science" and "objectivity" are more difficult, judgements of 'efficiency' less accurate, more controversial' (Waldo, 1984: 196).

In 1948, Waldo took the view that there were major problems involved when applying the so-called scientific method to the public sector, which had not been recognised by public administration. It seemed to him that the classical approach adopted a naive stance about the possibility of adopting the scientific method in a way similar to its use in the natural sciences. In his Foreword to the second edition in 1984, he remains uncertain whether: 'principles of public administration . . . exist or can be discovered' (Waldo, 1984: xlvii).

Waldo's criticism of public administration in 1948 was almost exclusively of a conceptual and methodological nature. It was a very negative argument, pointing in almost no direction whatsoever concerning how to overcome these difficulties. It seemed to imply that any general knowledge about public governance faces either the Scylla of naive acceptance of the method of inquiry used in the hard sciences or the Charybdis of practical science degenerating into a set of trivial normative maxims, or proverbs.

Yet, the social sciences, like the natural sciences, attempt to model reality. Although human behaviour is different from physical reality, the science of economics has shown that model building is a worthwhile and respectable effort. One may argue that the so-called principles of public administration did not constitute generally valid models, but it does not follow that it is impossible to conceive of a science of public governance based on model building.

Public administration has gradually lost its dominant position as offering models for understanding the public sector. Its decline begins with the head-on attack by Waldo. But perhaps Waldo was more correct in his criticism of the classical approach than in his general scepticism towards the possibility of model building in the social sciences. He was deeply concerned with understanding what the so-called principles of public administration were all about: behaviour regularities, instrumental efficiency recommendations or explicitly moral guidelines about the creation of the good society.

The Waldo criticism was no doubt effective in dismantling the claims of the classical approach. However, it contained little in terms of a positive contribution towards what public administration or public management could be if it were conducted in terms of the ordinary canons of the scientific method.

In order to arrive at new attempts at modelling the public sector we have to go to other scholars, who were less active about tearing down what the classics had built up and more eager to come up with a new foundation for the study of the public sector, namely Barnard, Simon and Wildavsky.

The politics/administration separation

The negative argument of Waldo may be contrasted with another book, published almost the same year, which also dealt a blow to public administration, using an empirical argument. I am referring to P. Appelby's *Policy and Administration* from 1949. It targeted the model (CM4), or the separation between politics and administration, but invalidated it by means of an examination of 'a full-dimensional picture of public administration' (Appelby, 1949: i).

Analysing the system of American government at the federal level, Appelby came to the conclusion that (CM4) was false, i.e. it did not model reality. Thus, the politics/administration distinction was not methodologically unsound as with Waldo, but it was not descriptive of anything real. On the contrary, the truth was quite the contrary, i.e. politics and administration were all the time interwoven to a very high degree.

Instead of requiring that politics and administration be kept separate, Appelby argued that all government bodies interact heavily, constituting a web of politics and administration:

> The courts influence legislation, legislation influences the courts, Courts and legislative bodies influence or control administrative agencies, and administrative agencies influence legislative bodies and courts.
>
> (Appelby, 1949: 51)

One could accept this description of how 'all of these political organs influence each other and are themselves products of a political climate and political institutions' (Appelby, 1949: 32), but still maintain that judicial, legislative and executive behaviour is not always quite the same behaviour.

Appelby, however, sharpens his argument considerably by claiming that all things in the executive branch of government are of the same nature, namely policy-making. He states:

> Public administration is policy-making. But it is not autonomous, exclusive or isolated policy-making. . . . It is policy-making subject to still other and various policy-makers. . . . Public administration is one of a number of basic political processes by which this people achieves and controls governance.
>
> (Appelby, 1949: 170)

If this description of the executive branch is true, then the model (CM4) does not apply. But is it true? The argument that one cannot make a separation between politics and administration became almost a dogma among scholars rejecting the classical approach.

The rejection of the distinction between politics and administration may be done by means of a philosophical argument, claiming that values and facts, ends and means as well as preferences and technology cannot be distinguished. Or the politics/administration distinction may be rejected by means of an empirical argument stating that administration is always policy-making, i.e. it involves politics.

The philosophical argument against the politics/administration separation is extremely weak, as it is not impossible to uphold a separation between the following entities:

- ends versus means
- values versus facts
- preferences versus technology
- objectives versus instruments
- norms versus existence
- directives versus reality.

One may adhere to a philosophy which denies all these distinctions, but I prefer to adhere to a philosophy maintaining them, albeit not dogmatically.

The empirical argument for collapsing the politics/administration separation may appear convincing when one looks at how one country is governed, from which it appears that 'everything is politics'. However, countries which adhere to the Rule of Law tradition operate a number of institutions which safeguard more or less a separation between politics and administrative behaviour. Thus, administrative jobs are separated from purely political ones. And various institutions, for example, courts and ombudsmen, regulate behaviour in administrative jobs so that they are free from political considerations. It may be true that in the final analysis 'everything is politics', but one may still insist upon that many countries do in fact have institutions which maintain a more or less clear distinction between politics and administration.

At the time when the classical approach started to be abandoned, there appeared a couple of new ideas that stimulated the modelling of public governance, inspired chiefly by private sector governance.

Organisational theory

Perhaps one could say that *The Functions of the Executive* by C. Barnard from 1938 implicitly contained the first coherent attempt to launch a quite new and very different approach to the analysis of the public sector after the classical framework had reached its peak. Barnard was, however, preoccupied with the analysis of all kinds of organisations, not specifically public ones.

Barnard not only integrated the informal and the formal aspects of organisations, but he also stated a crucial condition for successful organisations, namely management or as he called it: 'the executive function'. Bernard's emphasis upon the efficiency of organisations and the contribution of managers gave his analysis a distinctly dynamic tone, which set it off against the static orientation that characterised much of public administration. Where public administration scholars underlined rules, Barnard emphasised leadership.

Barnard does not start from authority as did the classical approach but he focuses upon cooperation, whether it takes place in the public or private sector. And cooperation between men and women in organisations presupposes objectives, whether they be formal or informal. Cooperation towards the accomplishment of objectives calls for management, i.e. the executive function.

Barnard conceived of cooperation in organisations as the most advanced or rational forms of human cooperation, where there is a strong emphasis upon the evaluation of accomplishments, measured by notions of effectiveness and efficiency. Organisational action is not static, but adapts to a changing environment and to the shifting demands from within the organisation. This flexibility or capacity to adapt is secured by organisations through the use of communication, involving the flow of information both up and down the hierarchy. Finally, cooperation in formal organisations calls for an explicit system of rewards, as incentives cannot only be handled by informal techniques.

Enter the managers, or the executive team, who handle the movement of the organisation along a path of external adaptation and internal cooperation. Barnard both underlined the crucial importance of the executive functions for an organisation and stated the limits of what managers can accomplish. Without leadership the organisation is lost. But without organisation leadership has no objectives.

Leadership as exercised by the executive team may rest upon formal rules – authority – or informal assets – personality. Both bases of executive action condition its capacity to achieve the objectives of the organisation. The steering of an organisation involves not only the mix of formal and informal features, but also the involvement of many groups, contributing to cooperation – i.e. the stakeholders of organisation effort consisting of the employees, the owners, the customers and the community. Could one speak of 'policy networks'? 'A purpose to be effective must be accepted by all contributors to the system of efforts', stated Barnard.

Yet, adherents of public administration often see Barnard as committing the sin of overemphasising management to the detriment of responsibility, leaning more towards the efficient achievement of objectives than upon the ethical requirements upon organisation, especially public ones. Thus, he is said to have privatised public leadership, subjugating the running of public organisations to the idea of management as practised in private organisation (Scott, 1995).

This criticism of *The Functions of the Executive* may be true, but that just makes Barnard all the more interesting from the point of view of public management, especially the NPM framework. It must be admitted though that Barnard did not present a coherent or systematic theory of public management.

The management approach

Herbert Simon's *Administrative Behavior* (1947) made the management approach, already anticipated in Barnard, the core framework for modelling the public sector. It did away with both (CM1) and (CM2) as well as (CM3) but retained (CM4). If (CM1), (CM2) and (CM3) are distinctive of classical public administration, then the management framework that Simon launched starts from other conceptions than roles, offices and rules.

Simon's position is that a management model is more relevant than an administration model. The concept of management focuses upon means and ends and they may be regarded as basic to any conception about the public sector as ongoing activities. Thus, we have as the basic model in the Simon approach:

(MM1)   Public sector activities = accomplishments of objectives.

(MM1) entails negatively a rejection of (CM1) and its focus upon roles and people as well as the distinction between these. Positively, the management framework refers instead to objectives and their accomplishment. (MM1) may sound innocuous, but it opens up altogether new ways of looking at the public sector. Especially, the focus upon rules is done away with, as objectives become the crucial starting-point.

(CM3), or the model about centralisation, now has to be assessed in relation to (MM1), which makes its status far from self-evident. How objectives are to be accomplished becomes the key issue in all debates about effectiveness and efficiency, where decentralisation may constitute a viable alternative to centralisation.

Achieving objectives requires that ends and means are properly related to each other, which calls for discretion or autonomy rather than hierarchy and extreme division of labour. Thus, we have:

(MM2)   Public governance = discretion about means in relation to ends.

(MM2) can be seen as a step away from the centralisation model that figured so prominently in the classical approach. However, it remains an open issue if centralisation or decentralisation is most in agreement with (MM2). If the objectives are identified at the centre and the technology is known, then public governance may be conducted in a centralised fashion. If, on the other hand, ends are to reflect local preferences or the choice of a technology concerning the means is to involve much flexibility, then decentralisation is to be preferred.

The classical framework focused upon the administration of a system of rules in order to minimise arbitrariness and increase predictability. Simon, on the contrary, when placing such an emphasis upon the accomplishment of objectives, points to the importance of discretion in relation to the legal system in order to find out which means truly accomplish ends. This process of finding the effective means in relation to ends as well as implementing them is the core of management, where the legal system is seen only as one restriction, albeit necessary.

Thus, we have by 1947 in the writings of Simon a new conception about public sector governance, i.e. public management as the accomplishment of objectives in public sector activities. Evidently, a variety of objectives can be chosen as well as different means be employed. How, then, are the ends and means decided upon in public governance?

Nature of public decision-making

The idea of public management as a dynamic process of pursuing ends by the employment of means is in accordance with the requirement of rationality that theories of organisation often accept as a starting-point. Yet, Simon gave this requirement a special twist by adding to his management model a special model of decision-making.

Perhaps one is a little surprised to be told by Simon that all kinds of decision-making are boundedly rational, given his identification of the public sector with management, which is decision-making about ends and means. Simon's model of decision-making does not have to be added to the management framework, as one could have a rational choice approach, i.e. a theory of decision-making which assumes complete rationality.

However, we must note that in addition to (MM1)–(MM2) Simon also favours a model of so-called incremental decision-making. Actually, Simon's importance depends not only upon his early conception of public management. Many scholars have regarded themselves as followers of Simon, because they have looked upon his theory of bounded rationality as more correct than the so-called neo-classical decision model, inherent in standard economics, especially when modelling the public sector.

Thus, we must add to (MM1)–(MM2) a model about decision-making which is outside of the public management conception. Let us formulate it as:

(MM3)   Public decision-making is bounded rationality.

(MM3), which deviates in specific ways from the rational choice model both in terms of its action requirements upon knowledge and preferences, has been employed to model various kinds of decision-making model in the public sector (Simon, 1957; March and Simon, 1958).

The so-called incrementalists maintained for some time that it was the true model of public decision-making. Not only did (MM3) more accurately describe decision-making, but public decision-making could never be more than bound-edly rational due to complexity, uncertainty and conflicts (Lindblom, 1959; Wildavsky, 1984). The model (MM3) was employed with predictive success in budgetary modelling for a long time, up until major shift-points were introduced in the politics of the early 1980s (Wildavsky, 1972, 1988).

Yet, the bounded rationality model of decision-making has received a renais-sance in the 1990s with the attention paid to the framework of so-called organisational failures, suggested by O. Williamson (1975).

Rationality or pathology

Simon's strong adherence to (MM3) is outside of his orientation towards the management concept focusing upon the attainment of objectives. This would suggest an emphasis upon what Weber referred to means–end rationality, leaning towards a rational choice model. Yet, Simon is sceptical about the strong ratio-nality claims that characterised not only the classical approach but also standard economics, as complete rationality is only feasible for God.

Yet, if management is the employment of means to accomplish ends, and if rationality is not achievable in organisations like those dominating the public sector, then what is the sense of looking at public governance as management? Simon's retreat from rationality was, however, only partial. Thus, as a follow-up model he suggested:

(MM4)   Decision-making is satisfying, not maximising.

A result is satisfying when certain ends have been considered and standard oper-ating procedures have been employed to accomplish these objectives. Whereas the concept of maximisation has a unique interpretation in the rational choice model of decision-making, the concept of satisfying could mean different things. What is satisfying to one actor may be quite unsatisfactory to another actor.

Many scholars still adhere to the bounded rationality model, because they consider it as empirically more truthful than the maximisation model of rational choice. Other scholars claim that a rational decision model should be used when modelling public governance, because its theoretical structure is clear and simple.

The independence of (MM3) and (MM4) in relation to (MM1)–(MM2) is seen most clearly when we move on to a third decision-making model, the garbage can model (March and Olsen, 1976). It underlines the opposite to ratio-nality, namely foolishness, claiming that it can more adequately analyse what happens in large organisations than any rational model, whether with complete or bounded rationality.

The garbage can model entails the idea that ends and means in the public sector are somehow sick (March and Olsen, 1976). A garbage can predicament in the public sector arises when the objectives are ambiguous and the technologies are uncertain. The key question is how probable is the occurrence of such processes. Will they occur frequently in all public sectors or are they dependent upon the size of the public sector in the sense that the larger the public sector, then the more probable the garbage can processes?

Is the garbage can model an individual or a collective decision model? It seems as if the model was developed in order to account for organisational pathologies. But if organisations tend to display garbage can symptoms:

- group leadership is luck
- the means are given, but which are the goals?
- participation is fluid

then such phenomena can arise even when the actors pursue rational choice. Although each actor behaves in a manner that is individually rational, the resultant group behaviour may be pathological, due to lack of coordination.

Such an irrational decision model seems adequate in relation to certain pathologies in the public sector, but its general claim to be a decision-making model in public governance cannot be accepted, as it contradicts the rationality requirement (Thompson, 1966). It certainly has empirical applicability, but its normative usefulness in relation to public management is practically nil. When garbage can processes occur, would not then everybody involved or concerned want to undo such activities or even remove the activities in question from the public sector and place them in the private sector, if possible?

The question of the choice of a decision-making model has been much debated since the appearance of Simon's contribution. In the policy approach, one has vacillated between a rational choice model and a bounded rationality model, but one also finds a line of thought which denies rationality.

The policy approach

Once the classical framework was abandoned, the search for new approaches could not be confined to the management framework, which is basically borrowed from the private sector. The public sector may be described as management but only to a limited extent, because one would not call decision-making by government 'management'.

The public sector, whether conceived of as the state or government, has an undeniable hierarchical feature in so far as it is governed by means of laws and budgets, enacted at the top and executed downwards. The classical framework modelled this aspect with the help of model (CM3). If this model is to be rejected, then what could replace it?

The policy framework was launched after the Second World War in an attempt to fill the gap after the classical framework. Its basic ideas, focusing upon policy or public programmes, are well outlined in a large literature. Here we only pin down its basic models (Hogwood and Gunn, 1992).

The policy approach starts from the idea of a policy cycle which includes the enactment and execution of so-called policies. Thus, we have:

(PM1)   Public governance constitutes a policy cycle moving continuously between policy making and implementation.

However, it fiercely rejects any sharp separation between policy-making and implementation (May and Wildavsky, 1978; Pressman and Wildavsky, 1984). On the contrary, scholars within the policy framework tend to reject (CM4) as a set of untenable distinctions.

In the policy approach, however, the basic separation is that between policy-making and implementation, the nature of which has become the target of much debate. Most policy scholars tend to agree that the enactment (policy-making) and the execution of policy (implementation) are so closely linked that they are almost indistinguishable. Thus, we have:

(PM2)   Policy-making and implementation are indistinguishable.

How then to separate policy-making and policy implementation, one may ask? The model (PM2) is often considered as related to the model (CM4) in the classical approach, although with the great difference that policy scholars tend to deny the model (CM4). Thus, to many (PM2) is the negation of (CM4).

Despite the adherence to the model (PM2), the public policy school came to display a clear bifurcation. On the one hand, there was a focus upon policy-making at the top level of government. On the other hand, there was a development of a focus upon what happened to policies after they had been enacted – the so-called implementation perspective. Sometimes, the link between the these two foci within the policy school was very weak.

The policy approach differed from the classical school in its insistence upon objectives as the key concept in public governance. And it differed from the management approach in its underlining of the constant presence of politics.

An issue in the policy school has been whether policy-making adheres to the rational choice model or the bounded rationality model. Few have placed their bets upon the garbage can model. However, what has given the policy approach much new blood is the evolution of the implementation perspective – the so-called missing link in public governance.

The implementation perspective

Once implementation in the policy cycle had been clearly identified as a non-trivial stage, then a huge literature was forthcoming about various aspects of this stage. One of these aspects was the choice of a proper implementation strategy. Another aspect included the discovery of the concept of a policy outcome, which invited the development of numerous approaches like policy evaluation, impact analysis and outcomes measurement. Implementation is conceptualised as both process and result. A model of policy implementation may target the proper implementation strategy or it may measure how outcomes relate to objectives.

Now, based upon the overwhelming opinion among scholars participating in the research within the implementation perspective, the policy framework added an important model to its policy models above. It suggests an answer to the question of a strategy of implementation. Thus, we have:

(PM3)   Decentralised implementation is more effective than top-down implementation.

This is the so-called bottom-up model of implementation, which amounts to a sharp rejection of model (CM3) within public administration. Moreover, the implementation perspective argues that policies are made when they are implemented, confirming the policy framework which often contained a rejection of a sharp distinction between the two stages in the policy process: (1) decision-making; (2) implementation.

It is considered that rejecting a sharp separation between policy-making and implementation is the same as denying that politics can be separated from administration, i.e. (CM4) is wrong. Yet, curiously enough the literature on implementation has developed a number of different strategies for effective implementation which assume that policies are somehow given.

If one accepts the model (PM3), then how is efficiency in implementation to be secured? Are there any yardsticks? The policy framework tends to underline the politics of the public sector, focusing upon the conflicts that surround the policy process. It comes close to asserting:

(PM4)   The policy cycle is more about politics than programme efficiency.

Only in its pathological version does the management approach come to a similar conclusion. Is the model (PM4) coherent with the model (PM3)? One could argue that if (PM4) is true, then the argument in favour of decentralisation in (PM3) is somewhat misplaced.

The policy network approach

Within the policy approach, it has remained a puzzle how policies decided by politicians are going to be put in practice by non-politicians. The more policy scholars reflected upon the implementation gap, the more serious the difficulties seemed to have become.

If the fundamental beliefs of the policy school, as they are outlined above, are true, then policy is not easily distinguished from implementation. Yet, the whole framework is based upon the gap between the making of policy and the putting into practice of a policy.

Reflection upon the implementation gap has resulted in a literature suggesting that policies can be put into practice by so-called policy networks. Thus, we have:

(PM5)   Networks are more efficient than hierarchies in implementation.

The policy networks model(s) is explicitly taking into account the stakeholders surrounding policy in order to make them legitimate participants in the process of implementing policies. Does (PM5) provide effective motivation?

The policy network model has been stated in many versions, from the British Iron Triangles over the American coalitions to the Dutch webs of contacts (Marsh and Rhodes, 1992; Sabatier and Jenkins-Smith, 1993; Klijn, 1996). Although the network model (PM5) receives much support from case studies of how social policies are run and how they develop over time, it remains a puzzle how to substantiate the efficiency claim of the model (PM5).

Policy networks exist and they do implement policies, but what about the efficiency claim? To resolve the status of (PM5), we seem to need more information than only descriptions of how networks operate. The efficiency argument entails the use of evaluation criteria about the outcomes of policy implementation (Ingram and Mann, 1980).

Yet, when the model (PM5) is combined with the other policy models – (PM1)–(PM4), then one arrives at the paradox that policy implementation is a never ending process where policies are made when they are executed and where policy implementation is lifelong learning. Then: what does the effective implementation of a policy amount to?

Summing up

We have identified the basic models in the three approaches to the public sector: traditional public administration, the management approach and the policy framework. The shift between these approaches in this century may be seen as Kuhnian paradigm changes. This is where we stand today. Yet, recent developments have stimulated the emergence of a new and fourth framework for public management, which build upon the changes in the public sector in the 1980s and 1990s – new public management (NPM). New public management challenges not only the classical approach but also the policy approaches and the bounded rationality or incremental model.

NPM should not be mixed up with the theory of public management that argues that government must be founded upon an ethical theory of public administration – what in the 1970s was also called 'New Public Administration' (Marini, 1971). The ethical theory of public management focuses upon questions about public responsibility, not public sector efficiency.

NPM focuses upon the employment of contracts in governing the public sector, being connected with the purchaser-provider model or the tendering/bidding model. In its most radical version, NPM as institutionalised in New Zealand transforms the entire state, placing the state under contract (Boston, 1995).

Conclusion

I dare to describe the public administration framework and the policy approaches discussed above under the label 'traditional public governance', however large the differences may be between them. These share certain characteristics which set them off against 'modern public governance'.

In traditional public governance there is an emphasis upon politics as well as upon the distinctness of public sector management in relation to private sector management. However, in modern public governance accomplishing objectives is in principle no different in the public sector than in the private sector. It results from contracting where the providers may be public or private organisations.

Table 1.1 presents an overview of the differences between traditional and modern public governance, where the differences between the two governance models will become apparent when we examine NPM in Part III.

Traditional public governance has lost much in relevance, both theoretically and practically. Institutional reforms in various countries and in the European Union and within the World Trade Organization push for the introduction of modern governance in as many countries as possible.

Vincent Ostrom describes the present predicament of public administration in his book *The Intellectual Crisis in American Public Administration* (1989). When a paradigm or major scientific approach runs into more and more problems, then it is often a better strategy to launch an entirely new framework than to try endlessly to sort out difficulties here and there, as new puzzles emerge as soon as old ones have been resolved.

Let me try to explain in more detail why traditional public governance is not considered theoretically sound today. I will do so by including in the overview of the main models of the public sector also the models that economists have

Table 1.1 Traditional and modern public governance

Traditional public governance	Modern public governance
(1) Emphasis upon politics	(1´) Emphasis upon getting the job done
(2) Use of public law mechanisms: (a) bureau; (b) public enterprise	(2´) Use of private law instruments: (a) the contract; (b) tendering/bidding
(3) Separation between public and private players	(3´) Levelling the playing field
(4) Separation between allocation and regulation	(4´) Integration of allocation and regulation

launched, especially within the public choice approach. Chapters 3, 4 and 5 present this economics-based criticism of traditional public governance.

Chapter 2 argues that despite the many reforms of the public sector in the 1980s and the 1990s being strongly influenced by market philosophy, public sector management remains extensive and relevant in all societies, whatever economic regime they adhere to.

2 Practical relevance of public sector management

Introduction

Could one predict that the role of the public sector will only diminish in the future, perhaps even to such an extent that there is virtually no need for public sector management? The call for privatisation has been so strong within the OECD set of countries that one would be prepared to guess that the future will see only the reversal of the major trend of the twentieth century, which has been the rise of the tax state, predicted by Joseph Schumpeter in 1918.

There would be a rationale for such a guess, only if the evidence from ongoing reforms of the public sector support the prediction that the public sector is indeed shrinking dramatically. But this is not true, at least not in relation to the countries of the world with an advanced economy, i.e. the OECD countries.

The purpose of this chapter is to examine how far public sector retrenchement has come after a decade of market inspired reforms. Despite massive deregulation and privatisation, the public sector in countries with a market economy remains truly large, and in many OECD countries the public sector is even slightly larger now than ten years ago. How is it that public sector reform does not reduce the tax state?

Shifting parts but constant overall size

I will argue that it is not the overall size of the public sector that has changed during the last decade but the size of the various parts of the public sector. Public sector management is still omnipresent, but it operates in new forms to a considerable extent. When some kinds of public activities decrease, then other types of public activities increase. What we have here is almost a law of the constant size of the public sector.

The two basic parts of any public sector are public resource allocation on the one hand and income maintenance on the other hand. Whereas the latter tends to increase, the former remains unchanged or shrinks. At the same time, one may distinguish between two different models of the proper size of the public sector, namely the welfare society on the one hand and the welfare state on the other hand.

In any advanced society, the average public sector stands at about 45 per cent of GDP. This average figure hides, however, the contrast between welfare societies and welfare states. The public sector is, it is true, lower in the welfare societies, where it may even go down to 30 per cent of GDP. In the welfare states, on the other hand, it may go up to 60 per cent of GDP. Table 2.1 presents the most recent figures for the OECD set of countries.

With an average public sector at 40–50 per cent of GDP, there is a need for public management in both welfare societies and welfare states, because public expenditures are big in both types of countries. One must always remember that an average public sector size of 40–45 per cent implies immense taxes or user fees and expenditures today, as the GDP in the OECD set of countries has more than doubled since 1950.

There is a whole literature on what has driven up public expenditures since

Table 2.1   Size of the public sector around 1995 and GDP 1996

Country	Current general government revenue (% of GDP)	Current general government expenditure (% of GDP)	Per capita at current prices using current PPPs[1]
Australia	34.9	35.6	20,376
Austria	47.4	48.6	21,395
Belgium	49.8	51.7	21,856
Canada	42.7	45.8	21,529
Czech Republic	43.3	40.5	—
Denmark	58.1	59.6	22,418
Finland	52.8	55.9	18,871
France	48.2	51.6	20,533
Germany	45.9	46.6	21,200
Greece	45.0	52.1	12,743
Iceland	36.0	35.1	23,242
Ireland	36.3	36.9	18,988
Italy	44.5	49.5	19,974
Japan	32.0	28.5	23,235
Korea	26.0	15.7	13,580
Luxembourg	52.9[2]	45.0[2]	32,416
Mexico	—	—	7,776
The Netherlands	49.3	50.0	20,905
New Zealand	—	—	17,473
Norway	50.9	45.8	24,364
Portugal	39.8	42.5	13,100
Spain	37.9	41.2	14,954
Sweden	57.5	63.8	19,258
Switzerland	53.8	47.7	25,402
Turkey	—	—	6,114
United Kingdom	37.2	42.3	18,636
United States	32.1	34.3	27,821

Sources: National Accounts, OECD, Paris, 1998; *Main Economic Indicators*, OECD, Paris, February 1998.

Notes: [1]PPP = purchasing power parities; [2]1986.

the end of the First World War. This trend of the increasing tax state, changing the balance between the public and the private sectors, has now come to an end. Which have been the forces – the push and pull so to speak – behind the expansion of the public sector, taking a macro perspective on the public sector? How can one account for the difference between welfare states and welfare societies?

Wagner's law of public policy

Does raising affluence increase or decrease the size of the public sector? This way of posing the question of the relationship between economic development resulting in a larger and larger GDP on the one hand and the need for the public sector on the other hand is distinctly Wagnerian. Adolf Wagner argued as early as 1871 that raising affluence must drive up public expenditures. Thus, economic development calls for public outlays (Wagner, 1877–1901).

The implication of Wagner's argument about a positive elasticity of public expenditures in relation to GDP is that the public sector will not only grow larger in absolute terms but also in relative terms. A large public sector is a characteristic feature of an advanced economy, claimed Wagner, as if there was no alternative to public sector expansion when countries attained higher affluence through industrialisation and urbanisation.

Wagner explained his law by a number of different reasons or needs for public expenditures: infrastructure, congestion, culture, safety, social justice, etc. Up until the 1980s, Wagner seems to have predicted things quite correctly. The public sector in rich countries began to increase as a percentage of GDP around 1900 and kept increasing up until 1980, although with varying speed during different decades. Since 1980 the public sector expansion process has come to an almost complete standstill. Yet, the public sector has not decreased to any significant amount during the same time on average, although a few OECD countries have made drastic changes in the mix of the public and the private sectors.

Wagner's law is of less relevance today, although it explained well the immense public sector expansion in the 1950s and 1960s. Other factors need to be taken into account when understanding the cross-sectional and longitudinal variation in public expenditures. The literature testing the relevance of Wagner's law is huge (Wilensky, 1975; Lybeck and Henreksson, 1988) but there seems to be no one single and definitive answer forthcoming about why the public sector in some countries sometimes grows sharply but at other times decreases considerably in other countries (Schmidt, 1997).

Demand or supply explanations

Wagner's law is basically a demand side explanation of the public sector, stating that people need a larger public sector in an industrial economy. In a poor country people are busy satisfying their most elementary needs for food and shelter. In an advanced economy, people can pay attention to other and 'higher' needs: education, health and culture. Government should according to Wagner play a major role in the economy in both promoting affluence through infrastructure and providing for the new 'higher' needs.

The enormous expansion of the public sector in Western Europe and in the market economies in North America, Japan and Oceania called forth a reaction to the effect that the public sector had grown too large. A set of theories were suggested that challenged Wagner's theory. They argued that public sector expansion tends to be supply side driven, involving the occurrence of the so-called Baumol's decease (Tarschys, 1975).

What has happened in the twentieth century is not that the quantity of public services has increased dramatically, as Wagner's law implies. Instead, it is the prices of the public sector services that have gone up, which explains why the public sector outlays have increased so sharply. The quantity of public services remains fairly steady, but the unit cost is up. The crux of the matter is the occurrence of a long-term negative productivity development trend, where public employees perform less and less but successfully demand more and more in salaries – the Baumol decease (Baumol, 1965).

Thus, the supply side argument claimed that there was government overload in the advanced industrialised countries. Wagner's law about the desired tendency of the public sector to replace the private sector was fundamentally flawed, because it did not take into account the forces on the supply side of the spending equation, involving not only the strong organisation of producer groups but also phenomena such as rent-seeking and fiscal illusions. Instead, public sector growth driven by supply side factors mean that the public sector will drive out the private sector.

This argument is entirely a supply side theory of the growth of government, focusing upon the bargaining strength of the people who supply public sector services. They carefully look at the wages of private sector employees, demanding all the time similar wage increases. Since labour can be replaced by capital in the private sector to a much higher extent than in the public sector, positive productivity gains in the private sector will be transferred to the public sector by means of taxation. Public sector growth is merely a figment of the imagination, resulting more from wage increases than from the supply of more services.

Figure 2.1 shows the two main theories of public sector expansion, the demand side theories on the one hand focusing on an increase in the demand for public sector services and the supply side theory on the other hand, explaining the increase in public sector expenditures by means of the rise in unit cost.

The demand side theories focus upon the shift from D1 to D2, which would explain why the public sector has expanded from Q1 to Q2, with the attending explosion in costs, from Q1 $\times$ P1 to Q2 $\times$ P1. However, the supply side theory can explain the same cost explosion by focusing upon the shift in price from P1 to P2, reflecting the change from one supply S1 (MC1) (marginal cost at P1) to another supply S2 (MC2) (marginal cost at P2). The public sector is as large today as it was forty years ago, but price has more than doubled, leaving the same huge bill to be paid for taxes or user fees, Q1 $\times$ P2 = Q2 $\times$ P1.

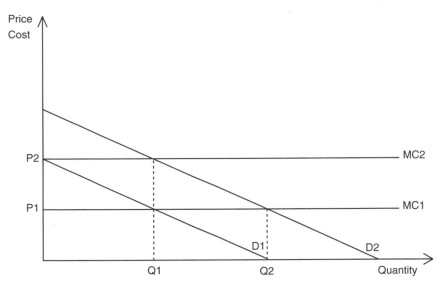

Figure 2.1 Demand and supply side theories of public sector expansion.

Note: D = demand; MC or S = supply; P = price; Q = quantity allocated.

Probably there is a grain of truth in both these explanations of public sector growth in this century. One trend has been to ask government to do more things – from D1 to D2, but another trend has been for unit cost to increase – from S1 to S2. We need to take into account both demand and supply in order to explain the cost explosion in some sectors of the public sector like health care. Perhaps the amount of health care produced has not changed that much, but the search for quality in treatment seems to require all the time more use of more costly equipment.

The expansion of the tax state

The average expansion in OECD countries of the public sector from around 15 per cent of GDP after the First World War to about 40 per cent of GDP in the 1990s involve both increases in the quantity of services supplied – from Q1 towards Q2, but it also reflects increases in unit cost – from P1 towards P2. One must remember that the base – GDP – increases considerably over time.

Interestingly, the quest for public sector reform in the 1990s has not changed the overall size of the public sector markedly. The trend towards public sector growth has come to a standstill, but it is not the case that the public sector has been reduced in any significant sense. Not even in countries that have been highly susceptible to the privatisation and marketisation philosophy, such as, e.g. the United Kingdom, has there been any sharp reduction in the size of the public sector in relation to the GDP.

There seems to be a steady need for public sector management in the advanced countries with democratic institutions and a market economy. Public sector management is also relevant in Third World countries. The public sector tends to be smaller in these countries, reflecting the Wagner mechanism that affluence is a necessary condition for public expenditures.

Thus, public sector management may have changed its appearance due to the extensive public sector reforms, but it has certainly not disappeared. Table 2.2 presents a picture of the size of the public sector in advanced and Third World countries around the 1980s and the mid-1990s.

Considering the fact that the GDP in the rich countries is about 5 to 10 or more times larger than the GDP in Third World countries, public management is a very prominent feature in the advanced countries, despite all the public sector reforms in these countries.

Much attention has focused upon explaining why some advanced countries have more public expenditures than other advanced countries. These explanations involve a rejection of both Wagner's law and the supply side theory.

The impact of politics and culture

Wagner's theory argues that affluence causes public expenditures, but it is not more accurate to say that affluence creates the possibility of a large public sector. Affluence is a necessary but it is not a sufficient condition. In order to start big public spending on the basis of heavy taxation, governments need not only a rich economy with a large enough GDP to be able to generate resources for public programmes. Governments must also have the inclination to support a large public sector, which is a question of preferences and not strictly resources. Thus, there must be something in addition to resources which drives governments to increase the public sector.

Table 2.2   General government expenditures

	1980	*1992*
Western Europe	47.3	51.1
Eastern Europe	41.7	42.9
North America	36.0	44.2
Central America	30.9	23.0
South America	22.6	20.8
North Africa and Middle East	42.6	31.4
Subsaharan Africa	32.8	28.7
East Asia	24.8	18.5
South Asia	35.1	30.9
Oceania	36.9	33.0
Mean	36.1	32.4
N	48	87

Sources: *IMF Government Finance Statistics Yearbook* (IMF 1984, 1994).

A number of arguments have been put forward as to the nature of the conditions which could drive up public expenditures. They all pointed to demand side factors, complementing the dominant demand side theory, viz. Wagner's law. Some argued that politics in a wide sense, including the power of trade unions, matter (Castles, 1998), whereas others stated that culture makes the difference.

According to one interpretation, preferences for a big public sector could derive from left-wing ideology, which characterises socialist parties and the trade union movement, or from a Christian democratic ideology. According to another interpretation, these interests behind public sector expansion are in general connected with an egalitarian culture, whatever its political expression may be (Wildavsky, 1986). This is still a demand side argument, explaining public sector expansion by reference to the wishes of citizens, not all of the citizens as with Wagner, but those with egalitarian preferences. If other political forces come to power, then public sector expansion may be halted, for instance by conservative parties or people adhering to libertarianism – 'marketers'.

Figure 2.2 presents a picture of the differences in overall public sector size in the 1990s among the countries adhering to the OECD. From Figure 2.2, we see that there is one cluster of countries that are well above the average size of the public sector in the OECD set of countries, namely the welfare states, scoring around or above 50 per cent. Here, we have almost all the Western European countries, with the exception of Ireland, Iceland and the United Kingdom. Another cluster of countries fall well below the average scores, namely the welfare societies, for which a public sector size of about 35 per cent or less is

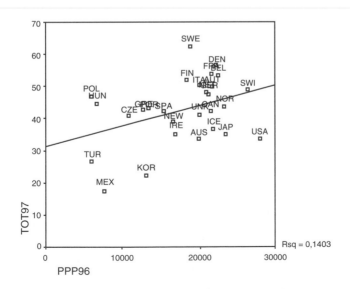

Figure 2.2   Total public outlays/GDP against affluence in OECD countries.
Source: OECD 1999.

typical: the US, Japan, Ireland and Oceania. Why is there this major difference in the role of public sector management in advanced societies?

Indeed, it seems difficult to account for the immense difference between the minimum size of the public sector in Japan – about 30 per cent – and the maximum size of the public sector in Sweden – around 65 per cent – within a Wagnerian framework. As a matter of fact, it would be almost equally difficult to account for the many country differences using a supply side approach. It has been attempted to use public choice theory in order to explain the fact that Switzerland had for a long time a small public sector by referring to its highly distinct set of political institutions, which would limit rent-seeking, as it were (Pommerehne and Schneider, 1978). However, Switzerland is no longer an exception to the continental European welfare state (see Chapter 6).

In the comparative analysis of public policy one has attempted to account for these cross-country differences in public sector size, measured mainly by means of public finance data, in terms of several demand factors, adding flesh to the rather meagre Wagnerian framework, suggesting only affluence as the predictor of public expenditure effort or welfare state size. As a matter of fact, almost all the countries in the OECD set can be designated affluent, meaning that Wagner's law would be of limited explanatory relevance when accounting for cross-sectional differences. The only countries with a low level of affluence are Turkey, South Korea and Mexico, relatively speaking, but these countries are of a limited interest in the debate about the 'politics matter' theme.

By looking at Figure 2.2 one may get hints at the kind of demand factors that would push up the size of the public sector. Among the countries with a level of total public spending higher than 50 per cent we find the Scandinavian countries and Finland. What they have in common is a strong trade union movement, which would welcome public expenditures in so far as they benefit their members. Among the big spenders we also find Austria, where again corporatism could be the explanatory factor.

The Nordic countries and Austria go together not only on trade union density and the acceptance of the legitimacy of corporatism, or the influence of hierarchically structured interest groups upon policy-making and policy implementation. They have in common also a party system where there is a large and often dominating social democratic party, often participating in governmental coalitions.

To the set of countries with a mature welfare state also belong Germany, The Netherlands and Italy. These countries seem to have less in common with the Nordic countries but more in common with Austria, or more specifically a strong position for Christian democracy, either in the party system or in social organisations. Public expenditures would be regarded as balancing the market in the subsidiarity philosophy of Christian democracy, as interpreted in major papal encyclias such as *Rerum Novarum* (1891) and *Quadragesimo Anno* (1931).

Christian democratic parties favour a market economy with social responsibility, meaning huge welfare state expenditures (Wilensky, 1976). But if social democracy or Christian democracy promote a welfare state, then why would

France have a large welfare state? Or, if strong hierarchical interest groups favour welfare state spending, then why would France belong to the welfare state set of countries?

At the other end of the scale measuring total public outlays as a percentage of GDP we have a cluster of countries that employ markets more than public programmes, the welfare societies as it were. Their public expenditures hover around 35 per cent of GDP. The distinction between welfare states and welfare societies is not stable, as countries may move from one category to the other. One could argue that the United Kingdom and New Zealand have left the set of welfare states and moved closer to the set of welfare societies, whereas the opposite would be true of Spain, Portugal and Greece. How would one account for such regime changes with demand arguments?

Castles (1998) argues that what matters is not the configuration of the left but the strength of a conservative party with a leaning towards Manchester liberalism. When such a party is strong as in Japan, Switzerland and the United States, then public outlays will be rather small. In France, only part of the Gaullist movement may be considered as a conservative neo-liberal party, as its left wing would belong more in the social liberalism camp. The Castles' argument seems to bypass the fundamental fact that the welfare state was supported also by the right-wing parties in many countries, for instance in the Nordic countries, except for the discontent parties and the ultra-right parties.

Wildavsky (1986) suggested that culture may account for the emphasis given to markets and to public policy. Welfare societies would basically adhere to libertarian values, underlining the virtues of competitive individualism and personal responsibility, whereas welfare states would focus upon egalitarianism and collective responsibility. Thus, the tension between liberty and equality occurring in the midst of culture shift would tend to be reflected in shifting preferences for the variety of mixes of state and market.

Welfare states and welfare societies

One may observe in relation to Figure 2.2 that some countries constitute anomalies in relation to the main theories about public expenditure determinants. In relation to Wagner's law, underlining affluence, one may note that several very rich countries such as the United States, Japan and Australia have small public sectors – the so-called welfare societies. With regard to the social democracy argument, one may point out that the transition from a welfare state to a welfare society in Australia and New Zealand was very much supported by social democratic parties. The hypothesis about a link between public outlays and Christian democracy may help us understand why many countries in Western Europe opted for the welfare state, but is not of much help in explaining why also other non-socialist parties support the welfare state strongly in France, The Netherlands, Switzerland and Belgium.

A welfare state is a politico-economic regime where the state is active in the economy in various ways though without extensive ownership, which results in a mixed economy instead of the system of decentralised capitalism where markets prevail and there is less income redistribution. The welfare state is active in public resource allocation, transfer payments and policies that promote full employment. In welfare societies markets handle many of these tasks.

Welfare states or welfare societies? This is the critical question in the debate in the 1990s about the size of the public sector, which was initiated by Chicago School Economics (Lucas, 1987; Barro, 1990) favouring the welfare society model. But what are the outcomes? Do welfare societies have better economic growth than welfare states? Can we speak of a performance crisis of the welfare state? It is well known that the welfare state no longer performs as it did in the heyday of Keynesian macro-economics in the 1950s and 1960s. We must enquire into whether it is the case that large public expenditures are counterproductive, meaning that they worsen performance on politico-economic outcomes.

The basic difficulty of the welfare states tends to be analysed by means of the concept of an efficiency–equity trade-off, meaning that the huge efforts in the public sector are driven by equity considerations which can only be effectuated with a cost in terms of total output. Thus, societies must decide where on the efficiency–equity trade-off they wish to place themselves, more towards efficiency as with the welfare societies, or more towards equality, as with the welfare states (Okun, 1975).

The efficiency–equity trade-off never rose under a pure Keynesian regime, as the argument for a large public sector was that it enhanced both economic efficacy and social justice. Acknowledging the existence of a trade-off between the size of the cake and its distribution, between total output on the one hand and social equality in distribution on the other hand, does not entail that one endorses the welfare society. One can argue that the efficiency losses are so marginal that the gains with regard to social solidarity outweigh the loss in total output, or average income. These questions may be researched by examining if the welfare societies really tend to outperform the welfare states in terms of macro-economic criteria as well as whether the welfare states perform better on equity criteria.

A few countries have switched from the welfare state format to the ideal of a welfare society, as for instance Australia, New Zealand and Canada. The United Kingdom under the Thatcher government partly remodelled the British welfare state on the basis of market ideals, whereas the debate about the future of the American welfare state became intense when the Republicans won the 1994 elections to the Congress.

Among the big welfare states, one may distinguish first between those that have large allocative expenditures as well as large redistributive expenditures. Second, we identify those that are large mainly on transfer payments. And third, we have a set of countries which are low on both allocative and redistributive expenditures, when military expenditures have been taken out. Table 2.3 contains a classification of the three types of public sectors.

There are, one may suggest, two kinds of welfare states, the allocative and the redistributive ones. Only to a limited extent are these the same countries, when

Table 2.3 Types of societies: public–private sector mixes around 1990

Welfare states		Welfare societies
Allocation	*Redistribution*	
Austria	Austria	Ireland
Denmark	Denmark	Spain
Finland	Finland	Portugal
France	France	USA
Germany	Italy	Japan
Greece	The Netherlands	Australia
Iceland	Norway	New Zealand
Norway	Sweden	Turkey
Sweden	Belgium	
Luxembourg	Luxembourg	
UK	Switzerland	
Canada		
Switzerland		

Source: Lane *et al.* (1996).

Note: Allocative welfare states use about 18 per cent or more of the GDP for general government consumption; redistributive welfare states employ 18 per cent or more on social security payments. Welfare societies include the remaining countries.

for instance the Scandinavian countries and Finland score high in both. The redistributive welfare state offers a larger space for markets than allocative welfare states where government is responsible for the supply of numerous services virtually free of charges. Transfer payments in the form of cash contributions to individuals play a major role in the redistributive welfare state as in Continental Europe.

The critical question is does it matter whether a country has one or the other kind of welfare state or adheres to the welfare society ideal. By 'matters' we refer to social and economic outcomes such as unemployment, economic growth and inflation as well as income equality. To connect a politico-economic regime with outcomes is far from a simple task. It requires methodological deliberations concerning the data to be employed as well as the specification of models to be tested. In Chapter 6 we take a few steps towards evaluating the welfare states and the welfare societies, looking at a series of average values on a few evaluation criteria as well as conducting a couple of regression analyses about the link between economic growth rates and public expenditures.

Now, even in welfare societies the state is by no means small. There is a lot of public policy and public management in so-called market regimes. What is the basic difference between a welfare state – 50 per cent of the GDP – and a welfare society – 35 per cent of GDP? Is it merely a matter of size, or do governments in welfare states do other things than governments in welfare societies?

Which are the public sector tasks?

The tasks in public sector management may be divided in several ways. Let us here contrast one policy-based typology with the traditional classification in the public finance approach.

How public management relates to public policy is an open question; this is also true of how public management is related to public administration. Partly we face here conceptual questions involving how key terms are used by various scholars as well as questions about how words like 'policy', 'management' and 'administration' may or should be used. Partly we speak about realities, i.e. how policy-making is related to management on the one hand and administration on the other hand. Public sector management tends to concentrate upon a few kinds of tasks.

The Lowi typology

In a well-known typology, T. Lowi has identified three or four types of public policies, each type focusing upon different things (Lowi, 1964, 1972):

1   Distributive: new resources
2   Redistributive: existing resources
3   Regulatory: control of activities
4   Constituent: setting-up or reorganising institutions.

There are a few difficulties in the Lowi typology, which have implications for the identification of public sector management tasks. Whereas one could argue that constituent policies do not really involve public sector management, it is easy to identify public sector management tasks within distributive, redistributive and regulatory policies. But how does one separate between constituent policies and regulatory policies? Regulating an area of the economy usually means setting up or reorganising an institution. Similarly, the distinction between distributive and redistributive policies is anything but clear. What is the difference between distributing new and existing resources?

Public management tasks could definitely play a major role in distributive policies. One could argue that redistributive policies focus more upon the administration of rules about income transfers and thus have a minor management component. Regulatory policies also seem to involve more of administration than management, as regulators do not really produce goods and services.

Yet, when redistributive policies involve other things than taxation and transfer payments, then redistribution involves public sector management, as when it covers redistribution in kind or the provision of certain goods and services to specified groups. Similarly, public regulation can involve managing a sector of the economy in the sense of enhancing objectives and not merely administering a body of rules.

The Lowi policy based classification is different from the classification in the public finance literature, which contains the economist's perspective upon the public sector.

The Musgrave system

In 1959 Richard A. Musgrave gave an authoritative presentation of the classical public finance approach to the public sector, which had emerged during the nineteenth century in the writings of various scholars in Italy, Germany and Sweden. Musgrave (1959) identified analytically three branches of government:

1   the allocative branch
2   the redistributive branch
3   the stabilisation branch

Since the stabilisation branch corresponds to the conduct of macro-economic policy, it falls in principle outside of the domain of public sector management, which is micro-orientated. The Musgrave system corresponds to a large degree to the public finance statistics of OECD, the public finances as represented in the National Accounts.

Thus, using the Musgrave system, although leaving the stabilisation branch outside of the schema, we have the fundamental and highly useful separation between two major kinds of public expenditure:

*   allocative expenditures
*   redistributive expenditures

This distinction cuts across the policy based categories. Public resource allocation, or final government consumption as it is called in the OECD statistics, is the provision of goods and services free or almost free of charge. Redistribution may be in terms of cash or goods and services. In the OECD system income redistribution involves only the transfer of money in various programmes, and not the provision of goods and services (in kind).

One advantage of the public finance classification is that it makes a sharp separation between production and income's policies. Public resource allocation involves truly large public management tasks, as numerous goods and services are provided without markets, or outside the private sector. Income transfers or transfer payments change people's behaviour in markets, but they do not replace markets. Another advantage of the distinction between allocation and distribution is that it is upheld in the official public finance statistics framework in many countries, especially in OECD countries. Thus, the distinction lends itself to reliable comparative study.

One major disadvantage of the OECD statistics is that they do not include the provision of goods and services which is fully financed by means of user fees or charges. Public enterprises involve huge public management tasks but they tend to operate under a requirement that they should not be tax financed, at least as long as they do not run deficits. Running public enterprises in one form or another is distinctly public sector management, but public enterprises tend to be placed outside of public finance statistics, i.e. within the private sector.

In addition, the public finance classification provides no separate space for public regulation, which is more about laws than allocation or money transfers. To the separation above between allocation and distribution, we will add another category, namely public regulation. Public sector management is basically about allocation and regulation through means of the government. It is less involved in income maintenance programmes, except when a workfare state is put in place. Let us explain why.

Management tasks and entitlement rights

Public sector management is both more narrow and more broad than the public finance view upon the public sector. It is more narrow, because income redistribution does not really belong with public sector management. The redistribution branch of government, or the state which pays various kinds of transfer payments to different social groups, engages in public management to only a very little extent. The entire movement of money through the redistribution apparatus, involving large-scale taxation as well as gigantic amounts of cash payments, concerns not basically management but citizen rights.

Public sector management is much focused upon public resource allocation. One may analyse the redistributive programmes from the efficiency perspective, examining their impact upon economic incentives both in taxation and in spending, but the perspective is not that of a manager. Policy-making concerning the overall size of redistribution as well as about the construction of the separate programmes involves consideration of justice together with macro-economics, not public sector management.

One could view the reforms towards a workfare state as a movement in the direction of introducing more management into redistributive programmes, but income redistribution is more a question of social justice – entitlements – than the efficient management of resources in order to reach objectives. Several programmes in the public sector are based upon rights that citizens have been given in legislation that has been in place for a long time (Chapter 5). The implementation of these rights is more a question of public administration, i.e. the meticulous respect for rules with the possibility of filing a complaint with a tribunal, than of public management. Where entitlements start to weigh heavily as a consideration, there we find the limits of the applicability of public management, especially new public management.

From Table 2.4 it appears that all governments in each group of countries around the world are engaged in public resource allocation. In the statistics, this is called 'Final Government Consumption' in order to distinguish it clearly from the redistribution of income from one group to another. In principle, the public enterprises in the infrastructure sector should be outside of Final Government

Table 2.4   Resource allocation: general government consumption

	1970	1980	1995
Western Europe	14.3	18.1	18.6
Eastern Europe	15.3	10.1	17.5
North America	19.2	18.5	17.5
Central America	10.7	13.3	10.5
South America	11.1	11.2	10.3
North Africa and Middle East	17.2	19.1	21.0
Subsaharan Africa	14.1	15.2	15.0
East Asia	11.7	11.1	9.9
South Asia	11.2	8.7	12.0
Oceania	16.0	17.2	13.7
Mean	13.8	14.7	15.4
N	107	112	126

Source: World Bank 1983, 1997, 1998a.

Consumption, although this is not always the case. The size of the allocative branch of government ranges from 10 per cent of GDP to 21 per cent in the 1990s, when average scores are examined.

In several rich countries income redistribution is now the largest of the two major functions in the public sector. And it is the function that keeps growing and thus maintains public expenditures at a high level of GDP. Table 2.5 shows the country group differences in the size of the transfer payments, ranging from 1 per cent to 24 per cent.

To understand the scope of public sector management, we must add public

Table 2.5   Social security transfer payments

	1975	1985	1994
Western Europe	17.9	21.2	23.8
Eastern Europe	12.8	13.6	14.5
North America	12.7	13.8	18.0
Central America	3.3	3.3	4.0
South America	5.2	4.1	5.7
North Africa and Middle East	5.9	3.1	3.0
Subsaharan Africa	2.0	0.6	0.7
East Asia	3.7	3.6	3.7
South Asia	1.6	1.2	1.1
Oceania	12.2	9.3	10.3
Mean	8.8	7.5	8.8
N	63	92	90

Source: *The Cost of Social Security* (ILO 1992, 1998).

regulation as well as the entire sector of public enterprises, whether they are organised in public or private law form. In the future, perhaps also parts of income maintenance programmes will be placed there, if the workfare concept spreads.

The workfare state

Managerialism could enter the redistributive branch of government, if workfare notions are introduced on a major scale. However, thus far we have seen various experiments with a rather limited range and mixed results. Workfare programmes replace first and foremost unemployment benefits and social care. They do not concern each and every income maintenance programme.

As R. Solow points out, the workfare programmes are based upon a conditional form of altruism on the part of society in relation to people who do not find stable work. Government declares itself prepared to help this group of voluntary or involuntary unemployed on the condition that they display effort in finding a job. Thus, there arises a kind of principal–agent interaction between the managers of these workfare programmes and the group of people seeking income support due to a lack of stable employment. Government as the principal will provide various kinds of support, only when effort is forthcoming on the part of those in need.

Whereas the direct income support of the welfare state involved altruism to an extent that was open to criticism which focused upon a lack of effort among people without stable work, the workfare programmes do not involve the opposite position – egoism, meaning that these kinds of income support could only be made in the short run if they pay off in the long run (Solow, 1998). Workfare programmes do not have to be economically sound in the sense that they will eventually cover their costs. As, for instance, when people benefiting from them do receive stable work and contribute to the economy and pay taxes. Yet, workfare programmes are less generous than welfare state programmes in that they condition the help given to the display of effort. They tend to favour self-reliance, meaning that people should look after themselves (Solow, 1988).

Two things stand out from the evidence about the outcomes of the workfare state: (1) Workfare programmes constitute only a part of the redistributional state, as it targets people in very great need. Many income maintenance programmes have the middle classes as the bulk of the recipients, but this is not the case with the workfare state programmes. Thus, a movement towards more workfare and less welfare will not substantially reduce the costs for social security. (2) The outcomes of the running of workfare programmes indicate that much more is needed than merely effort among those in need (Nathan, 1993; Evans, 1995; Rose, 1995; Gutmann, 1998).

The costs of a workfare state include expenditures for supporting activities for those who enter these programmes, especially day care centres for parents. The results show that only a small portion of those participating in these programmes manage to get a stable job. But the positive outcome is that many do get a temporary job experience. Workfare programmes appear to require much effort from managers which is costly at the same time as it increases the insecurity of the people who live on the margins of society.

Public sector reform and the welfare state transformation

Public sector management orientated towards efficiency requires a theory of governance mechanisms in the public sector, conceived in a broad sense. It is of great concern in the welfare states, which is understandable, given their large public sectors. But public management strategies are pursued with equal fervour in the so-called welfare societies. At the moment, new public management is stronger in societies with small public sectors than in welfare states. Thus, public sector reform and welfare state reform are not quite the same phenomena, although they are related.

Public sector reform can occur as part of welfare state reform, but need not do so. And welfare state reform can utilise public sector reform in order to accomplish a radical overhaul of the system, moving the country towards the welfare society model. Or welfare state reform can use public management strategies, for instance NPM, in order to revitalise and stabilise the welfare state. NPM is being tried in both welfare states and welfare societies. It may be employed as part of a strategy to reduce the public sector. But NPM could also enter a strategy of strengthening the public sector. Thus, NPM is neutral *vis-à-vis* the right and the left.

Conclusion

The relevance of public sector management has not diminished during the two decades of hegemony for the neo-liberal market philosophy. It is true that many countries have diminished the size of their public sectors, but the need for public sector management has not gone away, all state activities being handed over to the market, as it were. On the contrary, some public expenditures have increased whereas others have diminished, meaning that the overall reduction is in many cases not a large one. However, the techniques of governance have changed, both in countries reducing their public sector and in countries maintaining it.

Public sector management includes the government activities within public resource allocation, the state enterprise sector and in public regulation schemes. Outside of public management fall macro-economic policy-making as well as most of the entitlements in the income distribution branch of government.

Public sector reform has been hectic in the 1990s in many countries, government looking for new governance techniques. Why has there been this drive, which in a few countries has manifested itself as the introduction of new public management? I argue, it is because the traditional mechanisms for public management, the bureau and the public enterprise, have been considered as in need of institutional reform.

The criticism of the bureau and the public enterprise, stated in the public choice school, has met with acceptance in both welfare societies and welfare states. In addition, traditional public regulation theory has been abandoned and new regulatory regimes have been put in place, very much due to the criticism of Chicago School Economics upon the traditional regulation model in particular and state intervention in the economy in general (Friedman, 1964; Stigler, 1988). Let us examine these themes in Part II, so that we know where we are coming from before we begin to examine NPM.

Part II

From where we come

The reforms of the public sector in the 1990s have been driven by a distinctly economistic tone, which some call economic fundamentalism (Kelsey, 1995). The reason is that there has been a prevailing perception that the existing mechanisms for public resource allocation, income redistribution and public regulation have not worked well, meaning they produce inefficient outcomes.

The emergence of new public management would be incomprehensible without a background knowledge of the criticism of the traditional institutional mechanisms employed in the public sector: the bureau, the public enterprise and the traditional schemes focusing upon entry regulation as well as licences. The so-called public choice school has offered a number of models which question these mechanisms, used by government during the seminal process of public sector expansion (Mueller, 1989). Although the freshness of the public choice criticism of a large public sector has now faded to some extent, we still must take this criticism into account.

The public choice approach may be combined with other teachings in economics, e.g. from Chicago School Economics as well as from neo-institutional or new institutional economics (Eggertson, 1990). And the criticism of public sector mechanisms in allocation, redistribution and regulation may be regarded as a theoretical foundation for the search for new institutions, as with new public management, inspired by new ideas about principal–agent interaction, asymmetric knowledge, moral hazard as well as how law and economics depend upon each other.

Thus, in this part we ask what is wrong with bureau allocation and why public enterprises do not work well and what is the chief difficulty in income maintenance programmes or within public redistribution. Chapter 3 suggests an answer to the first question.

3 The bureau

Too much X-inefficiency

Introduction

The tasks of government have tended to be performed by a special type of organisation, especially if these tasks are paid for by means of taxes. When public activities are financed over the budget, then they tend to be given an organisational structure which follows the basic principles of Weber's ideal type of a bureaucracy. We will call this organisation the 'bureau'. The bureau is to the public sector what the enterprise is to the private sector, i.e. a governance mechanism that has proved highly suitable to the tasks given to it, at least most of the time.

The bureau is an organisation that is legally a part of government and thus lacks independent legal status. It is financed by government by means of an appropriation, based upon a request by the bureau. It has been given a special set of tasks, which it tends to perform over a long time, accumulating expertise in order to satisfy the requirement of efficiency.

The bureau operates on the basis of public law instructions, given on the one hand by government and on the other hand by internal bureau documents. Bureaux populate the whole public sector, whether the country has a unitary state or a federal state, whether it is centralised or decentralised. The names for the bureau vary: 'authority', 'board', 'commission', 'agency', 'tribunal' or 'crown entity' – to just mention a few alternatives.

The bureau mechanism is the most basic governance form in the twentieth century literature on public administration. We find it analysed by all the major scholars in the classical framework. The classical framework tends to be favourable to the bureau mechanism, on the whole. It seemed to score high on values that the classical framework emphasised such as impartiality, neutrality and the observation of rules.

On the one hand, there was the Weberian positive evaluation claiming that bureaucracy promotes efficiency. On the other hand, there was the more or less profound criticism from sociologists Merton, Selznick and Crozier pointing out that bureaux may operate in a dysfunctional manner which entailed a more negative perspective, sometimes equating bureaucracy with formalism and red tape (Merton, 1957; Selznick, 1957; Crozier, 1964).

But recently the bureau has been evaluated very differently. In the public choice approach, the bureau is rejected as a mechanism for service provision. The most radical criticism of the bureau was launched by William Niskanen in 1971. Let us discuss more closely the Niskanen model of the bureau, but first we must clarify the foundation of the Niskanen attack upon public administration, the starting-point being the requirement of efficiency. What does this norm entail?

The efficiency norm

The new management philosophy has one main objective for the public sector reforms that it recommends, and that is to raise efficiency in the provision of goods and services. The means employed to achieve this goal is considerable and includes, besides privatisation, incorporation of public enterprises, the introduction of internal markets, the employment of the purchaser–provider separation, contracting out, the use of massive contracting, bench-marking, restructuring of ministries or departments, increased use of user fees as well as increases in user fees, etc.

Focusing not upon the means but upon the single objective – efficiency – one may raise a question that appears to contain a few puzzles about public sector reform in the 1990s. First, what is nature of that key objective – efficiency – which so much is focused upon? Second, why are other objectives that have figured prominently in the public sector seldom mentioned, especially equity? Finally, one may enquire into the outcomes of public sector reform, relating the objectives above – efficiency and equity – to the actually accomplished results. One would, of course, want to know what are the signs, if any, that efficiency has increased as well as whether equity has been affected at the same time, either increasing or decreasing.

Talking about efficiency in the public sector, one may either take a *micro*-perspective, focusing upon how quantities, costs and qualities have developed within one sector or even within one ministry, department or production unit. Or one may take a *macro*-perspective, attempting to make an overall assessment of public sector reform with a measuring rod like efficiency, perhaps complemented by that of equity. In Chapter 5, we will pursue the macro-perspective, and in particular focus upon the argument about a trade-off between efficiency and equity.

Economic efficiency and the public sector

To call for more efficiency through public sector reform has become commonplace, but what does it really entail? Efficiency is such a general notion that it may mean lots of things or it may simply be used because it signals something positive. Who would not wish to have more efficiency? Yet, the words 'efficiency' or 'effectiveness' or 'productivity' mean something more than a positive signal. Some key social science concepts are value-loaded concepts, meaning that they have a theoretical core but at the same time they express a value. What we wish to distil here is a core meaning of efficiency, especially when the concept is used in public sector reform.

Efficiency in economics

One may identify two more precise definitions of efficiency in economics literature, referring to solutions to allocative problems, or questions about how goods and services are to be allocated and produced. First, there is the concept of allocative efficiency, meaning that the marginal utility (MU) of a good or service is equal to its marginal cost (MC) of production.

In economic theory, the concept of allocative efficiency is decomposed into efficiency in consumption, efficiency in production and overall social efficiency. The standard explanation of allocative efficiency is the model of Pareto-optimality. Pareto-improvements in consumption or production should occur if it is possible to increase the utility for one person without decreasing the utility of another person. The norm of efficiency requires such a Pareto-superior change, or if the production of one good can be increased without decreasing the production of another, then efficiency requires such a change, because it is Pareto-superior. All kinds of market analysis is based upon Pareto's approach to efficiency, where overall social efficiency occurs when MU = MC. Note that the concept of utility and costs covers more than what markets reveal, as the Pareto approach includes not only private utility or private cost but also social utility and social cost, as with the concept of positive or negative externalities.

Second, there is a much more limited concept of economic efficiency, targeting only production costs, i.e. the supply side. When average costs in production are minimised, then there is technological efficiency, given that there is real ongoing production. In market behaviour, firms need not necessarily produce at that quantity where average costs are minimised, i.e. where the marginal cost curve cuts the average cost curve from underneath, because firms may still earn huge profits. What has been sharply contested, however, is whether firms operating in competitive markets can avoid being technologically efficient. In the long run, competitive firms would be forced to operate close to the technologically efficient quantity. Only monopolies could afford to be what is called 'X-inefficient'. Yet, this dogma in market theory was challenged in an interesting theory about X-efficiency by H. Leibenstein, claiming that all firms seek slack, i.e. enterprises do not minimise their production costs (Leibenstein, 1966, 1978).

The relevance of the concept of X-efficiency and X-inefficiency to market theory was severely questioned by Chigaco School economists (Stigler, 1976), but it has certainly been much employed in the analysis of organisations facing a non-market environment. X-efficiency is close to the notion of technological efficiency above, but X-inefficiency may be developed to cover slack in general or rents and shirking, whether in private firms or in governmental departments.

Efficiency in organisational theory

In the theory of organisations, public, private or third sector type, a more embracing conception of efficiency in used, covering all kinds of organisations, market or non-market, but which also includes a crucial distinction between internal efficiency and external efficiency. What organisations do can be evaluated both from the perspective of the organisation – the productivity of activities – as well as from the perspective of society – the impact of the activities of the organisation – the effectiveness of activities.

In organisation theory, the key distinction is that between productivity as the relationship between inputs and outputs – internal efficiency, and the benefits that organisational performance brings about for others – external efficiency. Technological efficiency above would be much closer to productivity, whereas allocative efficiency would relate more to effectiveness. The concept of efficiency in organisational studies is broad enough to include organisations which are not active in a market environment. Thus, this approach is more encompassing or broader than the approach in economics.

Productivity is basically about performance and its costs. Thus, performance is to be measured by means of indicators on outputs of various kinds ranging from the numbers of hours worked, or the number of clients received or treated, or the size of a group rendered service to. The denominator to which output is to be related comprises all the inputs that are used in order to arrive at outputs. Inputs could be measured by various physical indicators, or they could be counted in money terms which would give the definition of cost productivity as output/costs. Productivity tends to be measured over time, which calls for methods to hold costs constant in money terms, i.e. control against the occurrence of inflation. Thus we have productivity as:

$$(P) \qquad \frac{\text{Output}}{\text{Input}} \times \frac{\text{Input}}{\text{Costs}} = \frac{\text{Output}}{\text{Costs}}$$

Effectiveness has been defined somewhat loosely as 'the extent of goal achievement' (Etzioni, 1964). Basically effectiveness refers to outcomes, or the results of organisational performance. Outcomes may sometimes be measured in terms of money value. It is basically about the benefits that people outside an organisation may derive from the output of the organisation, however these may be measured. *Effectiveness* would include:

$$(E) \qquad \frac{\text{Outcomes}}{\text{Outputs}} \times \frac{\text{Benefits}}{\text{Outcomes}} = \frac{\text{Benefits}}{\text{Outputs}}$$

Combining productivity as output/costs with effectiveness as benefits/outputs would allow us to arrive at efficiency = benefits/costs, or the cost-benefit approach to efficiency:

$$(C/B) \qquad \frac{\text{Output}}{\text{Costs}} \times \frac{\text{Benefits}}{\text{Output}} = \frac{\text{Benefits}}{\text{Costs}}$$

The strength of the cost-benefit approach is that it may embrace all kinds of organisations, in particular non-market organisations like public departments or bureaux. The weakness of the cost-benefit approach is that it is often difficult to measure the benefit component, especially when there is no evaluation by means of markets. Thus, what this approach gains in relation to the narrow approach by covering all kinds of organisations, it tends to lose in sharpness. It has proven difficult to find a method that reveals the true utility of something that an organisation provides for, especially in a non-market environment (Mishan, 1981).

In studies of organisational efficiency, one often sees a deliberate limitation of the ambition to cover only internal efficiency or productivity, because it tends to be measurable. Yet, the organisational approach to efficiency is a real extension of the limited focus of economists on organisations operating in a market environment.

Narrow and broad definitions

In economics and in organisational theory, the concept of efficiency refers to production or output and its value or the utility of the output. Either one measures how much output can be produced with a certain amount of input, or one measures the value of the output in terms of utility. In economics, the focus is upon market operations, meaning that costs and benefits can be measured by the same measuring rod, namely money. The efficiency of a market organisation would be revealed in its profits. For a non-market organisation, estimating efficiency is more difficult, because there is no common measuring rod to run through all the parameters. Thus, one tends to rely on measures of physical productivity on the one hand and surveys about consumer or client utility (U) or benefits (B) on the other hand.

One may distinguish between two Pareto concepts of efficiency. On the one hand, there is absolute efficiency as a static concept. On the other hand, there is a dynamic concept of efficiency, involving comparisons between two states, i.e. relative efficiency. The Pareto conception of efficiency leans strongly upon maximisation. It denotes a state as efficient if, and only if, it is not possible to either produce more of one single good leaving the production of all other goods unchanged or consume more of one good, leaving the consumption of all other goods unchanged.

Technological efficiency or productivity would be applications of the Pareto approach in supply, maximising output in relation to inputs. Allocative efficiency or social efficiency would go together with effectiveness focusing upon Pareto-efficiency also at the demand side of the economy in addition to the supply side. Thus, social efficiency requires that production is increased up until $MU = MC$ in allocative efficiency, or $MB = MC$ in cost-benefit analysis.

The Pareto approach is merely aggregative, and never distributive. Chapter 5 examines how distributional criteria enter the debate, as it matters not only how much is produced but also how the income is distributed, income and production being measures of the same underlying entity. After all, an efficient output or income has to be divided somehow – the so-called cake problem.

Gulf between financing and spending

Any allocation of goods and services in the public sector has a distribution of these goods and services attached to it. In addition allocation and distribution interact, meaning that certain efficient outcomes will not be satisfactory from a distributional point of view, or the other way around. Thus arises the possibility of an efficiency–equity trade-off.

A number of distributional criteria may be employed in relation to the public provision of goods and services. On the one hand, there are the user fee criteria of various kinds: charges, benefit taxes, involving an effort to have the people who get the goods and services pay in full for their utilisation. On the other hand, there are need criteria or rights criteria that distribute the goods and services not in accordance with the willingness to pay but on the basis of other criteria. When needs or rights are employed, then the allocation tends to be paid for by means of taxation schemes based upon the ability to pay. The applicability of these distributional criteria differs in relation to the kind of good or service allocated in the public sector, as benefit taxation seems reasonable in relation to divisible goods and services whereas ability-to-pay taxation would be more appropriate in relation to indivisible goods and services.

Efficiency reasons could be used against benefit taxation. Some goods and services cannot be priced and sold off to the purchaser due to the free rider problem. Other goods and services should not be priced at all, because enjoying them carries virtually no marginal cost. Finally, pricing goods and services the consumption of which leads to positive external effects may lead to an under-supply of these goods.

Government might wish to make certain goods and services – merit goods – freely available to special groups with needs that would not be properly looked after if prices were used to cover the entire cost for these goods and services. Government would definitely want to do so if groups were entitled to help in these respects. Ability-to-pay taxation is the means governments predominantly use to pay for the provision of goods and services in the so-called soft sector. The business sector is not problematic from this aspect, as it can in principle be fully financed by means of charges or user fees.

The gulf between payment and utilisation remains a typical feature of the public sector, especially the soft sector. Decisions about financing are taken separately from decisions about spending. The logic of decisions about taxation deals with matters that involve deliberations about how a spending total can be paid for by various revenues. The spending totals are decided elsewhere and at other times. Payment and benefits are only weakly coupled together in the public sector. Moreover, various forms of taxation placed upon different people and objects are on one occasion used to pay for a bundle of goods and services in the public sector that are on another occasion allocated to a variety of people.

Contracting and efficiency

New public management places a huge responsibility for public sector operations with politicians and managers, contracting between each other about the provision of goods and services. Whereas public administration created order by means of huge bulks of public law, administered by bureaucrats and professionals, new public management employs contracting because it will be conducive to efficiency. While the public policy school either relied upon top-down implementation – steering – or bottom-up implementation – discretion – new public management sees efficiency in service provision as forthcoming from voluntary contracting on the part of rational decision-makers. Thus, contracting for outputs is to result in allocative and technological efficiency.

In relation to new public management the crucial question is the connection between contracting in behaviour and efficiency in outcomes given the institutions of NPM. If that tie is not as tight as new public management claims, then contracting could fail as the great promoter of efficiency. What we face here is the problem whether rational politicians and managers will find and implement first-best contracts, or Pareto-optimal contracts. Thus, Chapter 11 asks: how would efficient contracts be forthcoming in new public management? This way of posing the question takes us into the logic of contracting, relating rationality of actors to efficiency in outcomes.

Niskanen's puzzle

The Niskanen model is a public choice theory, which assumes that the bureau mechanism is associated with the rational pursuit of self-interests among the administrators and professionals who supply the bureau activities – the supply side – in relation to the politicians who pay for the bureau activities – the demand side. Assuming merely that people working in the bureau maximise their self-interest, Niskanen derives a sensational result about the size of the bureau, it being the equilibrium outcome of the interaction between demand and supply (Niskanen, 1971).

Examining a model, one should distinguish between questions about the logic of the model and questions about the empirical applicability of the model. First, one may examine the consistency of the model in order to check whether it generates predictions that are coherent, harbouring some mechanism that explain why things are as they are. Second, one may examine whether the model is empirically true in the sense that its predictions are not only consistent with each other but are also confirmed by empirical research.

A phenomenon can be explained by alternative assumptions in various theories. Which theory is the correct one can only be decided by means of an examination of the test implications of the alternative theories. If the test implications are indeed true, then it is likely that the assumptions apply. Each and every set of assumptions in a theory can only be tested by means of the implications derived from the set. It is the predictions of a model that one tests empirically, and not the assumptions themselves (Friedman, 1953).

The bureau would be funded exclusively by tax money in the form of a yearly appropriation from the government to the bureau. The demand for the activities of the bureau thus reflects the utility function of the politicians in power, voting for the budget. Thus, we could have a demand function, i.e. the total benefits (TB) as a function of quantity according to the following function:

(1) $TB = 10q - \frac{1}{2}q^2$

TB or total demand is here modelled as a strict function of quantity q, which involves a normal form utility function, describing the value of the activities q of the bureau as involving the law of decreasing marginal value.

Assuming that such a utility function (1) is admissible, then it describes the total utility of the bureau as raising rapidly when the size of the bureau operations is small. When these activities have reached a certain size, then the increase in utility of additional new activities becomes smaller and smaller in order eventually to turn negative. Such a utility function (1) is standard in the theory of goods and services allocated in the market.

The supply function in Niskanen is equally simple. He assumes that total cost (TC) will rise with quantity produced, e.g. according to the following equation:

(2) $TC = 5q + q^2$

One can discuss whether the cost curve for bureau operations has one curvature or another. This depends on the various activities that bureaux may engage in. What is important for Niskanen is only to establish that the cost curve (TC) has an upward sloping curvature, which most cost curves tend to have in the short run, also for firms operating in markets (Niskanen, 1976). Figure 3.1 brings together the models (1) and (2), portraying the demand and supply for a bureau.

There is nothing exceptional about Figure 3.1. Actually, it could be a model about the demand and supply of a firm producing a standard type of good or service, involving no economies of scale. What is sensational is the equilibrium solution that Niskanen derives from the interaction between demand and supply.

The optimal quantity supplied in Figure 3.1 is where marginal utility is equal to marginal cost, or where the distance between total benefits and total costs is the largest. The Pareto-optimal quantity is at the quantity where marginal utility is equal to marginal cost. Taking the first derivative of (1) and (2), we arrive at the optimal output Q:

(3) $Q: 10 - q = 5 + 2q$
i.e. where $q = 5/3$.

Now comes the surprise. Niskanen denies that the Pareto-optimal output is forthcoming in budget allocation using the bureau mechanism. Instead, he claims that the outcome of the interaction between demand and supply will be an entirely different one, namely that quantity, for which total demand is equal to total cost, i.e.

(4) q nis : TD = TS,
which occurs where q = 10/3

At the Niskanen equlibrium the quantity supplied is twice the optimal quantity with attending huge efficiency losses. Something is badly wrong with such a mechanism for public sector determination.

How can Niskanen arrive at this stunning result? As it appears from Figure 3.2, showing the demand for public services and the marginal costs of supplying these services, the bureau activities would be much too large in relation to the Pareto-optimal output.

At the quantity q = 10/3, the Niskanen quantity, there is a heavy loss involved. The Niskanen outcome is always to the right of the optimal outcome Q, and can be as far away from the optimal output as twice that quantity. The Pareto-optimal output is at MB = MC, whereas the Niskanen output is at TD = TC.

If the Niskanen model is correct, then bureaux always run substantial losses. They tend to operate activities that are twice as large as necessary, resulting in what is referred to as 'allocative inefficiencies'. Thus, much of the resources spent upon the bureaux could be better employed elsewhere.

One can make a number of variations on the Niskanen theme by drawing the

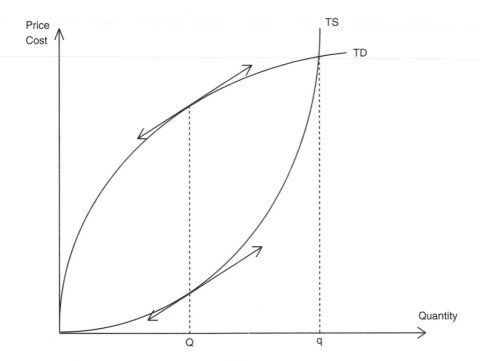

Figure 3.1   The Niskanen model 1.

curves in Figure 3.2 somewhat differently. What is essential, however, is to discuss whether the model is correct. This involves two different kinds of deliberations. First, we must discuss whether it is logically consistent. Second, we must look for empirical evidence in favour of the model.

Focusing first upon model consistency, we must discuss the following question: why would politicians end up demanding more, even double as much, than what maximises their gain, given that we assume that they also behave rationally, i.e. maximise their own interests?

Niskanen's error

Basically, Niskanen's argument is that the size of the public sector tends to be too large. This involves one type of inefficiency, causing losses to society, from mere oversupply. Notice that Niskanen is not saying that costs are too high or that unit costs are not minimised due to the accumulation of slack within the providers. Here, we have allocative inefficiency in the standard sense of MC > MB at the supplied quantity q.

At this quantity, the Niskanen equilibrium, society makes a loss from overproduction and the loss has to be borne first and foremost by the politicians, demanding too much activity from the bureau. The bureau makes a gain in the

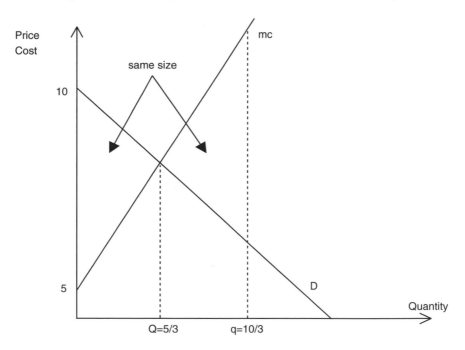

Figure 3.2   The Niskanen model 2.

Note: Figure 3.2 is derived from Figure 3.1 by taking the first derivative of the total demand curve, which gives MB, and the total supply curve, which gives MC.

sense that it can expand its output and be paid for all of its costs, including unnecessary employees. Evidently, the cause of what is wrong (social inefficiency) must be sought on the demand side, or more particularly how demand is forthcoming in the budgetary process.

The regular budgetary process that occurs on a yearly basis has been the object of different interpretations, which all focus upon the interaction between bureau requests on the one hand and parliamentary appropriations on the other hand (Fenno, 1966; Manley, 1975). That this interaction between request and appropriation involves strategic and tactical behaviour has been known for a long time, but it proved difficult to capture it by means of a simple model until Niskanen suggested that the appropriation is the demand side and the request is the supply side in a standard economic model sense.

The most well-known budgetary models derive from incrementalism (Wildavsky, 1964, 1972), which model the interaction between request and appropriation in accordance with the cognitive limits approach by Simon, i.e. assuming bounded rationality and not self-interest maximisation. Incremental budget models portray the use of standard operating procedures in order to construct requests and cut requests down to appropriations. Niskanen's model is much closer to game theory than the incremental budget models, assuming perfect rationality on the part of the players.

Now, why would politicians play this sort of a game where what they lose can be identified with the potential consumer surplus? It would clearly have been better for the politicians to appropriate a much smaller budget. Why do they not do just that?

It should be pointed out that Niskanen's result is so stunning and improbable given ordinary rational choice theory that one must really ask how he can reach such a surprising conclusion. It cannot be reached simply by ordinary demand and supply analysis, which after all informs us that there is a unique solution, i.e. the optimal Q at $MB = MC$. Why cannot politicians implement the efficient or the so-called first-best solution?

In order to arrive at the surprise result, Niskanen must add yet another assumption to his two equations, namely that public budgeting employs another decision rule than ordinary utility maximisation, which is $MB = MC$. Niskanen claims that in the public sector budgets are determined using the decision rule: $TB \geqslant TC$.

Only if this assumption about $TB \geqslant TC$ applies, can Niskanen derive his result that all public budgeting, funding in particular bureaux, involves allocative or social inefficiency. But why assume such an awkward decision rule that politicians set the budget where total benefits are equal to total costs? How could it be defended theoretically or made plausible empirically?

Assuming perfect information and self-interest maximisation on the part of all participants in the budgetary process, the equilibrium outcome is the first best solution, resulting from the use of the decision rule that $MB = MC$. Then, where does the decision rule that $TB \geqslant TC$ come from?

Asymmetric information

According to methodology, the test of a theory is the confrontation of its implications with the facts (Friedman, 1953). Thus, no matter how implausible the
Niskanen assumption about the decision rule employed in public budgeting may
be, the test of the Niskanen theory is whether it correctly predicts the size of the
public sector, stating that it tends to be twice as large as it should be.

Yet, although one cannot test the assumptions of a theory directly, it remains
to be explained why Niskanen uses an assumption that is at odds with his
rational choice starting-point. Why would utility maximising politicians not
employ the ordinary decision rule in economic behaviour? Politicians would gain
from optimising. Then, why not set quantity at MB = MC?

This counter-argument against Niskanen is a very serious one, because the
assumption about the use of a decision rule like TB $\geq$ TC is entirely without
foundation so long as other considerations have not been brought in. It has to be
backed by another assumption about the logic of public budgeting, i.e. we need
more assumptions in order to derive the surprise result.

Since Niskanen employs rational choice theory, then he cannot lean towards
bounded rationality or use theories that employ assumptions that are outside of
the rational choice framework. He can only resort to a rational choice theory
that starts from an assumption about information asymmetry or information
advantage, i.e. a theory about contracting between unequals like the
principal–agent model.

If one models the interaction between the politicians as paying for the allocation of a good or service by a bureau, where the latter is at the same time an
agent of the former which is a principal, then one may arrive at the peculiar
decision-making of politicians when appropriating a budget for a bureau. In
principal–agent interaction, which has a longer duration than merely so-called
spot-on contracting, agents tend to have more information than principals,
modelled as the occurrence of adverse selection and moral hazard (Stiglitz,
1989; Rasmusen, 1994).

What is crucial, then, is the assumption about the occurrence of asymmetric
information. If one does not assume asymmetrical information, then the
Niskanen puzzle simply does not arise, as politicians would use the normal decision rule of MR = MC. Asymmetric information may occur in any kind of
economic interaction, but it tends to be characteristic of principal–agent interaction due to the duration in time of the interaction.

If the politicians as principals face the bureau as an agent where the latter has
an information advantage over the former, then the bureau could use its advantage in order to capture a quasi-rent, as principal–agent theory predicts.
According to Niskanen, the bureau will search for this quasi-rent in an appropriation that is larger than the optimal one, because a larger budget will allow the
bureau to expand its activities and enjoy better conditions such as extra
employees and premises.

However, there is a decisive counter-argument: why would the rational strategy of the bureau be budget maximisation, given that the bureau as agent has an information advantage against the politicians or parliament as the principal? The quasi-rent could be captured by a much less onerous strategy than TB ≥ TC. What, if anything, does a bureau maximise?

The virtues and vices of bureaux

Let us first ask whether motivation is a real problem in bureaux. Niskanen's theory is the hard core public choice theory about bureaucracy. It is meant as the definitive refutation of Weber's famous argument that bureaucracy is the most effective institution for providing public services, especially in the soft sector.

Whereas Weber assumed that bureaucrats would have a special motivation to perform their tasks – vocation – Niskanen assumes a private utility function with bureaucrats, concerning salary, prestige, power, which are all linearly dependent upon the size of the bureau. The question of the motivation of bureaucrats has been much researched, especially in organisation theory, focusing either upon administrators or professionals. One finds several versions of the two themes: vocation or the public interest on the one hand and egoism on the other, as well as other alternatives too, as e.g. with Kaufman, 1976, in Wilson, 1989 or with Dunleavy, 1991.

The Niskanen conclusion that bureaucrats seek as large bureaux as possible has been challenged by pointing out that it is not in agreement with one often observed fact about bureaucrats, namely that they dislike uncertainty and risk. Rapid growth of a bureau along the Parkinson model of bureaucratisation is, strictly speaking, not in the best interests of the bureaucrats themselves.

Assuming instead that bureaucrats avoid uncertainty and risk, one may arrive at an entirely different conclusion from Niskanen. Thus, Wilson, using organisational theory, argues that bureaux search for stability:

> All organisations seek the stability and comfort that comes from relying on standard operating procedures – 'SOPs'. When results are unknown or equivocal, bureaus will have no incentive to alter those SOPs so as to better achieve their goals, only an incentive to modify them to conform to externally imposed constraints. The SOPs will represent an internally defined equilibrium that reconciles the situational imperatives, professional norms, bureaucratic ideologies, peer-group expectations, and (if present) leadership demands unique to that agency.
>
> (Wilson, 1989: 375)

Both the assumptions and the implications in the Wilson model of bureaucracy are far apart from the Niskanen model. Wilson's image of bureaucracy is much closer to the well-known analysis of Kaufman than to the public choice image of the bureau.

H. Kaufman examined bureaucracies in a few empirical studies, the findings of which hardly support the conclusion of Niskanen about bureau maximisation.

They do not lend credibility to the assumption about the realisation of self-interests in the form of budget maximisation (Kaufman, 1976, 1981).

It has been suggested that what matters to bureaucrats is not the size of the bureau but the status of the bureau, which tends to be linked more with its tasks than with its number of sections or the total size of its employees (Dunleavy, 1991). Bureau shaping would be the basic motivation, not bureau maximisation.

One may explain a phenomenon by using alternative assumptions in different theories. At the end of the day, what counts is the confrontation with the empirical evidence. One can never test the assumptions of a theory directly, but one can test a theory indirectly by investigating whether its test implications receive empirical confirmation (Friedman, 1953).

Yet, let us assume that bureaucrats are driven by the ambition to maximise their self-interests, and capture quasi-rents whenever possible, meaning we accept the Niskanen starting-point and not the Weberian claim about vocation as a peculiar motivation in the public sector. However, the conclusion about budget maximisation does not follow, strictly speaking.

Bureaucrats could find it easier to capture quasi-rent by simply raising unit costs. Why expand output? Producing up to twice as much as the optimal size would put enormous pressure on bureaux to deliver huge quantities of services. The same private objectives can in fact be secured simply by delivering a smaller amount but not producing at the lowest possible cost.

Niskanen cannot answer that unit costs that are significantly higher than the lowest feasible ones, including considerable amounts of fat or slack in the organisation, would tend to be revealed by the politicians. If there is asymmetric information, the agent knowing more about marginal costs and marginal benefits than the principal, then the politicians as principal cannot find out or reveal that there is slack.

The basic problem in bureau supply is not budget maximisation or the delivery of too large a quantity of services. It is the occurrence of X-inefficiencies. In addition, if one assumes the occurrence of asymmetric information in order to explain the existence of X-inefficiency, then one may wish to point out that it could result from the mere lack of competition.

X-inefficiency

Whereas allocative efficiency focuses upon the quantity of services where marginal benefits equal marginal costs, technological efficiency investigates whether the use of inputs results in the largest possible output. Harvey Leibenstein identified the concept of X-efficiency to denote that use of inputs which maximises the outputs. The skill that allows an organisation to minimise its costs and thus reach the highest possible ratio between inputs and outputs is this X-capacity that everybody speaks about but nobody knows exactly what it is – as Tolstoy spelled it out once in his novel *War and Peace* (1867–1869). This X-capacity to employ the inputs in the most efficient manner is what characterises the winner among organisations, in peace as well as in war.

Now, the Leibenstein theory about X-efficiency in organisations from 1966 implies that organisations, private or public, do not achieve X-efficiency. Organisations for various reasons feed upon X-inefficiency, or the generation of slack (Leibenstein, 1966). Slack helps organisations in various ways to survive. Let me quote from a recent book on X-inefficiency, distinguishing it from allocative inefficiency:

> another type of inefficiency that is manifest as excess unit costs of production among firms sheltered from competitive pressure. Being of an unknown nature, Leibenstein referred to it as X-inefficiency. He believed then, as evidence has shown since, that the costs of X-inefficiency exceed those of allocative efficiency.
>
> (Frantz, 1997: 2)

Bureaux are perhaps the kind of organisations that are most protected from market pressures of all kinds of organisations, at least if they are funded through general taxation as in the standard budgetary process. Due to the absence of competition, we may thus expect unit costs or prices to be substantially higher than the minimisation of costs implies.

When there is fat in the organisation, life tends to be easier and more agreeable – doing less, feeling better. Not only are there redundant resources that can be used to increase long-term survival, but slack can also be spent upon the employees in the form of fringe benefits. Figure 3.3 portrays the occurrence of X-inefficiency, assuming constant marginal cost curves, where in this example $MC1 = 6$.

Figure 3.3 shows that raising the unit price of a public service and thus effecting a considerable X-inefficiency could generate the same amount of extra money for the bureau as the Niskanen budget maximising strategy. Bureaux will achieve at least as good a position if they add to unit costs putting prices high while doing little, or at least not more, as when they budget-maximise.

In order to inflict upon the politicians a similar loss as in Niskanen budgeting, the bureau needs only raise costs from $MC1$ in Figure 3.3 to $MC2$, i.e. it must determine quantity such that the two areas indicated in Figure 3.3 have the same area size.

The X-inefficient quantity of output is similar to the monopoly position in market allocation, involving too little output and too high costs, whereas the Niskanen quantity of output simply involves too much output. In both cases, there is loss that the politicians must cover. At the Niskanen quantity the loss arises from too large a quantity supplied, whereas when there is X-inefficiency the loss arises from too high unit costs. Which theory is correct: the X-inefficiency theory or the Niskanen theory? Let us examine the empirical evidence about efficiency, internal and external, of the bureau.

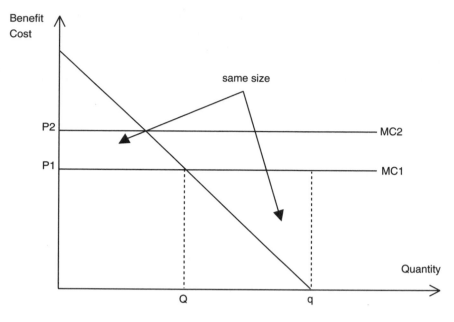

Figure 3.3   X-inefficiency in budget allocation.

Evaluating the evidence

Frankly speaking, we know of no empirical study that has been able to corroborate the Niskanen effect, i.e. that public supply is in reality twice as large as the optimal supply. However, numerous studies indicate the occurrence of X-inefficiencies or too high prices (P2–P1) (Borcherding, 1977, 1984; Borcherding *et al.*, 1985; Mueller, 1989; Boyne, 1998; Hodge, 2000).

Evaluating efficiency in bureau supply, one may target either the productivity of the bureau or the effectiveness of the bureau. Whereas productivity is to be observed in the analysis of outputs/inputs, effectiveness can only be revealed by looking at the outcomes benefits of the bureau operations. Now, Niskanen predicts that the standard bureau will be twice as large as the optimal bureau. It is thus basically an argument about the size of the bureau outputs, not their unit costs.

However, almost all productivity studies of bureaux indicate that they have a cost disadvantage. The X-inefficiency of bureaux appears in two kinds of studies. First, there are the cost comparisons between bureaux delivering the same kind of services. In such relative cost comparisons, one tends to arrive at huge differences in unit price, which can only to a certain extent be explained as a variation in service quality or quantity.

Second, there are the comparisons between public and private providers when this is possible and the public provider is a bureau. Such cost comparisons reveal almost always that the bureau does somewhat less at a higher unit cost price. However, such comparisons do not disclose much differences in service quantities or that the bureau would allocate twice as much as its private counterpart.

Conclusion

During the seminal process of government growth in the twentieth century, one relied very much upon the Weberian mechanism of a bureau, providing the services demanded by politicians in the first place and the electorate in the second place. Weber identified the institutional requirements of a bureau, which were entered into administrative law in various ways in different countries. The bureau was what the firm represented in the private sector, i.e. the basic mechanism for service provision.

Doubts about the efficiency and rationality of the bureau mechanism were soon raised within the theory of organisations, but it was not until the public choice school launched its attack upon the Weberian model that the bureau model began to be regarded as in need of revision. The key critique came from the Niskanen model of the bureau, though this involves a grave exaggeration.

The problem of the bureau is instead to be found by its constant tendency to display X-inefficiency, i.e. higher units costs than necessary. The bureau is simply not cost effective, running slack or simply accumulating waste. The basis weakness of the bureau model is its reliance upon long-term contracting, which together with opportunistic behaviour or asymmetric knowledge open for the possibility of shirking.

The Niskanen model is not plausible. Assuming that actors maximise their self-interests, the supply side interests could be satisfied in a more simple fashion by raising unit costs and reducing quantity supplied. The key concept is not allocative inefficiency but X-inefficiency according to the Leibenstein interpretation. This concept is also very relevant when it comes to understanding the failure of the traditional public enterprise.

4 The public enterprise

Not socially useful

Introduction

One of the most conspicuous reforms of the public sector has been the restructuring of public enterprises. Since public enterprises tend to be huge in the infrastructure sector where they serve large numbers of customers, major reforms of them become politicised quickly, creating highly divisive issues. When public enterprises are incorporated or privatised, then the restructuring means that thousands of employees have reason to fear that they may lose their jobs sooner or later.

Yet, despite all the controversy surrounding the reforms of the public enterprises, this type of public sector reform has been very successful in almost all countries that embarked upon restructuring their public enterprises. The traditional public enterprise hardly exists any longer, at least not within the OECD countries. In some countries, the huge state enterprises have been privatised completely, meaning that they have been sold off to private investors. In other countries, governments have been less inclined to divest themselves once and for all of these firms, instead reforming their institutional identity by means of the incorporation strategy, or the creation of public joint-stock companies, where government is a majority owner of the equity (Thynne, 1994).

Actually, various countries have different legal ways of identifying the status of corporations. This institutional variety cannot be covered or analysed here. The aim of this chapter is to provide an understanding of why the traditional public enterprise has been done away with, regardless of the new institutional form of recognition. What has happened in almost all OECD countries is that public enterprises have been transformed into joint-stock companies, which is not a category in public law but in private law. Why is the public joint-stock company a superior governance form to the traditional public enterprise?

Rationale of the public enterprise

Many of the traditional public enterprises employed huge numbers of people, operated on the basis of massive physical investments and often ran yearly deficits. These characteristics set these firms off from other businesses. And they constituted at the same time their rationale, because only government could provide the needed capital and cover the losses at the same time as government could use these 'giants' for employment purposes, for instance in regional or industrial policy efforts.

The traditional public enterprise was active in the business part of the public sector, i.e. in the sector where revenues are raised through user fees. In practice, this meant that they were engaged in infrastructure activities where traditional economic wisdom recommended state intervention in order to undo monopoly tendencies (Sherman, 1989; Spulber, 1989; Tirole, 1993). The traditional public enterprises included the postal service, railroad and buses, airlines, telecommunications, energy as well as water and sewage. Some of the enterprises handling these services were very large indeed.

The traditional public enterprise had a few distinctive characteristics, including: (1) The employment of low prices in order not to make profits but to decide prices so that they covered costs only; (2) Numerous employees in order to provide work for regions or localities where private initiatives were weak; (3) Subsidies or yearly contributions from the budget in order to cover losses; (4) The lack of rate of return criteria on either assets or operating activities; and (5) The dependency upon a ministry for the making of major decisions. How these features were institutionalised in various countries reflected their legal traditions, as some countries allowed for more enterprise discretion than others.

The public enterprises in the business sector may be separated from government-owned industries in the market sector. In most countries, governments own and operate some firms which adhere to the logic of the market, i.e. they are profit-making enterprises. Thus, governments have run car industries as well as coal and steel industries. Their logic is a different one from the traditional public enterprise, as they had to base their strategies upon operating in competitive markets.

A large payroll is hardly an end in itself, especially if it results in substantial deficits, meaning a negative rate of return on massive capital investments. Public enterprises must have a rationale, i.e. an argument stating that their pros outweigh their cons. The positive argument(s) in favour of public enterprises were outlined in two different theories.

Infrastructure

First, there is the argument that the advantages of the public enterprise are to be found within the theory of infrastructure. Here, it used to be stated that a need for huge and long-term capital investments as well as the rationality of accepting prices that did not cover average costs implied the need for public enterprise, at least so the traditional theory of public regulation argued (Viscusi *et al.* 1992; Tirole, 1993).

If there was no public enterprise put into place for handling infrastructure services, then they would be taken over by private firms, using their market power to create a natural monopoly. Thus, the choice was either private sector inefficiencies or the use of the public enterprise, which would allow government to steer away from a private monopoly. According to this theory, public enterprises were extrinsically good because they avoided an even worse evil, namely private monopolies. This argument for public enterprises has been used in almost all countries.

Firm excellence

Second, there was the notion of public enterprises as an intrinsic good, because they would be the ideal type of an enterprise in a country, on which private firms should model themselves. This argument used to be central in the industrial policy theory (Johnson, 1984).

Public enterprises as the leading businesses in a country was an idea developed within economic nationalism, or the theory that gave the state a major role in economic development. This argument in favour of public enterprises has been employed in the countries that were attracted to economic nationalism as a politico-economic regime, e.g. France, Italy, Spain, Portugal, Latin America, India and South East Asia including Japan (Lane and Ersson, 1997).

I now spell out why these two arguments in favour of public enterprises are no longer accepted. The new theory about public joint-stock companies may be seen as a response to globalisation.

The first argument public enterprises undoing private monopolies was undermined by the new ideas about regulation that Chicago School Economics initiated (Stigler, 1988). The second argument about public enterprises as models of excellence proved difficult to uphold even in the country where it was driven to its most logical conclusion, i.e. France. Globalisation sets limits to the applicability of a politico-economic regime like economic nationalism, especially if the country is part of a regional integration mechanism with explicit rules against state intervention in enterprises, be these public or private.

Let us develop the criticism of these two basic arguments for the public enterprise a little bit more.

The case for monopoly intervention

The occurrence of private monopolies presents a challenge to government, because it involves inefficiencies. Theoretically, resource allocation could be improved upon, leaving all parties involved better off. Then, why should government not intervene? Perhaps because it is practically difficult to accomplish this Pareto improvement. Let us explain.

Private monopolies occur when firms have market power, which is only forthcoming in certain market structures, if the state has not introduced a legal monopoly. Real monopolies or so-called natural monopolies arise where there are economies of scale, and economies of product scope. When these two conditions apply, then one firm can supply the whole market at the lowest possible unit price. But will the firm do that? The answer is no.

Given the situation outlined in Figure 4.1, firms have no incentives in pricing the quantities supplied at the Pareto optimal price, i.e. where MC = D. At the optimally supplied quantity, Q, the firm would make no profits, but instead run at a loss, since price does not cover average cost due to the huge investments that are connected with the phenomenon of decreasing marginal cost. At marginal cost equals demand, firms cannot recover their huge investments, as price is lower than average cost.

The firm faces the problem of maximising its revenues, which it solves by finding the quantity where the marginal revenue equals the marginal cost. Suppose that demand and supply can be described as in Chapter 3, i.e. with the following functions of q:

(1) $TD = 10q - \frac{1}{2}q^2$

and

(2) $TC = 5q + q^2$

Then, the firm calculates total revenue as q times price:

(3) $TR = q(10 - q) = 10q - q^2$

as well as marginal revenue as:

(4) $MR = 10 - 2q$

Then, it decides q, or the amount to allocate, by the decision rule:

$MR = MC$, i.e.

(5) $10 - 2q = 5 + 2q$

which results in a quantity, q = 5/4, which is different (and less) than that given by the decision rule which gives the Pareto optimal quantity Q.

The quantity supplied under monopoly will be sharply lower than the optimal quantity, and price will be sharply higher, resulting in a huge profit for the firm (see the shaded area in Figure 4.1).

Monopolies present two allocative problems. First, there are dead-weight losses, which concern both the producer and the consumer, implying that the quantity allocated must be Pareto-inferior. Second, there is the economic rent that the producer captures in the form of an excessive price, cutting deep into the consumer surplus. This is a distributional matter which is outside of Paretian considerations. What, if anything, should government do?

Enter the mechanism of a public enterprise. Government could look upon the public enterprise as a tool for removing the private monopoly, which is embarrassing from the point of efficiency as well as distribution. There are two possible solutions, both involving the public enterprise achieving a Pareto-improvement. Either the public enterprise is instructed to supply the optimal

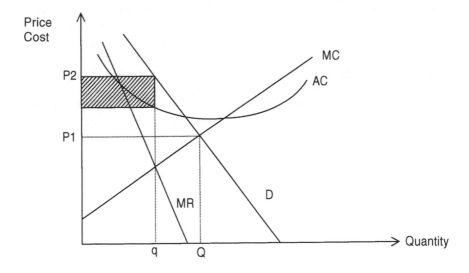

Figure 4.1 Monopoly allocation.

quantity, government covering the loss to the firm by means of a subsidy over the budget. Or government orders the public enterprise to choose a so-called second-best solution, i.e. failing to reach a Pareto-optimal or first-best solution, one tries something as close as feasible to that, i.e. where price = average cost.

The theory of second-best solutions to allocative problems argues that a second-best solution involves more than simply changing one parameter, meaning that second-best solutions can become very tricky (Lipsey and Lancaster, 1956). The standard second-best solution using a public enterprise to remove private monopoly is to employ so-called Ramsey prices, which would be a price where average costs are covered but not more – see Figure 4.1.

Public enterprises exist because they are socially useful. This is the implication of the analysis above. Public enterprises could dramatically lower the cost to the consumer, allocating the Pareto optimal quantity or close to that quantity Q. This is all theory though. We must discuss whether the implementation of such an ideal solution is at all feasible.

Traditional regulation and the argument against monopoly intervention

In practice, the public enterprise will move close to the monopoly point because it is the best solution for the enterprise. At this quantity it may maximise its X-inefficiency. The government may argue that it could accept this solution on the condition that it receives the excessive profits, i.e. the rent is transferred from the enterprise to the state. But why would the enterprise do that? In reality, there will ensue a struggle between government, the public enterprise and the public over how the consumer surplus is to be divided. Three solutions are conceivable:

1 The consumer takes all: if government instructs and achieves that public enterprise uses the Ramsey price, then one would employ cost prices, meaning that the allocated quantity would be large and the price low.
2 The enterprise takes all: if the enterprise can use a scheme of perfect price competition over the entire quantity allocated, then it would maximise its profits, the producer rent seizing the entire consumer surplus.
3 The government takes all: government could require that the public enterprise transfers all of its rent to the state, for instance stating that the enterprise must pay a high dividend on the capital that the state has placed with the enterprise.

The likely outcome of these three possibilities is that the public enterprise takes the huge part of the gain, due to the occurrence of asymmetric information. The public enterprise will capture this rent by the use of strategies that entail running up X-inefficiencies.

A private enterprise would benefit from a monopoly position by having windfall profits. Thus, it would still be interested in keeping running costs as low as possible, because the profits can be transferred to the owners of the enterprise. However, a public enterprise would have a somewhat different incentive structure, as the potential profit would go to the public, i.e. to each and everyone. The difficulty involved is typically analysed by means of principal–agent theory (Stiglitz, 1989).

Public enterprises and principal–agent interaction

The relationship between government and its public enterprises is a classical case of principal–agent interaction. The principal (government) wants the agent (enterprise) to accomplish a mission for it, but where the agent will demand compensation in one form or the other, which reduces the utility for the principal (Ricketts, 1987).

In one respect, the public enterprise is totally different from a private firm. All its profits belong to the state, i.e. there are no individual owners of equity. Thus, it does not make sense for the public enterprise to maximise its profits, because they would automatically end up with government as the residual owner.

Public enterprises, accordingly, should use the economic rent for its own purposes, i.e. it should run slack. The logical strategy of the enterprise is to maximise X-inefficiency, allowing itself waste as long as it benefits its employees. Public enterprises will never be efficient, because it is not in their interest to be so.

Public enterprises will not minimise their costs, because they do not stand to gain from such a strategy. Government can order the public enterprise to produce at a quantity q where P = minimum MC or where P = minimum AC, but how can government know what is the minimum MC or the minimum AC? Here, the asymmetric information assumption enters the explanation of why public enterprises may succeed in running slack.

Suppose that the principal has full information and can order the agent what to do. Given that the principal pays the agent a compensation or salary for his effort (E) that is over what the agent can secure by him/herself, and that the effort of the agent gives the principal an economic gain (G), then principal–agent interaction has a unique solution (see Figure 4.2).

However, if there is asymmetric information, then both principal and agent would engage in various strategies to advance their interests, meaning that the exact nature of the curves in Figure 4.2 are not known (Macho-Stadler and Perez-Castillo, 1997; Molho, 1997). For a given wage *w*, which effort is forthcoming, E1 or E3?

The principal–agent problem involved in motivating the managers of an enterprise to run the company in the best interests of the owners of the capital arises in any form of enterprise, not only in public enterprises but also in big private enterprises or in joint-stock companies where there is a distance between

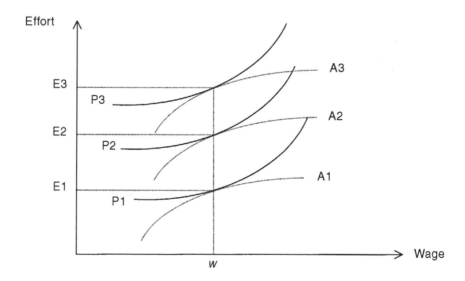

Figure 4.2 Principal–agent interaction: alternative preferences for effort and wage with different principals (P) and agents (A).

owners and managers. Thus, when new public management recommends incorporation of public enterprises, then the principal–agent problems will not go away. They surface also in the conduct of an industrial policy.

Against industrial policy

The second major argument for a public enterprise derives from the so-called industrial policy reason. The adherents of an industrial policy claim that the state should be active in not only guiding the economy by means of macro-economic policy-making but also through the active ownership of key industries. This argument appears in for instance the infant industry hypothesis or the idea of state enterprises as the spearheads of the economy. What I wish to point out is that the principal–agent problem, especially when combined with the asymmetric information assumption, is as applicable to the industrial policy context as to the monopoly context.

Let us take an empirical example, viz. French state enterprises. Perhaps no other country has emphasised the extent to which these firms are the excellent enterprises in the entire economy. French enterprises constitute the model enterprises, upon which all firms should focus. In reality, the French model seems to have worked reasonably well, at least in so far as the reputation of the state enterprises is concerned. High prestige seems to have been the carrot used to pull skilled management towards the state enterprise sector. Yet, what seems to work well in the short run, could turn out badly in the long run. This is actually what happened with some French state enterprises, such as Credit Lyonnais and Air France.

The crux of the matter is that reputation works only just so far. Not even high salaries for management can make sure that public enterprises remain well run. If there is asymmetric information, then the agent can hide the real situation of the public enterprise for a long time, while at the same time receiving a high remuneration for his/her work.

The occurrence of asymmetric information opens up the possibility of short-term opportunistic behaviour on the part of the agent managing a state enterprise. Why care about the long-run development of the firm, since working to that end is producing a public good that may be reaped by anyone? If, in the long run, we are all dead, then the actors will focus upon the short run.

Principal checking agents

The management function in a public enterprise involves a principal–agent problem that is worse than the corresponding problem for a private firm, where the standard strategy is to make the agent part of the ownership of the firm (Rasmusen, 1994). This strategy is not available in relation to a public enterprise. The only way to ensure that the public enterprise is truly a leading firm, well managed and economically soundly run is either to conduct monitoring in the short run or to employ reputation-based strategies in the long run, involving the use of the threat to fire.

Monitoring

The traditional public enterprise used to be closely monitored by government. There was limited discretion for the managers to act on their own, with key decisions taken by a ministry (finance, industry) or even parliament. Thus, the traditional public enterprise could not make large investments without approval of the ministry of finance. Often the objectives of the traditional public enterprise included political goals such as regional development and employment, decided in a ministry of industry.

Monitoring is, however, efficient only up to a certain level. Actually, the marginal gains from monitoring decline rapidly whereas the marginal cost of monitoring tends to rise rapidly. Often, public commissions or investigations were trusted with the task of monitoring a public enterprise. But such teams work slowly and are highly vulnerable to pressure from special interest groups. The effort to lay down long-run objectives for public enterprises faltered upon the impossibility of predicting how events would turn out. And enterprise costs could not really be understood by outsiders.

How the traditional public enterprise was to be run often created confusion. On the one hand, a certain degree of managerial discretion was considered vital for the proper management of the enterprise on the basis of firm criteria. On the other hand, the public enterprise did not have legal autonomy in relation to the state, which implied that whenever sensitive matters cropped up, then a ministry would become involved.

Public enterprises used to present a need for a yearly subsidy, besides their requirement of investment funds in order to maintain themselves and grow. At first, government used to accept that public enterprises were loss-making units with the argument that they were socially useful. However, governments soon began to try to cut back the subsidies, partly for financial reasons and partly for competition reasons.

Yet, governments were not content with simply stopping to pay subsidies, they also wanted a certain rate of return on the capital handed over to the public enterprise. Thus, there developed a strategy of financial steering targets related to the public enterprise involving the payment of a reasonable rate of return on its capital. However, such a strategy could only imply that user fees or charges had to go up, working against the social objectives of the public enterprise of providing cost plus prices only.

Faced with financial steering targets on the part of the owner, public enterprises began to transform themselves. In order to increase rentability, managers started to cut the number of employees and to raise user fees. Sometimes this new style of management caused conflict, either with the trade unions or with a regulatory board who supervised prices. Sometimes this process went smoothly meaning that managers could claim that the public enterprise was ripe for incorporation, or the transfer of it to another legal form: the public joint-stock company.

How much monitoring should government do in relation to its enterprises? And which types of monitoring are most effective? Running the traditional enterprises involved reflecting upon these two questions, but they are not easily answered. At first, governments attempted ex ante control, steering their organisations by means of budgetary instructions. However, it was realised that ex post evaluation is more effective.

Monitoring can be done by detailed examinations of how an enterprise is run. But it is a very costly type of monitoring, which basically targets whether standard operating procedures have been followed and not whether these procedures are effective or productive in themselves. Monitoring can be done against a few major criteria, set up in advance of a budgetary year. But it is often far from clear what these targets meant at the implementation stage, or whether enterprise effort really mattered much for their achievement.

This difficulty can be seen in Figure 4.3, which shows the marginal benefit and cost curves involved in monitoring from the point of view of the principal or the owner of the enterprise.

Government, when conducting monitoring, must know where the optimal

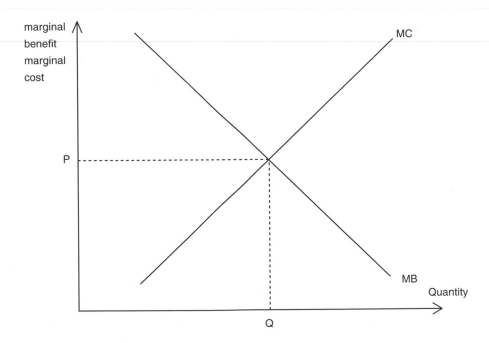

Figure 4.3   Marginal benefit and marginal cost in monitoring.

amount of monitoring occurs. When little monitoring has been accomplished, then the marginal benefit from increasing monitoring is large whereas the marginal cost from increasing monitoring is rather low. However, monitoring benefits go down and monitoring costs go up as monitoring expands.

Once detailed monitoring was given up and standard financial targets were employed instead, then the rationale of the public enterprise institution was gone. Placing a rate of return objective upon a firm is most easily done by using another institution, or the private firm, especially in its joint-stock company version. The transition to the public joint-stock company form was eagerly sought by the managers in the public enterprises. Why?

In many traditional public enterprises, the salaries of managers tended to be lower than that of private managers at the corresponding level, reflecting the circumstance that their discretion and thus responsibility was lower. Why would managers try hard in such an environment? Any efficiency-promoting change would probably not benefit them. In a public joint-stock company, discretion is much more substantive and efforts to reduce costs could be rewarded by higher salaries.

Yet, reputation has played a not insignificant role in motivating the managers of public enterprises to try hard, at the same time as politicians have had a certain space of manoeuvring in the manipulation of presenting and withdrawing this prestige-enhancing reward that reputation constitutes. Is reputation more efficiency-enhancing than monitoring?

Reputation

To use reputation as the governance mechanism for a public enterprise involves a risk for both government and the managers. Since reputation comes and goes quickly, reflecting not only the day-to-day continuous hard work but also the occurrence of spectacular events taking place randomly, both government and managers have an interest in attempting to bend it to their advantage.

Reputation is something stored, like capital, to be used when the time is ripe. It takes a long time to build up reputation but it takes little time to lose it, if things go wrong. Managers can spend a lifetime's work in building up a reputation just to lose it overnight. Governments may consider that they have their public enterprises in order, but unpredictable events take place which reveal that their firms are out of tune.

The reputation of the firm creates both a conflict and a common interest between government and the managers of public enterprises. When things go well, the reputation of both parties are enhanced. When things go badly, they start to blame each other.

Reputation is a strategic asset which can be manipulated for the purposes of gaining advantages. When reputation is questioned, then opportunistic behaviour tends to set in in order to bolster reputation and prevent it from being ruined. The great problem when reputation enters opportunistic behaviour is that cheating could pay off handsomely, if not in the form of the telling of straightforward lies, perhaps more so in disguising facts.

Again we come back to the condition of asymmetric knowledge in combination with opportunistic behaviour. In relation to public enterprises, asymmetric knowledge works for the managers and against government, but both may engage in opportunistic behaviour in relation to reputation building or reputation destruction. For reputation to work it must be used in tendering/bidding schemes recruiting public managers competitively.

Entry regulation and rent-seeking

As stated above, the traditional theory of public regulation, focusing upon entry regulation, employed licences which government would issue to firms, either private or public, that stated the conditions under which they were allowed to operate in a sector. Such licences would lay down prices and quantities, which the firm had to respect in order to receive the sole permission to be active in this regulated sector of the economy. Sometimes also quality standards that had to be met were specified.

Traditional public regulation thus conceived of some amount of reciprocity between government and the firm, the latter accepting being regulated against receiving a legal monopoly, based upon the licensing power of the state as part of its legal authority. However, the occurrence of asymmetric knowledge undoes the reciprocity, when public regulation is approached as a principal–agent relationship.

We need to reflect first on why traditional public regulation could not make this reciprocity work. Second, we need to explore whether reregulation can handle this reciprocity. Once the difficulties in creating a reciprocity between government as regulator and the regulated firms were realised, there followed a search for deregulation. But here the key question becomes: how far should or could deregulation go? Is there perhaps a fundamental need for reregulation, i.e. the invention of new forms of regulation that could successfully supplant traditional regulation?

One may examine the argument by G. Majone (1996) suggesting that Europe needs a new regulatory state and that the European Union is very much a response to this need. Before we discuss the need for a new regulatory state in general and for Europe in particular, we examine the argument against the old regulatory state.

One may distinguish between two types of regulation, entry regulation and product regulation. Since the aim of public regulation is to promote socially useful ends, one may identify the different standard objectives of entry regulation on the one hand and of product regulation on the other hand.

First, when government issues licences, stating the conditions for entry into a sector of the economy, then the objective is to promote economic efficiency. Licences and entry regulation have been used in relation to infrastructure and capital intensive industry. Traditional entry regulation is considered a policy tool to undo the occurrence of monopoly in the market, when contestation is not naturally forthcoming due to economies of scale or scope. The rationale of entry licences is the economic theory of economies of scale or scope, which argues that one sole producer minimises unit costs.

Second, product regulations target risk, or the reduction of the probability of the occurrence of accidents. Thus, such regulatory policies consist in the specification of product standards about quality. During the last decade, the amount of product regulation has increased considerably as measured by the number of new rules about the quality of products or how they are to be handled. The rationale of product regulations is consumer vulnerability or the search for safety (Wildavsky, 1988a).

Government, it was argued, could undo private monopolies by regulating them. Thus, there was strictly speaking no need for the use of a public enterprise because government could interact with a private firm, using its power to legislate in order to lay down the conditions for the operations of the firm. Thus, firms would accept rules of how to be socially useful, receiving from government as a reciprocity the licence to be the sole enterprise active in a sector. Private firms accepting such a trade-off between accepting regulation and receiving entry protection would constitute so-called public utilities.

Traditional public regulations theory models government as the active part in setting up regulatory schemes, supervised by a public board of some kind. Yet, the criticism of public regulation portrays government regulation as a so-called endogenous phenomenon, i.e. it is determined by the market and it does not determine the market, i.e. it is not exogeneous.

Public regulation may be the outcome of so-called rent-seeking, which benefits the regulated firms first and foremost. Regulation is a valuable good or service which firms are prepared to invest in order to capture the government regulators (Stigler, 1975). Government creating licences become captured by the firms seeking favourable public regulation of the market, limiting competition.

Since licences can be extremely lucrative, there is plenty of money available for rent-seeking. Moreover, product regulations may enter into rent-seeking, as regulation may favour certain producers.

The standard model of rent-seeking, as developed within the public choice school, is shown in Figure 4.4 (Tollison, 1982). The potential gain from rent-seeking is the entire consumer surplus in Figure 4.4. If a private firm can receive favourable regulation from government, then it could restrict the quantity supplied and engage in price discrimination. Thus, the quantity supplied would be less than the optimal quantity – Q – and price would be raised, allowing the private firm to receive an economic rent, or excessive profits. If price is raised from Pe to Pm, then the firm takes a huge chunk away from the consumer surplus, or the shaded area in Figure 4.4.

However, the capture of government comes with a cost to the firm. It must engage in lobbying in order to get the favourable regulation. This rent-seeking behaviour can become very costly, as government must be paid attention to in many ways – the firm accumulating transaction costs. These costs for rent-

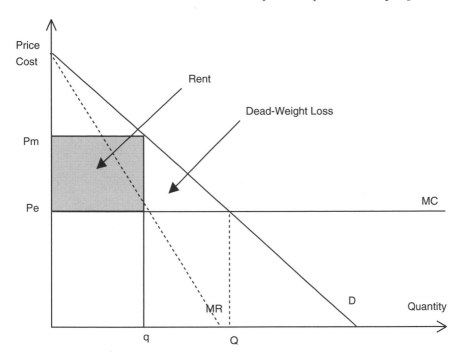

Figure 4.4   General rent-seeking model.

seeking can run so high as to dissipate the entire consumer surplus, i.e. the shared area in Figure 4.4.

Thus, public regulation may not only cause a huge burden to the economy (dead-weight loss, abnormal profits), but it may actually result in no gain whatsoever for anyone. If that is the case, the entire producer surplus being dissipated, then entry regulation is only socially wasteful. In the case of entry regulations, it would be better to let a private firm operate a private monopoly, because there would be no rent dissipation, although the standard monopoly costs would have to be incurred by society. In the case of product regulations, it is perhaps possible to use only strict liability rules (Posner, 1992).

Legislative markets for public regulation and procurement

If governments creating regulation are not acting exogeneously, i.e. independently, in relation to the economy, then how is public regulation forthcoming? Widening the concept of public regulation to cover any kind of state intervention in the economy, the model of rent-seeking must be developed to take into account the possibility of competition for legislation that regulates the economy. Besides, there are all the government contracts.

It is not only entry regulation that is interesting for the players in the economy. Lots of other kinds of state intervention have economic consequences. Thus, private as well as public firms, interest organisations or consumer groups seek to influence the state intervention by framing legislation to their advantage. There will be competition in the demand for state intervention or government contracts from various players.

What about the supply of state intervention? One may argue that the initiative does not rest entirely with the players seeking state intervention, but that one should in addition take into account the willingness of politicians to supply state intervention in the form of licences or product standards.

One may generalise the analysis of government-creating regulatory schemes to cover not only entry regulation or product regulation but all kinds of state intervention in markets, including also public procurement, or government purchasing things by means of state contracts. Such a generalisation should include both supply and demand, with the consequence that we arrive at a model of legislative markets for state intervention (Peltzman, 1988).

Government contracts may be subsumed under the general model of the demand for and supply of state intervention. Such contracts favour certain groups, firms, regions, employees and consumers, and disfavour others in the same manner as legislation works to the benefit of some and brings about costs for others. In all countries, rich and poor, government contracts tend to be of substantial size and quite lucrative for some.

Government contracts used to be mainly concerned with the purchase of equipment and the construction of buildings and roads. However, with the advent of contractualism in the entire public sector, government contracts are omnipresent. Here, we deal with so-called public procurement.

Once one opens up for competition in the demand and supply of state intervention, then the losses from rent-seeking can be substantially reduced. Politicians stand to gain from allocating legislation, if they can establish a quid pro quo for the services that they provide, i.e. the legislative acts or the contracts, receiving votes or money. On the other hand, politicians may lose in a grim fashion if they supply state intervention that the electorate does not want, resulting in loss of votes. Evidently, there is both push and pull in legislative markets. A general way of modelling legislative markets is outlined in Figures 4.5 and 4.6 (Stevens, 1993). Politicians may receive different support from various interest groups for the same supply of legislation (Figure 4.5). Or politicians may allocate different kinds or amounts of legislation to various groups, all searching legislation (Figure 4.6), for instance for different regions of the country.

Conclusion

The traditional public enterprise has almost ceased to exist in many countries. Governments have chosen another governance form for their business activity,

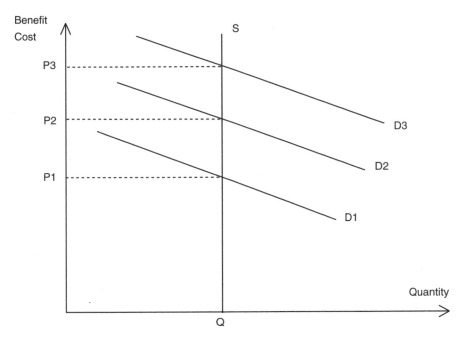

Figure 4.5   Legislative markets 1.

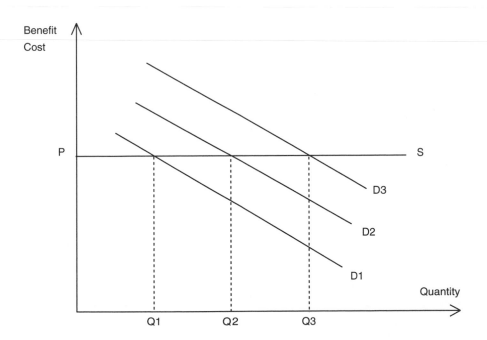

Figure 4.6   Legislative markets 2.

namely the public joint-stock company. In addition to its advantages for running business activity it offers to the government, as the owner, also the possibility of privatisation, partially or completely, by simply selling out the equity.

There are two highly contradictory images of the public enterprise as it has tended to operate in real life. On the one hand it is seen as socially useful. The negative image is that it is inefficient and that runs yearly losses. The final image is that disadvantages seem to have carried a larger weight than the advantages in offering employment and cost plus prices.

The basic difficulty with the public enterprise is the occurrence of X-inefficiency (Leibenstein, 1966). It destroys the entire argument about the social usefulness of the public enterprise. Even if public enterprises uses cost plus prices, there is no guarantee that it will minimise costs. On the contrary, the public enterprise has no self-interest connected with being X-efficient.

The key problem concerns who is to gain from increased X-efficiency in the public enterprise: the principal (government), the agent (the enterprise) or the client (the customers)? The transformation of the public enterprise into a public joint-stock company or incorporation implies that government has won, at least over the public as consumer/customer. Incorporation entails higher user fees, less employees and larger profits, to be partially repatriated to the state. The advantage with the public joint-stock company for the public or the citizens is that subsidies and losses are easily discovered. Thus, they may also be eliminated.

Government may try to promote X-efficiency by means of two strategies: (1) monitoring the enterprise and (2) affecting the reputation of managers. Monitoring is not cost-less. Transaction costs may start running high after a certain minimum level of monitoring has been accomplished. And reputation is not strategy-proof, meaning that both government and managers of the public enterprise may invest in strategies that impact upon reputation, which would actually be a form of rent-dissipation.

5   Redistribution
The efficiency–equity trade-off

Introduction

There is one large part of the public sector that seems to be outside of the scope of public management. The vast and often highly costly programmes which transfer money to people do not appear to bend themselves to the logic of public management with its focus upon efficiency. Social security is not about the provision of goods and services but concerns citizens' rights, so-called entitlements. Few question the justice inherent in entitlements, but what is contested is the size of the transfer payments as well as how they are to be financed.

If entitlements belong to the domain of social justice, then deliberating about these rights requires a theory of justice. Yet, such a theory is not available in the social sciences, as the concept of justice remains an essentially contested notion. However, transfer payments may be examined from another angle, namely economic efficiency in a macro-sense. What are the costs to the economy of large transfer payments, either on the income side (taxation) or on the expenditure side (subsidies)?

Could it be the case that entitlements are inversely related to economic efficiency in the sense of total output? A number of hypotheses in both expenditure and taxation theory have suggested that this is the case. Here, we find the Okun efficiency–equity trade-off, the Laffer curve, the leisure–work reaction curve and the excess burden argument from tax wedges. If some of these hypotheses are correct, then a government distributing entitlements must take into account the costs of redistribution, which may go prohibitively high. Let us look at what is involved here.

If it is true that income redistribution runs into conflict with economic efficiency, lowering total output, then why do governments operate such programmes? We must search for the basic rationale of all the transfer programmes that loom so large in the budgets of rich countries. Brian Barry suggests that justice implies that governments redistribute in order to achieve equality. Director's law suggests another answer (Stigler, 1970).

Income redistribution

Wagner's Law about the impact of affluence upon public expenditure seems particularly applicable to transfer payments. Whereas poor countries are largely unconcerned with this type of public expenditure, the case is entirely different in rich countries. In the OECD set of countries, all governments pay huge sums of money for income maintenance. And the share of the GDP going to income maintenance is rising, slowly but seemingly inexorably.

The Wagner effect, or the positive elasticity to spend publicly any increase in GDP, seems to make sense in relation to income maintenance. Even poor countries must pay for basic state necessities, such as public goods and infrastructure. But only rich countries can afford income maintenance programmes. In his original statement of his hypothesis about the future size of government, Wagner actually separated the need for infrastructure from the need for income maintenance, although he argued industrialisation and urbanisation would increase both kinds of expenditures (Wagner, 1877–1901).

Yet, Wagner's Law has its limits. The so-called welfare societies have a much lower level of income maintenance than the welfare states. And whereas the latter employ pay-as-you-go schemes, the former have introduced more actuarial principles. Affluence is a necessary but not a sufficient condition for huge income maintenance programmes.

Income maintenance is a concept that covers a variety of programmes. What is characteristic is that they constitute rights, i.e. they are part of public law, meaning that governments must respect them even when they face financial difficulties. Entitlements can only be changed through law, and this has happened in the 1990s because governments have found the task of paying for all promises made in income maintenance too burdensome.

Transfer programmes give money to many groups of people, collected in principle by means of taxation. Some countries employ only taxes, while other countries also use social security charges. Income redistribution arises when transfer programmes are not based upon so-called actuarial principles, i.e. rules that guarantee that what one person pays in he/she can also collect. Thus, public income maintenance which is based upon pay-as-you-go schemes is not an insurance scheme.

Public maintenance schemes build upon the fundamental separation between the income side of the public household and the expenditure side of the same household. Although governments have tried to limit the gap between what a person pays in and what he receives, it remains the case that income maintenance is basically a pay-as-you-go system where there are winners and losers.

But who is money being transferred to in public redistribution schemes and from whom is it coming? The naïve opinion is that money is taken from the rich and given to the poor, but income maintenance schemes do not operate that way. Much of the money in these programmes concerns redistribution from and to the same individual, i.e. they constitute redistribution over the life cycle of the same individual. One and the same person pays into the system during certain years but takes out from the system at other periods of time.

Now, there is in principle no limit to the demand for income maintenance. The remuneration could always be made more generous and programmes could always be extended in various forms. In addition, real life developments push expenditures upwards due to demographic changes. The situation is such that governments have reason to be worried about the transfer payments.

Expenditures for income redistribution have increased much faster than the GDP, and more rapidly than the allocative expenditures. Transfer payments are today larger than allocative expenditures in most OECD countries. Sometimes one type of income maintenance is left outside the entitlements, namely poor relief, because in some countries it is more a discretionary expenditure than a right. However, when included in the income maintenance sector, then the redistributive branch of government becomes clearly larger than the allocative branch almost everywhere.

If it is certain that income maintenance costs more and more not only directly but also indirectly, then it is uncertain what the outcomes of transfer payments are. There are two problems involved. First, there is the excess burden question, i.e. whether the true cost of transfer payments is significantly larger than the nominal cost. Second, there is the problem of the effect of redistribution, i.e. whether such schemes really lead to more income equality.

Efficiency versus equity

The new management philosophy has one main objective for the public sector reforms that it recommends, namely to raise efficiency in the provision of goods and services. The number of means employed to enhance this goal is considerable and covers, besides privatisation, incorporation of public enterprises, the introduction of internal markets, the employment of the purchaser–provider separation, contracting out, the use of massive contracting whether provision is inhouse or outhouse, bench-marking, restructuring of ministries, use of executive agencies, increased use of user fees, etc.

Focusing not upon the means but upon the single objective efficiency, one may raise a question that appears to contain a few puzzles about public sector reform in the 1990s. First, what is nature of that key objective, efficiency, which is so much focused upon? Second, why are other objectives that have figured prominently in the public sector never mentioned, especially equity? Finally, one may enquire into the outcomes of public sector reform, relating the objectives concerning efficiency and equity to the actually accomplished results. One would, of course, want to know what are the signs, if any, that efficiency has increased as well as whether equity has been affected at the same time, either increasing or decreasing.

Talking about efficiency in the public sector, one may either take a *micro*-perspective, focusing upon how quantities, qualities and costs have developed within one sector or even within one ministry, department or production unit.

Or one may take a macro-perspective, attempting to make an overall assessment of public sector reform with a measuring rod like *macro*-efficiency, meaning the maximisation of output. Below, we will pursue the macro-perspective, and in particular focus upon the argument about a trade-off between efficiency and equity.

Relevance of a distributional perspective on taxes and expenditures

The public sector allocation of goods and services cannot be approached only from the efficiency perspective. Such goods and services are distributed to consumers or citizens. Distributional matters are unavoidable when one looks at public finances. The minute that a supply of goods and services is forthcoming, one can ask: who gets what, when and how?

Each allocation of services has a distribution of these attached to it, but there is in addition the large set of transfer payments, i.e. the income redistribution branch of government, or as it is also called: social security. In advanced countries, social security is larger than public resource allocation on both the income and expenditure sides. Redistribution can be in kind or in money.

Moreover, allocation and distribution interact, meaning that certain efficient outcomes may not be satisfactory from a distributional point of view – the equity perspective – or the other way around. The possibility of an efficiency–equity trade-off arises not only in the income maintenance programmes, but also in the allocative programmes. What, then, is the equity perspective that may compete with the efficiency norm?

Distributional criteria in relation to the public provision of goods and services (in kind) or in relation to transfer payments (in money) are not easily specified. From an efficiency point of view, there are the user fee criteria of various kinds: charges, benefit taxes, which mean that people who get the goods and services pay in full for their utilisation. From an equity point of view, there are need or want criteria as well as rights criteria so that distribution of the goods and services is not in accordance with the willingness to pay but on the basis of criteria derived from social justice theory.

When needs, wants or rights are employed, then the allocation (in kind) or redistribution (transfer payments) is basically paid for by means of taxation schemes based upon the ability to pay. Taxation has immense distributional implications, as the choice of a finance scheme faces alternatives, which relate to the kind of good or service allocated in the public sector. Benefit taxation seems reasonable in relation to divisible goods and services (mainly private goods) whereas ability-to-pay taxation would be more appropriate in relation to indivisible goods and services (mainly public goods). Redistribution in the social security system can be paid for by means of a benefit approach or the ability-to-pay approach, where the latter allows much more interpersonal redistribution whereas the former is more conducive to intergenerational redistribution for one and the same person.

The widespread employment of schemes for ability to pay in combination with public resource allocation entails redistribution in kind. It seems impossible to satisfy by means of a realistic mechanism the Wicksell requirement for efficiency in the public sector, where MB = MC for all individuals over all goods and services, when there is lots of allocation paid for by means of the ability-to-pay approach. It is true that benefit taxation schemes enhance the Wicksell requirement, but not all benefit taxation schemes fully implement the rule that the individual who benefits also pays the cost for the good or service that he/she consumes (Wicksell, 1967).

Actually, a number of efficiency reasons could be used against benefit taxation. Many public goods cannot be sold due to the free rider problem. Some goods and services should not be priced at all, because enjoying them carries hardly any marginal cost, such as roads. Finally, pricing goods and services the consumption of which leads to positive external effects may lead to an under-supply of these goods.

Moreover, an equity argument against benefit taxation could be stated, as government sometimes wants to make certain goods and services freely available to groups with needs that would not be properly looked after, if prices were used to cover the entire cost for these goods and services – redistribution in kind or true merit goods. Government would definitely want to do so, if groups were entitled to help in these respects.

Transfer payments are often considered to be entitlements which people have because they are citizens in a country. The concept of an entitlement is critical in social justice theory and cannot be derived only from the efficiency framework, focusing upon Pareto-optimality. Entitlements play a major role in welfare state theory as well as in nationalism (Miller, 1997).

Ability-to-pay taxation is the income type that governments predominantly use to pay for the provision of goods and services in the so-called soft sector. The business sector is not problematic from this aspect, as it can in principle be fully financed by means of charges or user fees – benefit taxation. However, no government has ever accepted the proposal to put a price tag on all its goods and services, if it were at all feasible from a practical point of view, in order to arrive at the Wicksell efficiency condition, or MB = MC also for the public sector.

As already underlined in Chapter 3, various forms of taxation are placed upon different people and objects on one occasion in order to pay for a bundle of goods and services as well as transfer payments that on another occasion are distributed to a variety of people. Thus, arises the gulf between payment and utilisation, which remains a typical feature of any public sector, i.e. especially the soft sector. Decisions about financing are taken on separate occasions from decisions about spending.

The inverse law of concentration of benefits and diffusion of costs appears very much true of the public sector, especially the soft sector. Benefits tend to be concentrated on certain groups of people whereas costs tend to be spread out upon all groups of people. In the social security system this seems almost to be unavoidable in a modern public sector, given that they are founded upon the pay-as-you-go idea instead of upon only an actuarial mechanism.

Distributional aspects of public sector services

When goods and services are claimed to be in the public interest or the national interest, then they should benefit in principle each and everyone. Yet, one could argue that so-called public goods like defence or Rule of Law benefit some groups more than others, although they would be in the public interest. However, it seems exaggerated to emphasise the distributional implications of the allocation of all kinds of goods and services, especially pure public goods or common pool goods. Only in relation to the types of goods and services in the public sector that are not classified as pure public goods, such as infrastructure, environment and education as well as health and social care, the question, who gains by it, seems highly relevant.

Semi-private or semi-public goods and services do not provide benefits that are entirely for one group of people. Society as a whole – each and everyone practically – benefits from good communications, a clean environment and a high average standard of living of the population with regard to education, health and social care. There are externalities involved, meaning that private utility is smaller than social utility. Yet, some groups benefit more than others.

The distributional consequences of the allocation of services in the public sector appear in a clear manner in relation to goods and services which are characterised by full appropriability and very little jointness, such as education, health care and social care. On the other hand, benefits tend to be less concentrated on certain groups and more widespread in their distributional implications when goods and services are characterised by considerable jointness such as with communications or positive externalities such as with various aspects of the environment. Yet, one can argue that distributional consequences occur everywhere, in roads for instance there are groups that are favoured such as motorists or people who use trucks and buses primarily. Urban areas favour their populations concerned with the protection of the environment in a very wide sense of that concept including all kinds of pollution, clean water and sewage.

Distributional implications of social security

As we move to the core of the redistributional branch of government, viz. social security, distributional considerations loom really large. Both on the payments side and the expenditure side social security is very much focused upon redistribution. Social security in an advanced country costs so much that it is vital to establish the distribution consequences of such large flows of money. Several welfare states have devised special forms of taxation – social security charges – in order to pay for the immense expansion of the transfer payments system characteristic of the last twenty years. A key question is whether the person who pays these charges is the same person who benefits from the transfer payments as well as whether there is proportionality in the system.

Transfer payments include a number of items of expenditure: pensions, unemployment benefits, sickness insurance, maternity leave, child allowances, accident and handicap insurance, student support, social care, etc. Due to a combination of political pressures and demographic changes, the total sums of money passing through social security have skyrocketed. There is little demand for a reduction in the size of these programmes, as they are considered to be entitlements.

Obviously, much social security is the transfer of money from one person to the very same person with only a difference in time. The same person pays social security charges during his active time in occupational life and then collects much of the same money when he/she is no longer active occupationally. However, social security is not the same as insurance.

First, social security is obligatory, as the social security system covers people by means of public law regulations. Individuals have to pay the social security charges and they are entitled to the social security payments. Second, there is no guarantee whatsoever of proportionality, or any automatic relationship between the amount paid and the amount received. There are losers and winners in the social security system meaning that some people pay more than they receive whereas other people receive more than they pay.

The rationale of social security is more concerned with equity than efficiency. Although for reasons of opportunism or negligence not all people would buy insurance against the unfortunate and unpredictable events that might hit them during their life time, social security is motivated less by consumer myopia and more by the argument that many people cannot afford such insurance.

Since the income and wealth distribution among people is always more or less skewed, there is a need for state intervention after markets have distributed resources in accordance with the basic criterion that factor (labour, capital, land) payments are equal to their marginal contribution or value:

(MP)   Factor compensation = Marginal productivity

In principle, people who are not working will receive nothing when (MP) is applied. Thus, there is a demand for state intervention in the distribution of income and wealth after markets have been in operation. This is *ex post* redistribution.

Yet, there is also an argument in favour of *ex ante* redistribution stating that equity requires that there is equal opportunity for each and everyone. Markets should start their operation of rewarding the talented and punishing the unfortunate from a starting-point that is just – i.e. there should be equal opportunity. Thus, social justice requires state intervention both before and after the operation of markets. To make things more complicated still, justice is also employed as a criterion for the evaluation of market operations, requiring inter alia contractual honesty and the mutual fulfilment of obligations.

To sum up, social justice or equity is a normative conception that can be applied to several different things:

1   Ex ante: the starting-point for human interaction, especially markets
2   Process: the process of interaction, especially contractual behaviour
3   Ex post: the end product or result of human interaction, especially market outcomes.

When equity theory requires state intervention in relation to (1) or (2) or (3) above, then which criteria of evaluation may be employed in order to complement or correct for the application of the market criterion of (MP)? These criteria would define a desirable distribution of income and wealth. But we must ask whether they can be fully implemented and what costs are involved?

Distributional criteria

Government faces some key alternatives about how to distribute the goods and services in the public sector as well as how to frame the social security system. For the business sector, it seems reasonable to adhere to the principle that the user pays fully for the use of the goods and services in this sector. For the soft sector, government may wish to mix a number of criteria stating who should use the goods and services allocated in that sector. Finally, in the social security sector government has some degree of freedom about how to construct the basic principles, covering on the one hand the levying of charges and on the other hand the payment of cheques.

Examining social justice theory, one may distinguish the following different distributional reasons or relevant criteria in distribution (Miller, 1976).

1   utilitarian criteria or wants
2   rights
3   needs

The application of these three criteria for the distribution of goods and services as well as money cheques in the public sector will not result in the same distributional solutions. Thus, government must make up its mind which criteria are to be applied for which goods, which services and which type of pay cheques. Only in relation to a set of very special goods and services – pure public goods – is it possible to argue that they benefit all people. Concerning several goods and services in the public sector as well as concerning transfer payments, distribution policy has the characteristics of a zero-sum game. When one group benefits, then others do not. Thus, government must decide which criteria to apply in distributional conflicts.

The trade-off between equity and efficiency

The efficiency–equity trade-off arises when rights are allocated by the government in such a manner that total output is decreased. Rights do not always have to conflict with the efficient allocation of resources, but they may do so. Rights may comprise the free access to goods and services or the participation in social security programmes.

Arthur M. Okun has identified a number of ways in which rights and economic output may conflict. He states:

> In short, the domain of rights is full of infringements on the calculus of economic efficiency. Our rights can be viewed as inefficient, because they preclude prices that would promote economising, choices that would invoke comparative advantage, incentives that would augment socially productive effort, and trades that potentially would benefit buyer and seller alike.
>
> (Okun, 1975: 10)

The interaction between output or money maximisation and rights works both ways, however. Thus, Okun pays much attention to what he calls the transgression of dollars on rights, which should be stemmed: 'But the basic transgression of the marketplace on equal rights must be curbed by specific, detailed rules on what money should not buy' (Okun, 1975: 31).

Since rights tend to be created through the democratic process, the transgression of dollars upon rights may be interpreted as a threat from the market towards the democratic system of government. Rights occur not only in the redistributive branch of government but also in the allocative branch of government. When, as in a welfare state, citizens are provided with rights to a number of services almost free, then the efficiency–equity trade-off also arises in public resource allocation.

Yet, the debate around the efficiency–equity conflict is also relevant in the redistributive branch of government, identifying the extra costs of redistribution both on the income side and the expenditure side. These costs are the additional costs to the economy from income maintenance schemes, besides the transfers themselves.

The income side

When transfer payments start to loom large in the public budgets, then governments face the problem of deciding what instrument to use to raise the necessary money. This is the choice between taxes or social security charges, since deficit spending is only a possibility in the short run. Some countries mainly use taxation whereas other countries rely chiefly upon charges levied upon the employer. Moreover, some countries use invisible taxes to pay for part of the transfer payments whereas others rely mainly upon visible taxes, such as income taxation.

There is no one single best method to raise the resources needed for transfer

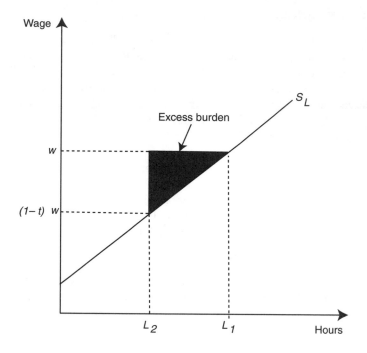

Figure 5.1   Excess burden in taxation.

payments, except that deficit spending is a dead-end, at least in the long run. The theory of fiscal illusion focuses upon invisible taxes and their capacity to allow for expenditure levels that are not clearly recognised by the electorate. However, the critical problem concerns the estimation of how large is the excess burden that occurs in taxation. In order to raise $1 in taxation, how much extra will this $1 cost to society in lost production? Reply: between $1.3 and $1.6.

Excess burden in taxation is the cost to the economy from lost output, or lost work or profit opportunity (Figure 5.1). The estimation of the costs of tax wedges varies somewhat, as its weight is contested in economics. But in general one may say that the cost in lost production ranges between 20 to 50 cents for each dollar raised. Generally, the higher the marginal rates of taxation, the more serious the excess burden. Excess burden occurs, however, not only on the income side of the public household.

The expenditure side

When government provides cheap money by means of various transfer programmes, then it may impact upon the functioning of markets, causing inefficiencies, often in the form of too much quantity allocated. One may give an example from the subsidisation of housing costs, as in Figure 5.2 involving a

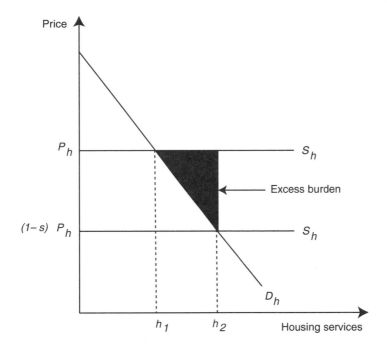

Figure 5.2   Excess burden in subsidies.

direct subsidy lowering the rent paid by a person, which causes too much housing to be consumed (the shared area).

Perhaps the most debated form of excess burden refers to unemployment benefits and sickness benefits and their impact upon the incentives in the economy. The key question is the rate of remuneration as a percentage of the normal wage of a person. If such remuneration rates are put very high or close to one hundred per cent, then there is a substantial risk for double excess burden occurring in the economy at large.

First, raising the money for paying for these costly transfer payments involves using high tax rates, which entails the risk of excess burden in taxation. Second, paying out generous transfers entails the risk of stimulating unemployment and sickness leave by changing the preferences for work as against leisure. In combination, such transfer programmes could become so costly that it costs almost $2 to pay out $1.

Now, whatever estimate one makes of excess burden in income maintenance programmes, one cannot deny the problem of tax wedges and incentive effects from the operation of such schemes, combining the excess burden on both the income and expenditure sides. Why, then, do governments commit themselves heavily towards income maintenance, when the private sector offers insurance schemes which could in principle substitute for the transfer programmes?

To minimise the conflict between economic efficiency and equity one could employ the Wicksell recommendation to keep allocation and redistribution clearly distinct. Knut Wicksell did not deny the relevance of distributional considerations when he stated his theory of just taxation in 1896 (Wicksell, 1967). On the contrary, he argued for the use of inheritance taxation in order to create more equality at the starting-point for each and everyone. What he insisted upon was that distribution and allocation be kept separate, meaning that after the starting-points had been more equalised by state intervention, then the market should rule unfettered. Thus, Wicksell would reject redistribution in kind which seems to be such an omnipresent phenomenon in welfare states.

The reason for income redistribution: what is equity?

Justice is rapidly becoming a very important measuring rod in public sector reform. Yet, there is little agreement in identifying a definition of the concept. Justice has an inherently institutional ring, which makes it important also in the institutionalist drive in the social sciences at the moment. How are just institutions to be identified?

The maturing of the welfare state has provoked an intense debate about the concept of justice. Today welfare state programmes are often less grounded in efficiency considerations but are mainly defended because they are believed to enhance social justice. In the trade-off between efficiency and equity distributional matters tend to be decisive. When justice plays such a major role for determining the size of the public sector, then it is little wonder that there is a search in the social sciences for a definition of the concept or for criteria that identify what enhances justice.

Actually, the old discipline of normative political theory has been rejuvenated largely as a response to the attempts at identifying justice. The debate during the past twenty years has resulted in a number of definitions of 'justice', but there is little agreement among scholars about necessary or sufficient properties of the concept, if indeed there exists an unambiguous single one.

Actually, justice seems to be one of the most difficult of all the concepts that are relevant to the concerns of the social sciences. This reflects the fact that the concept of justice in the political economy of the welfare state is called upon to solve two different problems: first, it is supposed to deliver institutions that define fair play between interacting players. Second, it is asked to bring forward rules about compensation.

Justice theory as institutional theory

The analysis of various conceptions of justice leads to the conclusion that 'justice' refers to institutions (Barry, 1989, 1995). The search for a definition of the concept of justice involves looking for general norms of human conduct. Just institutions may be either institutions that are of intrinsic value such as human rights or extrinsic value such as transaction cost-saving mechanisms.

One may find in the literature at least three alternative approaches to justice: (1) mutual advantage; (2) reciprocity; and (3) impartiality. According to Barry's well-known analysis of mutual advantage: 'we are to imagine people with different conceptions of the good seeking a set of ground rules that holds out to each person the prospect of doing better than any of them could expect from pursuing the good individually without constraints' (Barry, 1995: 32). With regard to reciprocity: 'the criterion of justice is that any mutually advantageous deal that is agreed on is to be deemed just – exactly as in the theory of justice as mutual advantage. What is different from that theory is that, if the parties believe the deal to be fair, that in itself gives them a motive for upholding it' (ibid.: 49).

Barry's argument in relation to these two approaches is very similar to the Wicksell distinction between efficiency and justice. Institutions that derive from agreement among the players will be efficient but not necessarily just, because the positions from which negotiations take place could be unjust. Barry states: 'The baseline must itself be fair, and the parties must be well informed and well matched' (ibid.: 50).

Thus, institutional arrangements can only be just if they 'can be freely agreed on by equally well-placed parties' (ibid.: 51). Wicksell in a similar vein called for ex ante or ex post changes in the baseline positions of the various players as a complement to the efficiency framework which is basically reciprocity or mutual advantage. Instead Barry argues that the following approach to impartiality is the one to be preferred: 'The basic idea here is that just rules are those that can be freely endorsed by people on a footing of equality' (ibid.: 52). Just institutions are thus the rules that equal players would endorse for social interaction. Still, the concept of justice entails a profound institutional emphasis.

However, the basic problem of social justice remains unresolved as we do not know which institutions these players will endorse when they are on an equal footing. Asking people which institutions they agree upon will not do, because that would see justice as mutual consent or reciprocity. In any case, the players in existing societies are hardly on a footing of equality. What, then, are the institutions that equal players can endorse? Barry suggests: equality.

Impartiality seems to be a relevant criteria when evaluating institutions from a normative point of view, but is impartiality really the same as equality? What would a definition of justice look like and how would one go about accepting or rejecting various proposals? If someone suggests that an institution or rule is a likely candidate for being just, and another person disagrees, then how does one go about settling the issue? What is the logic of arguments about social justice?

Is justice what is reasonable?

The problem of defining 'justice' is to come up with a set of criteria that if present in institutions then justice would be enhanced in social life. One may wish to make a distinction between a set of rules on the one hand and their application in concrete cases on the other hand. Thus, one may talk about the rules of chess as the presuppositions for playing the game. Another matter is the application of the rules to an ongoing real life game. One can discuss whether the basic rules of the game are reasonable as well as raise the question whether they are implemented in a just manner in a tournament.

The same distinction is important when one evaluates any social institution: (1) Are the rules in themselves just? (2) Are the rules being applied in a just manner? The second question (2) has a legal ring whereas the first question (1) raises an ethical question. We will deal with (1), but here we focus first upon how arguments about (1) may be decided. Is the choice of just institutions an arbitrary one reflecting merely different values?

Let us discuss whether the preference for one set of institutions as being more just than another set of institutions can be challenged on rational grounds. It does not really add much to demand that the criteria be accepted by one group or another. If institutions are truly just, then maybe they are just for each and every group. Thus, we are led to the 'Scanlonian approach' after a proposal by T.M. Scanlon about how matters pertaining to right and wrong are to be decided in an ethical argument. Let us quote from Scanlon:

> An act is wrong if its performance under the circumstances would be disallowed by any system of rules for the general regulation of behaviour which no one could reasonably reject as a basis for informed, unforced general agreement.
>
> (Scanlon, 1982: 110)

One may note that Barry accepts the Scanlonian approach to the search for the criteria for justice as the choice of criteria that no one would wish to reasonably reject. Yet, accepting Scanlon does not entail accepting Barry's starting-point which requires a 'footing of equality', because one could reasonably reject the imposition of such a starting-point.

Barry claims that Rawls' well-known difference principle is a rule that no one can reasonably reject. Why? Surely, one can think about other objectives for the redistributive branch of government than maximising the lot of the least advantaged such as, e.g. maximising total output, which conceivably may form the basis for 'informed, unforced general agreement'.

At the same time it is readily recognised that the Scanlonian approach in no way solves the problem of identifying the criteria of justice. Which criteria would reasonable men/women not reject? Impartiality? Equality? We need to discuss the relationship between impartiality and equality in ethical matters.

Fairness and institutions

Fairness refers to how people are treated under a set of institutions. To treat someone fairly implies that the actions taken under the institutions or the outcomes that a set of institutions result in for people are reasonable. Since no one could reasonably reject what is fair, it would seem that the fairness criteria must be the same as the justice criteria or constitute some subset of the criteria of justice. We have to discuss the concept of fairness in relation to institutions. What is at stake is not whether the institutions are being applied in a fair manner but whether the institutions themselves are fair.

A definition of fairness would have to specify how two groups of people, X and Y, are to be treated in terms of rewards W with respect to characteristics Z. 'W' may range over benefits, costs, rewards, punishments, burdens, favours, permissions and so forth. And 'Z' may stand for such things as abilities, needs, desires, endowments, capacities, accomplishments and so forth.

The criteria for fair treatment are conceived of in a different way from one sphere of human interaction to another (Walzer, 1983). Thus, athletes are treated fairly in one way and chess players in another. The institutions of the economy and the political system offer in a similar way different criteria for how people are to be treated. Fairness requires not only that a single individual be treated fairly, but also that each and everyone be treated in the same way. Fairness implies universalisability. All people that may fall under 'X' and 'Y' are to be treated in the same way with regard to Z and W.

Looking at the different criteria that are used for treating persons one may ask whether there are any criteria that would occur constantly across different forms of human interaction. Barry suggests that impartiality is such a criterion in so far as there is fair treatment for the two groups, X and Y, of persons.

Thus, criminals may be treated impartially with regard to punishment or permissions Z in relation to the crime committed W, and job applicants may be treated impartially with regard to job promotion W based upon their achievements or abilities Z. What is crucial in the impartiality concept is to come up with the criteria in terms of which people are to be treated, if they are to be treated truly fairly, i.e. to decide upon the content of 'Z' and 'W' and how W is to relate to Z.

Impartial treatment seems to meet the Scanlonian test. In many circumstances no one would reasonably reject that two groups of people A and B are treated in a just manner when they are treated in an impartial way with regard to Z and W. However, Barry takes the argument one step further by claiming that impartial treatment is the same as equal treatment. He states:

> A society with a norm of universal impartiality, however, would be one in which everybody was supposed to show equal concern for all.
>
> (Barry, 1995: 204)

Yet, to treat people in an impartial manner does not imply to 'show equal concern for all'. The impartial treatment of two groups X and Y depends upon the Z and W involved. If X and Y differ with regard to W, then impartiality may require different treatment on Z. Not making such distinction would in some cases raise objections of partial treatment. Thus, criminals with different histories W may have different treatment Z. People with different abilities W must be given different rewards Z, because otherwise they are not treated in an impartial way. Impartiality is not the same as equality.

Fair play, institutions and impartiality

One may employ the model of the chess game in order to identify two concerns for public policy derived from a theory of justice. If human interaction is approached as a game of chess, then justice would require that the institutions of chess are fair and that the set of rules are implemented by fair umpires. Justice would certainly not be the only requirement upon the rules of the chess game. A number of other requirements are very much at stake such as for instance technical considerations of various kinds, calling for an exciting game as well as a feasible game. But as to the requirement of fairness, impartiality would loom large. X and Y would have to follow the same rules, implemented in the same way for both players, have the same pieces and the same amount of time for play, but fairness also entails that there be a clear connection between Z and W: the winner takes all on the basis of his/her successful completion of the game in accordance with the institution of chess. The players are equal under the rules, but they are certainly not to be treated equally in terms of rewards or outcomes.

The economy resembles a game of chess. Various players interact under more or less clearly specified institutions governing the interaction in various markets for labour, capital, equity, goods and services. Justice requires that the interaction is fair.

Impartiality could hardly be both a necessary and sufficient condition for fairness in human interaction. Fair games would require additional things such as feasibility, measured among other things by means of transaction costs. But the requirement of impartiality would be a necessary condition, both with regard to the institution itself and with regard to its implementation.

Can markets satisfy this condition for a fair game? Can markets be impartial? Barry denies that this may be the case, stating about a so-called Nozickean society or the ideal type of a market society:

> Strict impartiality will in such a society be an obligation almost entirely confined to people acting in juridical and bureaucratic capacities, whose functions will be very limited.
>
> (Barry, 1995: 202)

Partiality will be the characteristic feature of a market society, because:

> People would be free to do anything they chose to do provided only that they did not overstep the boundaries set by the persons and property of others. However, against this advantage have to be offset the disadvantages of leaving people on such a loose rein, and these tell conclusively against it.
>
> (Barry, 1995: 202)

This is not the place to discuss whether market regimes are correctly described here. What is important to emphasise is that markets do have institutions which operate under a requirement for impartiality which is policed in various ways (Williamson, 1985). Whether the institutions of the market economy can be improved upon is certainly a very important matter of public policy-making, as one may wish to argue the case that state intervention could be expanded in quantity or strengthened in quality.

A quite different matter of justice concerns whether the outcomes of market operations are acceptable. The institutions of real life games just as the game of chess separate winners and losers. No one would reasonably reject these institutions as long as they are impartial in themselves and they have been implemented in an impartial manner. But once the game is over and X has been declared the winner to receive the prize W, then what to do with Y who lost the game and received nil?

Justice as fairness in human interaction is one thing, whereas justice in income compensation or maintenance is another. Scoring the right winner requires certain institutions, but the amelioration of the predicament of the losers calls for other kinds of institutions. Impartiality is certainly a very important feature of the first kind of justice institutions, but what does impartiality entail for the construction of the second type of justice institutions? Barry writes furthermore in his rejection of the market society:

> To begin with, almost everyone would have reason to fear the prospect of being reduced to destitution by the operation of an economic system in which the only sources of money were inheritance, gift, savings, selling one's labour power to an employer, and providing goods and services to the market. . . . At the very least, the parties to the hypothetical contract would insist on a 'safety net' to avert destitution.
>
> (Barry, 1995: 203)

Here there is talk about an entirely different matter, namely the maintenance of income or compensation against losses in the face of adversity, poor performance or merely bad luck. Such demands may be just even if the operation of the institutions has been fair. The critical question for the welfare state is here: how much security or compensation should government provide? What levels of income maintenance would no one reasonably reject?

Barry's mistake

Searching for a just solution to the problem of income and wealth distribution we turn back to the threefold distinction between justice as mutual advantage, justice as reciprocity and justice as impartiality. If we reject the first two approaches to justice when it comes to the identification of institutions for fair play, then they would presumably be equally deficient when it comes to redistribution. But can impartiality really provide redistributional criteria?

The difficulty is to identify the criterion C, or the set of criteria C, if one wishes to employ several ones. In order for C to be just it must be the case that: the distributional criterion C is one that no one could reasonably reject, as long as we follow the Scanlonian approach. There is no lack of candidates: need, desert, aggregate utility, liberty, endowments and equality. But which one is it that no on can reasonably reject when these criteria have different implications? Barry suggests that impartiality is a strong candidate for C as the criterion on a just income distribution. Really?

Although few have spoken about impartial distributions of income and wealth or an impartial redistributional income policy, it is still possible to conceive of a definition along the following lines: (DF) 'The distribution of income and wealth is just in society S' = 'In S income and wealth are distributed impartially'. Yes, but impartially in relation to what?

DF is elliptic or opaque, because it leaves out the crux of the matter, viz. the norm against which impartiality is to be tested. Incomes and wealth may be distributed in an impartial manner according to a lot of criteria: achievement, wants, endowments, and so on. Impartiality is a powerful criterion – that is true, because it prohibits discrimination. But it is not powerful enough to identify a necessary and sufficient condition for a distribution of incomes and wealth to be just, since it is basically elliptical or opaque.

Barry strongly links impartiality with equality. This is erroneous. A distribution of income and wealth can very well be impartial but comprise sharp income differences as long as there is no discrimination involved. Successful tennis players are better paid than university professors simply because their accomplishments have a higher market value. Should government tax tennis players sharply and redistribute to the lower income strata? Is that a policy no one could reasonably reject, meaning that it is just? Why? Perhaps such a redistributional policy would entail a partial treatment of the achievers?

Barry claims that justice = equality through the third link impartiality. Thus we have: Justice = Impartiality; (2) Impartiality = Equality; (3) Justice = Equality. It is the link (2) that does not hold. Barry's mistake about impartiality and equality cannot be explained by his starting-point for people to agree upon what is justice:

> The essential idea is that fair terms of agreement are those that can reasonably be accepted by people who are free and equal.
>
> (Barry, 1995: 112)

But people are not equal. People have different tastes, skills, ambitions and accomplishments. In any case, even if the differences between people could be minimised, it does not follow that people 'who are free and equal' would necessarily agree on an equal distribution of income. They would most certainly favour impartiality but they need not underline equality.

There is a fundamental misunderstanding in Barry of what the concept of impartiality is all about. This is how a society where impartiality would be maximised is described:

> In an attempt to secure strict impartiality in all areas of life a huge number of decisions would have to be turned over to public officials; and all decisions left in private hands would be open to scrutiny and censure on the basis of the hypertrophied positive morality of the society.
>
> (Barry, 1995: 205)

Surely each and everyone could reasonably reject such a conception of a just society. The error here is that impartiality can only be maximised with regard to some norm of criteria such as skill in playing chess, seniority in promoting bureaucrats or the payment of income compensation according to a fixed policy. Without the norm or the criterion, impartiality cannot be applied.

The inefficiency of income redistribution

Now, does income redistribution work? This is quite another question. It does not ask whether transfer programmes reduce total output in the economy. Instead, it asks whether income maintenance programmes have any redistributive effect, whatever the excess burden involved – low or high.

Calculating the total impact of the redistributive branch of government and also taking into account the occurrence of redistribution in kind in the allocative branch of government, the findings tend to come close to Director's Law. Redistribution in kind occurs when services are provided free of charge to very particular groups, while the financing of these services is based upon taxes that all have to share.

Director's Law states that all in all income maintenance programmes have only a slight redistributive impact, favouring the middle classes. Interestingly, the amount of real redistribution accomplished from the rich to the poor is very seldomly substantial. The middle classes benefit from most of the redistributive schemes, whether redistribution in kind or in money, at the same time as they take on the bulk of the taxation burden. The middle classes tend to use the free allocative services heavily, which is not true of the rich and the poor.

The evidence in favour of Director's Law – equality of income can only be achieved when poverty is shared by all – seems universal. It is supported not only by US studies but also by evidence from welfare states, such as Scandinavia (Stigler, 1970; Jakobsson and Normann, 1974; Musgrave and Jarrett, 1979).

Conclusion

Public management theory has not much preoccupied itself with income maintenance programmes. The reforms introducing a so-called workfare state imply that transfer programmes may also enter the domain of management, at least to some extent. It would definitely hurt the prevailing conception of the redistribu-tive government as a set of entitlements (Gutmann, 1998).

Yet, governments may be very tempted to launch a workfare state, because the income maintenance programmes are very costly. Besides the direct cost, there are the excess burden costs, on both the income and the expenditure sides of the economy. In many OECD countries, the redistributive branch of govern-ments is now larger than the allocative branch of government. The expansion of the costs for transfer programmes has been quite substantial in most countries during the last two decades. This is true not only of the welfare states but also of the welfare societies.

The argument that impartiality is the core concept in justice has been anal-ysed, because income maintenance or income redistribution tends to be based on justice. The critique made here against the Barry theory of justice is that one should make a couple of critical distinctions in the concept of impartiality as well as separate it from the concept of equality.

Social justice theory would be helpful for public sector reform if it could deliver solutions to two distinct problems: (1) Which institutions are fair in rela-tion to competitive human interaction? (2) Which institutions are just when it comes to compensating those who do less well in competitive interaction? Justice as impartiality is not enough to solve both these two urgent social questions.

The discussion about justice in the social sciences could employ the following distinctions, which have been analysed above:

1   Impartial institutions versus an impartial application of institutions.
2   Impartial institutions for the competitive interaction between persons versus institutions that compensate those who would fare less well in competitive interaction.

The aim has been to emphasise how important it is to make the distinctions in (1) and (2). Linking impartiality to equality is far more problematic than believed by many (Nagel, 1991).

6 Welfare states or welfare societies?

Introduction

I wish to argue that the basic political choice that confronts the advanced societies in the world is to choose between a welfare society and a welfare state. This amounts to a regime choice that has profound implications for the distinction between the public and the private sectors in a society. It is the welfare societies that have been keen upon engaging in public sector reform, especially the approach associated with new public management.

The way a country makes the distinction between the public sector and the private sector is highly relevant from both political and economic points of view. It is a commonplace that political parties to the right favour the private sector, whereas parties to the left often wish to increase or maintain the public sector. This is the classical distinction in political economy, as it is connected with the separation between two different mechanisms of coordination: the state and the market (Hayek, 1935; Friedman, 1964; Brus and Laski, 1990).

The demarcation between politics and economics tends to reflect the prevailing values in a democracy, because voters may express their preferences for the mix of the public and the private sectors in elections or in referenda. Decisions on items of taxes or expenditures may be linked to such overall preferences for the state or the market. Sometimes entire elections or referenda are fought upon the issue of whether the public sector should be diminished, increased or simply maintained.

The aim of this chapter is twofold. First, we wish to discuss how one identifies a welfare society or a welfare state. This distinction pertains to the OECD set of countries, i.e. to the countries with a democratic regime and with a market economy. These countries all have more or less public programmes that provide protection for individuals against the vagaries of the capitalist system. When can one say that a country has a sufficiently large public sector to warrant the designation 'welfare state'? Let us focus upon Switzerland, which – all used to agree – was to be classified as a welfare society.

Second, we must examine the implications of the choice between these two kinds of politico-economic regimes. Their pros and cons must be found in the social and economic consequences that they promote, one would be inclined to assume. The standard image of the choice between welfare societies and welfare states is that it involves choosing between different trade-offs between efficiency and equality. Let us again pursue this idea of two different outcome configurations in relation to welfare societies and welfare states in relation to Switzerland examining its socio-economic performance during the last three decades.

The public/private sector distinction in Switzerland

The standard image of Switzerland, launched with fervour by the public choice school of the country, used to be that it has a politico-economic regime favouring markets, very much due to its exceptional political institutions that would limit rent-seeking and reduce the power of fiscal illusions (Pommerehne and Schneider, 1978; Kirchgässner and Pommerehne, 1997; Feld and Kirchgässner, 1999). However, this picture of Switzerland is not correct today and has perhaps been inaccurate for quite some time. Already in 1980 Blümle and Schwarz published an article which showed that the Swiss public sector was of considerable size, measured from the income side.

Yet, it must be emphasised that how the politico-economic regime of Switzerland is to be described remains a contested issue in international research. Can Switzerland today be classified as a welfare state with its typical 50–50 per cent mix of the public and the private? The classification of Switzerland in relation to the distinction between the public and the private sectors has implications for the social sciences, especially for research on the outcomes of the public sector. It is highly relevant for the comparative enquiry into the welfare state (Castles, 1998; Obinger, 1998; Esping-Andersen, 1999).

Is Switzerland a welfare society?

In the contemporary debate about the welfare state, as it occurs in the OECD set of countries, the separation between the public and the private sectors has been considered to be of great importance when different politico-economic regimes have been identified. In 1990, G. Esping-Andersen suggested a much discussed regime classification, covering three types: (1) High de-commodification = social democratic type; (2) Medium de-commodification = Christian democratic type; (3) Low de-commodification = liberal type. The larger the public sector, the more likely de-commodification, he argued (1990: 51).

Esping-Andersen placed Switzerland into category 2. But he also pointed out that in relation to pensions Switzerland entered into the 'residualist systems, in which the market tends to prevail at the expense of either social security or civil-service privilege' (1990: 86). In a recent publication, Esping-Andersen identifies Switzerland as a liberal regime (1999: 77, note 7).

Another well-known researcher on the welfare state states that it is difficult to place Switzerland in one category. Thus, F. Castles in 1998 distinguished between four types of politico-economic regimes: (1) English-speaking; (2) Scandinavian type; (3) Continental Western-Europe; (4) Southern European type. He states that Switzerland and Japan form a residual type of their own (1998: 8–9): 'The Swiss case is certainly unusual in a variety of ways, but Switzerland's non-inclusion in the family groupings here is essentially arbitrary' (ibid.: 9). Perhaps the use of classifications like that of Esping-Andersen or that of Castles is somewhat confusing, because it is not transparent today how a social democratic welfare state differs from a Christian democratic one, or how the welfare state varies from Northern to Southern Europe. What is de-commodification? A real or moral conception?

This image of Switzerland as the main exception in Western Europe, so often encountered in the international research on the welfare state, should be questioned. One needs to examine both international and Swiss data on the size of its public sector.

Is Switzerland a welfare state?

We suggest that one only employs a clear dichotomy, operationalised in relation to the standard items used in the international public finance statistics: (1) The welfare state with a public sector of about 45–55 per cent of GDP; (2) The welfare society with a public sector of about 30–35 per cent of GDP (Lane and Maeland, 1998).

In the OECD set today, all countries with a stable state have a public sector larger than the minimum size that characterised Hong Kong before the transfer of authority to China, and no countries have the tiny private sector that characterised the communist countries. However, the alternative mixes of the public sector and the private sector in the form of a welfare state or a welfare society constitute a true variation in the OECD set, which is also a highly contested political issue in rich countries that are democratic and adhere to the market economy, i.e. the OECD set of countries.

One set of countries favours the state, or government at various levels, whereas another set emphasises markets much more when it comes to the allocation of goods and services or the redistribution of money. The first set, the welfare states, tends to have about 50 per cent of GDP in the form of general receipts or in the form of total outlays, depending upon which side of the public household one focuses upon. The second set, the welfare societies, tends to score considerably lower, or around 30–35 percent of GDP. How is Switzerland to be classified?

In the comparative study of the welfare state, it is absolutely vital that one applies the same criteria in the same way to the different countries in the OECD set, although one may have different ideas about which criteria to apply. However, the OECD has itself contributed to the confusion about Switzerland, as it has only recently changed its classification of the country. It used to place Switzerland among the countries with very low public expenditures.

The OECD reclassification

The OECD has erected an impressive data base on National Accounts. It has for a long time stated numbers for Switzerland that indicate that it is a welfare society. However, the OECD has now changed its numbers for Switzerland, realising that they have been calculated in a manner that is not correct, i.e. the figures for Switzerland have not been comparable to other member countries of the OECD, including the same items of public expenditures.

The OECD revision of the Swiss numbers is mainly a matter of rendering the Swiss statistics fully comparable with the data on other countries. It is a well-known fact that the OECD system of National Accounts faces difficult problems of both validity and reliability. Actually, Switzerland may itself have contributed to the confusion, as it decided to employ the current international system for National Accounts only in 1997.

Recent figures concerning Current Receipts and Total Outlays for the OECD set are stated in Table 6.1, covering all levels of government or the so-called consolidated public sector for the late 1990s. These figures can be regarded as being as close to the correct picture as one can come when using an international data series, where figures always have to be rearranged in order to satisfy comparability between countries. They indicate that Switzerland is a welfare state, both on the income side and the expenditure of the public household, i.e. total public sector revenues and expenditures, when excluding the public enterprises within infrastructure.

From Table 6.1 it is clear that Switzerland is closer to the standard continental Western-European welfare state regime than to the Anglo-Saxon welfare society regime that is dominant in the peripheral democracies, i.e. the United States, Canada, Australia, New Zealand, Japan and Ireland. But can these numbers be trusted entirely?

As a matter of fact, these most recent OECD statistics predict that Switzerland will have the largest public sector in the year 2001, measured from the income side, or almost 57 per cent of GDP. On the output side, Switzerland will have the third largest public sector, according to this estimation. However, the 1999 figures do not seem to be entirely accurate, for instance with regard to Luxembourg.

Let us consider data taken from a classical Swiss source, which employs the standard public finance categories, namely the statistical yearbook of the country, which now has data for the 1950s up until 1996.

The Swiss data

To grasp the overall structure of the Swiss public sector, we will use one Swiss publication that renders exact definitions of its measures besides stating series that may be used for longitudinal purposes. We are referring to the publication: *Statistisches Jahrbuch der Schweiz (SJ)*. It is as a matter of fact extremely instructive

Table 6.1 General government current receipts (% of nominal GDP)

	1970	*1980*	*1990*	*1995*	*2000**
Australia	24.9	29.3	32.3	31.8	33.0
Austria	38.8	45.4	46.2	47.5	46.6
Belgium	39.3	48.1	47.9	49.2	49.1
Canada	34.6	36.5	42.1	42.0	42.5
Czech Republic	–	–	–	41.5	40.0
Denmark	–	–	55.0	56.8	56.3
Finland	34.3	40.3	49.9	50.7	49.6
France	39.1	45.6	47.7	48.0	49.8
Germany	37.4	43.7	41.8	45.0	45.6
Greece	27.2	32.0	34.9	44.5	47.2
Hungary	–	–	48.3	42.8	39.4
Iceland	–	–	33.3	36.0	36.7
Ireland	–	34.1	35.0	34.0	32.9
Italy	28.8	33.5	42.1	44.2	45.9
Japan	20.6	27.6	34.2	32.0	30.5
Korea	16.8	19.3	21.8	23.5	24.8
Luxembourg	–	–	–	–	–
Mexico	–	–	–	–	–
The Netherlands	35.6	46.2	43.7	43.6	43.0
New Zealand	–	–	44.0	41.9	40.3
Norway	40.0	49.3	52.3	51.1	51.4
Poland	–	–	–	44.4	40.0
Portugal	22.1	28.7	35.5	38.8	42.5
Spain	20.8	28.0	35.6	35.5	36.9

Source: Analytical Databank, OECD (http://www.oecd.org/).

Note: *Estimates and projections (*Economic Outlook*, no. 66, December 1999, OECD).

in these matters, as it is clearly structured in accordance with the basic distinctions in public finance theory (Musgrave, 1959; Musgrave and Musgrave, 1980).

First, the basis for all estimations of public sector size will be stated, namely the nominal GDP. We will use current price estimates of the gross domestic product at market prices – see Table 6.2 for a series from 1960 to 1996, covering ten-year periods at first and five-year periods later on.

Table 6.2 indicates that GDP growth in Switzerland has been slow in the mid-1990s, whereas the GDP increased in a steady and strong manner in the 1960s and 1970s (see *Statistisches Jahrbuch der Schweiz* 1998: 172). If GDP expansion is mediocre but public expenditures grow fast, then the relative share of the public sector could change rather dramatically.

One has discussed the causes of the stagnation of the Swiss economy with almost zero average real growth in 1990–1995 and 1 per cent average growth for

Table 6.2   Switzerland: GDP at market prices (current prices, million Swiss francs)

1950	1960	1970	1980	1985	1990	1993	1996
18,270	36,810	88,850	177,345	241,345	327,585	357,130	363,815

Source: Statistisches Jahrbuch der Schweiz, 1960–1996.

1996–1998, but without coming to any definitive conclusion. I will dare to suggest a new answer to this much debated (both domestically and internationally) puzzle, after I have stated correct numbers for the public sector.

Second, the size of the Swiss public sector will be estimated using the distinction between public resource allocation and income maintenance. Speaking of the Swiss public sector, we follow the excellent distinctions that the *Statistisches Jahrbuch* employs, which correspond fully to both the theoretical distinctions in public finance and the OECD system for calculating the National Accounts of each member country.

The *SJ* makes it crystal clear that the entire sector of public enterprises – federal, continual or communal – falls outside of the concept of the public sector in the Swiss statistics (*SJ*, 1998: 476). And this sector is not small in Switzerland, as most infrastructure (roads, railroad, electricity, telecommunications, water, sewage) has been handled by means of public enterprises.

The key distinction in the *SJ* for the Swiss public sector is that between (1) Finances publiques (öffenliche Finanzen) and (2) Securité sociale et assurances (Soziale Sicherheit und Versicherung), which corresponds in an almost exact manner to the classical separation in public finance theory between: (1) public resource allocation and (2) public resource redistribution or income maintenance.

Table 6.3 presents the absolute and relative numbers for public resource allocation, using the above figures for GDP as the basis. We may indeed observe a quick expansion of the allocative side of the public sector, i.e. the costs for the provision of public services that are almost free of charge.

Between 1960 and 1980, the allocative public sector increased step by step, or almost seven-fold in current prices and 10 per cent relatively. From 1980 and onwards the rate of expansion has again been staggering in absolute numbers,

Table 6.3   Switzerland: public finances 1950–1996 (expenditures, current prices, million Swiss francs)

	1950	*1960*	*1970*	*1980*	*1990*	*1993*	*1996*
Absolute	3,897	6,478	20,285	47,524	86,614	110,244	114,520
Relative to GDP	21.3	17.6	22.8	26.6	26.4	30.3	31.5

Sources: Statistisches Jahrbuch der Schweiz, 1960 – (öffentliche Finanzen).

the public sector almost tripling in current costs between 1980s and up to now. In relation to the GDP, there is a considerable 5 per cent increase in fifteen years.

These numbers indicate clearly that the allocative part of the public sector is growing faster than the GDP. Actually, these numbers indicate that the public sector is virtually driving out the private sector. In relative terms, the expansion is considerable, from 17 per cent in 1960 to 32 per cent in 1996.

To these allocative numbers, we must add the costs for income maintenance, as these programmes are not only numerous in Switzerland but belong under public law, as *SJ* declares correctly (*SJ*, 1998: 340). The whole set of transfer payment programmes is obligatory. The major programs are various pensions (AVS, BV), sickness and accidents payments (KV, UV), unemployment benefits (ALV) and family allowances (FZ). It appears that Switzerland has a full-scale supply of welfare state programmes in the redistributive branch of government.

Table 6.4 states how the costs have developed for income maintenance, with the exclusion of the item social assistance, which in the *SJ* enters the item Finances publiques. Under the item Assurance sociales are all the costs for the programmes that belong under social security regulated by means of public law. Social assistance falls under the discretion of the various governments in the Swiss federal system and thus enters Finances publiques and not Assurances sociales.

One may list the distinguishing features: 'Les assurances sociales se distinguent par: (1) leur caractère obligatoire (2) leur statut d'institution de droit public; (3) l'existence de prestations minimales; (4) leur vocation non lucrative; (5) redistribution; (6) les cotisations supportent seulement une part du cout' (*SJ*, 1998: 340). Table 6.4 shows the expansion of the Swiss transfer state.

The redistributive state in Switzerland has almost exploded in size during the last four decades. The growth in income maintenance obligations of the Swiss state against its population has been spectacular, transfer payments rising from 6 per cent of GDP in 1980 to 20 per cent in 1996.

To derive the entire size of the public sector today we need only add the figures from Finances publiques – the costs for provision of public services – to the numbers from Assurance sociales – the costs for income maintenance, besides including also the interest payments upon the public debt. These two items – allocative and redistributive expenditures – add up to a public sector of the average Western European size of about 50 per cent of GDP.

Table 6.4 Switzerland: social security 1960–1995 (expenditures, current costs, million Swiss francs)

	1960	*1970*	*1980*	*1985*	*1990*	*1993*	*1995*
Absolute	2,297	9,626	25,278	33,463	54,188	69,565	75,508
Relative to GDP	6.2	10.8	14.7	13.9	16.5	15.5	20.8

Source: Statistisches Jahrbuch der Schweiz, 1960– (Soziale Sicherheit und Versicherung).

Switzerland as a full scale welfare state

Switzerland now presents a full-scale comprehensively sized welfare state that is in no way different from the average Western European model. There are some special features in the Swiss welfare state, as for instance the use of private insurance companies to pay for publicly provided health care services. But these special features do not change the overall image of Switzerland as a comprehensive welfare state of the Western European type. It is, after all, obligatory to pay private insurance fees for health care. And the amount of actuarial principles in the pension system is not much, because the AVS is to a large extent basically a pay-as-you go system.

Let us look at the present structure of the Swiss welfare state from the expenditure side, using an alternative way of presenting the structure of the public sector. Table 6.5 covers the major budgetary items aggregated for all

Table 6.5   Switzerland: structure of the public sector (current expenditures 1995, million Swiss francs)

Items of expenditure	Absolute cost	Percentage of the entire public sector
Allocation (1995)		
Public goods	22,089	12.2
Education, culture and leisure	24,542	13.5
Health care	14,224	7.8
Social care	6,738	3.7
Infrastructure	11,209	6.2
Environment	4,482	2.5
Sum	83,284	45.9
Income maintenance (1995)		
Agriculture etc.	5,973	3.3
Pensions (AVS)	24,416	13.4
Pensions (BV)	14,200	7.8
Disabled (AI)	6,571	3.6
Sickness insurance (AM)	14,754	8.1
Accident insurance (AA)	3,160	1.7
Unemployment insurance (AC)	4,154	2.3
Family Allowances (AF)	3,832	2.1
Social care	13,115	7.2
Sum	90,175	49.5
Debt service	8,383	4.6
Total	181,459	100

Source: *SJ* 1998: 343 and 483.

Note: This estimation of the size of the Swiss public sector amounts to a share of GDP of roughly 50 per cent. The cost of administration has been excluded from Assurances Sociales. It is slightly lower than the figures in Tables 6.3 and 6.4 reflecting the possibility of minor double calculations in Tables 6.3 and 6.4.

levels of government, i.e. whether they occur at the federal, cantonal or communal level.

This way of presenting the structure of the public sector is related to but not entirely similar to the system employed in Tables 6.3 and 6.4. All the income maintenance programmes have been among the insurance categories, although social care and support for agriculture are placed under public resource allocation in the *SJ*.

On the basis of Table 6.5, it seems undeniable that Switzerland has such a large public sector at 50 per cent of the GDP or more that it is to be characterised as a welfare state.

Understanding Switzerland: how exceptional is the country?

Stating how Switzerland relates to the distinction between welfare societies and welfare states is one step towards a new analysis of the Swiss public sector.

The classical argument in the Swiss public choice school was that Switzerland owed its small public sector to its special political institutions. Now that we have shown that Switzerland's public sector is by no means exceptional in Western Europe, then we may also question the theory: if the special Swiss political institutions could not prevent a major process of public sector expansion, then perhaps they do not help explain the small public sector size in the 1950s and 1960s?

Switzerland is an interesting case in the comparative research on the welfare state and the distinction between the public and the private sector, especially when Switzerland is placed correctly in relation to the standard Western European model of a welfare state with about 50 per cent of GDP going to government. A few well-known models may be examined in the light of the revision of the Swiss numbers (Lane and Ersson, 1997).

First, arriving at a correct estimate of the overall nature of the Swiss public sector would be a step towards understanding how Switzerland relates to the crucial choice between a welfare state and a welfare society. It must be pointed out though that the level of affluence in Switzerland at an average of 25,000 US dollars (purchasing power parities) is extremely high, comparatively speaking. In the OECD statistics, only Luxembourg (32,500) and the US score higher (28,000) (Table 2.1). Yet, Switzerland faces a growth problem that appears more and more grave.

Second, one needs to conduct research on the implications of a large public sector in Switzerland upon its rate of economic growth. Countries with huge public expenditures run sooner or later into what I have dared to call 'Swedish disease', which stands for the experience of Sweden with excess burden from tax wedges, disincentives from various generous subsidies and mounting deficits and accumulating debts (Lane and Ersson, 1997).

That Switzerland does not suffer from Swedish disease is evident from its strong currency (Swiss francs), but its dismal growth record may be caused by the very rapid expansion of the public sector since 1980. A few cantons have engaged in rather staggering forms of deficit spending, even sanctioned in referenda.

Finally, according to the new figures Switzerland follows the well-known Wagner's law about modernisation driving up the size of the public sector, instead of being researched as an exception to this law. Yet, Switzerland does not achieve much income equality despite its huge income maintenance programmes, although it is a well-known fact that large public expenditures are conducive to income equality.

Summing up

The OECD revision of the size of the public sector in Switzerland should be seen not only as a truthful correction, but also as a stimulus for public sector research. Switzerland is no longer an exceptional welfare society in the centre of Europe, but may be analysed in accordance with the Wagner model, affluence promoting public expenditures. The puzzle of the low growth rate in the Swiss economy also becomes more understandable.

The figures presented in the tables above challenge the image of Switzerland that the Swiss public choice school has propagated for a long period. Switzerland certainly has exceptional political institutions, but Switzerland is not an exceptional country when it comes to the choice of a politico-economic regime. Switzerland is actually very close to the standard Western European welfare state model, and it is very far from a welfare society model like for instance Australia and New Zealand. The analysis of the Swiss public sector in the Swiss public choice school (Frey and Bohnet, 1993) is, I dare to say, erroneous.

Accomplishing a revision of how Switzerland relates to the distinction between welfare societies and welfare states brings about a new picture of the Swiss public sector. Now, it is time to connect up with welfare state theory and the distinction between a welfare society and a welfare state.

Welfare society or welfare state: the regime consequences

Let us examine three basic theories of the welfare society–welfare state distinction in the light of the above revision of Switzerland. Placing Switzerland correctly affects, it will be seen, the evaluation of our theories of the outcomes of the two basic regime alternatives, the welfare society and the welfare state. Three key theories may be consulted when it comes to interpreting what it means for a country to be a welfare society or a welfare state, or to change from one to the other.

Theory 1: Wagner's Law

Economic advancedness drives up the relative size of the public sector. Switzerland used to be considered an anti-Wagnerian case, being high on modernisation (GDP) and low on public sector size. With a totally revised number for Switzerland, Wagner's Law will most probably receive a higher level of empirical support.

At the same time it becomes more clear that the basic distinction between welfare states and welfare societies concerns the separation between Western Europe on the one hand and the European settler countries outside of Europe on the other hand. Why are the US, Japan, Canada, Australia and New Zealand different from Western Europe in terms of the choice between a welfare state and a welfare society? Wagner's Law fails to provide an answer to this question.

When Switzerland is reclassified, then the confrontation between continental Western Europe and the Anglo-Saxon countries appears much more transparently. There is simply no longer one major exception in the centre of Europe that is more similar to the Anglo-Saxon democracies than to the standard European model of a welfare state. In continental Europe, all countries except the former communist countries are welfare states. The United Kingdom and Ireland are perhaps more akin to the peripheral democracies than continental Europe, when it comes to the mix of the private and the public sectors.

Theory 2: Lane's Law

The larger the public sector, the lower the rate of economic growth. Although one cannot find one particular author who has suggested this theory, it is well known in the literature. Perhaps one could call it 'Lane's Law', due to the simple reason that I have advocated it on several occasions (Lane and Ersson, 1997).

Switzerland used to be considered a counter-case to the inverse relationship between public sector size and economic growth, because it was seen as low on both public expenditures at the same time as it really has scored low on economic growth since about 1980. With the revised Swiss figures the hypothesis of a direct impact from public sector size upon economic stagnation would receive support also in the case of Switzerland.

Actually, one would then be able to explain why Switzerland has displayed such a dysmal growth performance during the last decade. Other factors have been suggested: the protection of markets, the changing status of migrant workers, and the growing isolation of the country in relation to European integration. However, public sector size seems a more adequate explanation.

Theory 3: Director's Law

Huge public expenditures will have an overall mild redistributive consequence upon income inequalities. This is the general hypothesis suggested by Director, in an attempt to explain why the total effect of several redistributive programmes often is rather meagre (Stigler, 1970).

Income inequalities tend to be substantial in poor countries, but affluence is only one of many predictors of income equality. A large public sector could drive down income inequalities by two mechanisms, one referring to the income side (taxation) and another referring to the expenditures side (income support, goods and services free).

However, the redistribution impact will be a mild one, tending to benefit the middle classes as being in a median voter position. Thus, one may expect that the public sector impact slightly reduces income inequalities, holding constant the negative impact of the level of affluence upon income inequalities (the trickle-down effect).

Let us now test these three models of the causes and consequences of the public sector by means of a cross-sectional regression analysis, relying upon most recent available data about the OECD countries and considering Switzerland as a normal Western European case.

Test of the models

What are the consequences of a large public sector? Table 6.6 contains the results of three regression analysis, corresponding to the three models specified above.

The findings from the three regression analyses indicate support for all three public sector models, discussed above. The estimates of the key parameters in the three equations show an interaction between key factors that is in accordance with the models in terms of both direction and strength.

The findings in Table 6.6 show also that another factor, trade union density, is of great importance for explaining public sector size. It is even more important than affluence when it is a matter of accounting for the variation in public sector size among the OECD countries. As a matter of fact, it helps us to account for why continental Europe has a different mix of the public and the private sectors than the Anglo-Saxon democracies.

Table 6.6 Regression analysis of public sector models

		Growth 1980–1995	Public sector size	LIS	GINI
Public sector	coeff	−0.05		−0.37	−0.34
Size	t-stat	−1.82		−2.75	−3.99
Affluence	coeff	0.00	0.00	−0.00	−0.00
	t-stat	0.79	2.05	−0.90	−0.37
Trade union	coeff		0.20		
Density	t-stat		2.32		
const	coeff	3.24	26.52	49.57	49.84
	t-stat	2.63	3.99	6.63	12.58
adj rsq		0.05	0.19	0.24	0.39
N		26	29	20	27

Note: Economic growth 1980–1995: *Human Development Report* 1998; PPP 1996: World Bank 1998b, World Bank Atlas 1998; Trade Union Density 1985: ILO 1997; LIS: Luxembourg Income Study; GINI: World Bank Data.

Public sector size appears to be a better predictor of income equality than affluence. This is an important finding which has relevance for the choice of alternative mixes of the public and the private sectors, opening up the possibility of trade-offs between macro-outcomes. Let us portray one such trade-off, namely that between low economic growth and large income inequalities, by looking at the most recently available data for some OECD countries.

The welfare societies have the edge

If the findings in Table 6.6 really hold, then there will occur two contrary effects in countries with a large public sector. On the one hand, the rate of economic growth will definitely be low. On the other hand, the extent of income equality will be rather high. By opting for a large public sector, a country would by entailment choose a trade-off between economic growth and income equality that is entirely different from the trade-off chosen by a country that favours the private sector ahead of the public sector.

Let us examine what is involved in this trade-off between economic efficiency as total output and equality as small income differences. Again, we look at the case of Switzerland.

Figure 6.1 shows the clear negative association between total public outlays and economic growth among the OECD countries. The negative association applies, it seems, with a vengeance to Switzerland, when its public sector has been correctly estimated at over 50 per cent of GDP. However, at the same time

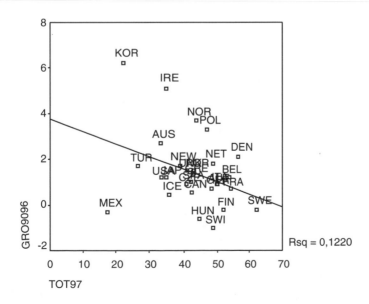

Figure 6.1 Economic growth 1990–1996 and public sector size.

Switzerland is very affluent, which, according to Wagner's Law, will put pressure upwards on public expenditures.

Thus, Switzerland sits in a jam, being squeezed from two sides. Since it is affluent, it tends to have huge public expenditures. But since it has a large public sector, its growth record is meagre.

Switzerland cannot improve its growth record by increasing its public sector. It has actually a public sector size that is in accordance with its level of affluence, if Wagner's law is to be trusted. To improve its meagre growth, Switzerland would have to embark upon public sector reform, moving towards an alternative public–private sector mix.

The connection between total public sector size and income inequality is persistently and significantly negative whatever measure we use. Among the OECD countries, there is clear evidence for the occurrence of a positive impact of the public sector upon income equality, high levels of affluence driving down income inequalities.

Figure 6.2 shows the relationship between public sector size and income inequality. It may be pointed out that the GINI-indices for Switzerland place the country at almost the highest level for Western Europe. In order to arrive at higher income inequality scores than the Swiss figure, we need to turn to the peripheral democracies like Australia and New Zealand or to the USA.

Since Switzerland has a high level of affluence, we might have expected that income inequalities are not excessive. When Switzerland is reclassified in terms of its public sector size, then we would have strong reason to expect that Swiss

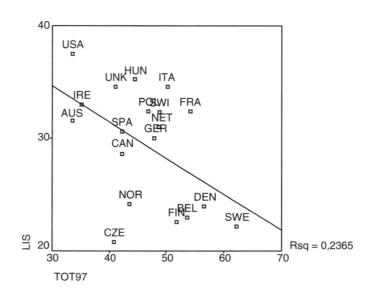

Figure 6.2   Income distribution and public sector size.

income inequality measures are lower than the scores for the Anglo-Saxon or peripheral democracies, i.e. the USA, Australia and New Zealand. Whereas Switzerland sits in a jam regarding economic growth, public sector size and affluence, Switzerland actually cannot fully reap the benefits of a huge public sector in the form of much income equality. It does somewhat worse than expected according to Director's Law.

Perhaps this trade-off can be related to the basic confrontation between two values in a democratic regime, namely freedom from government and equality by means of government?

Two performance profiles of democracies

Democracy is considered at the start of the twenty-first century to be the system of institutions that basically triumphed over its competitors, communism and fascism. To some, this is the end of a long process of institutional choice, but to others it is the beginning of a new period of institutional deliberations. The relevant question now is whether one type of democracy performs better than another type, or in our way of formulating the problem: does one democratic institution result in different outcomes than another?

Institutional superiority or institutional improvement may be based upon political, social or economic outcomes. In the theory about two types of democracy – Westminster democracy (WD) and Consensus democracy (CD) – all three types of evaluation criteria play a role. Lijphart claims that CD institutions tend to outperform WD institutions on all three evaluation criteria. At least CD institutions never do worse than WD institutions (Lijphart, 1999). We wish to argue that it is much more a question about a trade-off.

Examining data about policy outputs and economic and social outcomes in the 1990s, there are a few interesting differences between countries that score low and countries that score high on power sharing, which point at the existence of a major institutional trade-off in the set of stable democracies, i.e. the OECD countries.

The countries that score low on power sharing are the countries with strong institutionalisation of majoritarian institutions in the form of the election system or the executive. These countries include for instance the UK, the USA, Canada, Australia and New Zealand. On the other hand, there are countries which score high on power sharing, for instance the small European democracies and the Scandinavian countries, which countries favour PR election techniques and consociational or corporatist institutions.

What is striking is that the policy output and outcome configuration connected with the Anglo-Saxon democracies tends to be different from that of the continental European countries. These differences refer especially to the following three dimensions:

- public sector size
- economic growth
- income inequalities

The Anglo-Saxon democracies favour low public expenditures whereas the continental European democracies favour a large public sector. And the former countries are characterised by the combination of high economic growth and considerable income inequalities, whereas typical for the latter is an more even distribution of income, especially in the Nordic countries, and low economic growth (Jones and Schedler, 1998; Rouban, 1999).

Welfare states tend to be less dynamic than welfare societies, because they have large public sectors. Since WD institutions favour the welfare society more than CD institutions, the WD countries tend to be more dynamic than the CD countries, including Switzerland.

Conclusion

Behind much public sector reform there has been an ambition to change the mix of the public and the private sectors in a country. The choice between two alternative politico-economic regimes, the welfare state or the welfare society, is at the core of much of the political debate in the countries adhering to the institutions of a democratic society and a market economy.

Choosing between alternative mixes between the public and the private sectors involves taking a stand on a fundamental trade-off between economic efficiency interpreted as maximising total output or affluence on the one hand and income equality on the other hand. Choosing a public sector size is the instrument variable in this choice of a regime, because a large public sector has a negative impact upon economic growth but a positive impact upon income equality.

The OECD revision of the size of the public sector in Switzerland should be seen not only as a truthful correction, but as a confirmation of a few basic models in public sector research. Switzerland is no longer an exceptional welfare society in the centre of Europe – the outlier *par préférance*. But Switzerland may be analysed in accordance with the three models about public expenditures. The puzzle of the low growth rate in the Swiss economy becomes much more understandable than earlier, as a large public sector drives down economic growth, all other things being equal.

To vitalize the economy, both welfare states and welfare societies may turn to new public management. NPM, when fully implemented, breaks down the institutional separation between the public and the private sectors. It can be used in both welfare societies and welfare states. Let us turn to the analysis of this new theory of public management.

Part III

Where we are heading

The public sector reforms in the 1990s aimed at a basic change in the mix of markets and bureaucracy in society. They may be seen as reflecting an institutional choice between two different kinds of institutions that may be employed for providing goods and services: long-term contracting versus short-term contracting. This distinction has consequences also for regulative reforms and social security.

New public management suggests that contracting should become the basis for new institutions in the public sector. A contracting regime could be employed in all three branches of government: allocation, redistribution and regulation. What, more specifically, is involved in the preference for contracting rather than authority as the mechanism for handling matters in the public sector?

In the five chapters below, the pros and cons of new public management will be stated. The argument is basically that the positive contributions of NPM are a decrease in costs, increased efficiency and more transparency in objectives. At the same time, one should be aware of the limitations of NPM, as it in no way offers a complete substitute for other approaches, for instance bureaucracy.

One can look at the arrival of new public management and the extensive public sector reforms inspired by this theory from many angles. Here we examine the shift from long-term contracting, typical of bureaucracy and traditional enterprises, to short-term contracting, borrowed from private sector governance methods. Short-term contracting has three principal uses in the governance of the public sector: (1) contracting with service providers after a tendering/bidding process; (2) contracting with the CEOs of the incorporated public enterprises; and (3) contracting with executive agencies about what they should deliver.

Theoretical analysis, supported by substantial empirical evidence, suggests that short-term contracting eliminates the extensive post-contractual opportunism connected with long-term contracting, but is vulnerable to pre-contractual opportunism. Short-term contracting is not just another public sector reform fad, but constitutes a new tool for government which increases efficiency when handled with prudence. A contracting regime must, however, resolve certain contradictions that arise from the fact that government will play several roles: contractor, owner and umpire.

Contracting regimes reduce costs, especially the occurrence of X-inefficiencies, but they increase transaction costs. There is a risk for organisational failures also in NPM.

7 From long-term to short-term contracting

Introduction

The ongoing reforms of the public sectors in the OECD countries present a true challenge for theoretical interpretation. New public management presents a paradigm shift in the conduct of public sector activities. What is involved in the public sector reform in the United Kingdom, in Scandinavia and in Continental European countries as well as in Australia, New Zealand and Canada is a general reconsideration of how government may use and mix markets and bureaucracies in order to achieve its objectives with regard to the provision of goods and services with a special emphasis upon the employment of tendering and contracting out (Halligan and Power, 1992; Boston, 1995; Naschold *et al.*, 1996; Coulson, 1997; Budaus, 1999; Choi, 1999).

The 1990s public sector reforms have been vast and painstaking and they may certainly be analysed from the stand-point of several social science paradigms. Within public administration, it has been argued that the 1990s have brought about a hollowing out of the state (Rhodes, 1994; Campbell and Wilson, 1995; Peters, 1997). However, reforms in the allocative and regulative branches of government may be interpreted as the search for a new model of public sector governance.

Although the characteristics of such a new regime are far from clear or entirely known, they involve governments seeking to substitute short-term contracting for long-term contracting. Here we will employ a contractual perspective and view public sector reforms as responses to contractual failures, which may be ameliorated by the design of new institutions by means of which governments make arrangements for the provision of goods and services.

New public management, or NPM, is certainly not a coherent set of principles that replace public administration. Several commentators have called attention to the fact that new public management lacks a core set of ideas, combines different reform strategies and gives the impression of fad and fashion (Hood, 1991, 1995). While not denying that the public sector reform strategy of tendering/bidding cannot be traced back to a single body of theory, I still wish to pose the following question: to what extent is it possible to view the ongoing public sector reforms in capitalist democracies as a search for optimal institutional design?

Public sector reform, mechanism design and transaction costs

Posing a question about optimality involves the danger of committing the sin of teleology, or naïvely believing that if one can identify optimal solutions to social problems, then actors will automatically implement them. The theory of the design of institutions is orientated towards finding the rules of human interaction, which promote the achievement of optimal social outcomes (Ledyard, 1989; Meyerson, 1989). But the institutions designed must also be implementable, given the assumption that behaviour is predominantly egoistic.

Mechanism design theory looks upon the institutions that govern contractual interaction (Molho, 1997). It was basically developed for analysing contractual difficulties in the private sector, but we must ask whether it is not also applicable to the public sector. As mechanism design theory asks which institutions promote socially acceptable outcomes and reduce at the same time the incentive to cheat or lie, we may apply it to public sector reform issues, asking how governments would go about finding optimal contracts for service provision and implement them.

In order to understand public sector reform conducted in accordance with the NPM paradigm, we will focus upon the distinction between long-term contracts and short-term contracts and state what it implies in terms of a principal–agent approach to the public sector. Work upon the principal–agent framework has been progressing since the 1970s regarding problems in private sector interaction (Stiglitz, 1989), but it is nowadays often employed in modelling public sector problems, e.g. bureaucracy behaviour (Miller and Moe, 1983). The distinction between long-term and short-term contracts has, however, not been used frequently.

The principal–agent framework is highly applicable to human interaction that takes places over a considerable time horizon, involving an agreement between at least two persons according to which one (the agent) is instructed to take action on behalf of another (the principal) against money compensation (Ricketts, 1987). Agency type relationships characterise the work of professionals such as lawyers, stock-brokers and doctors, but the principal–agent framework is in a general way applicable to the employment relationship, i.e. it models the interaction between employer and employees not only in the private sector but also in the public sector (Milgrom and Roberts, 1992).

The key problem in agency relationships is to devise a contract that motivates the agent to work for the principal at the same time as the principal pays a compensation that corresponds to the effort of the agency. Since effort tends to be non-observable, there arises the problem of fully and correctly specifying the contract guiding the interaction. Post-contractual difficulties can occur when an agent shirks – moral hazard problems concerning hidden actions. Or pre-contractual opportunism can occur when an agent hides information that is relevant to the negotiation and signing of a contract – adverse selection problems resulting from asymmetric knowledge (Macho-Stadler and Perez-Castillo, 1997).

At the basis of the contractual difficulties modelled in advanced game theory (Rasmusen, 1994), we have the fundamental fact of contractual incompleteness, or the impossibility of writing a contract that covers all contingencies. Negotiating, signing and implementing a contract results in so-called transaction costs. When contracts have a short-term duration and deal with standardised goods and services, then transaction costs can be kept low, as they can be quickly arrived at and effectively enforced in court by litigation. However, when contracts concern agency relationships, then matters are different.

In the conventional transaction cost approach, the occurrence of massive transaction costs gives raise to non-market types of institutions, so-called hierarchies (Williamson, 1975; Coase, 1988). Yet, one needs to broaden the analysis of transaction costs to include also the contractual difficulties encountered in hierarchies, namely monitoring costs. Basically, contracts may be of two types, short-term or long-term, and the use of each type results in principal–agent problems. Short-term contracts are optimal when transactions costs are non-existent and long-term costs are optimal when transaction costs start running high. Add monitoring costs, however, and the analysis will be different.

Each type of contracting, long-term versus short-term, poses problems in transacting between principals and agents. Since the NPM framework proposes the massive employment of tendering/bidding, the key question for public sector reform today becomes the pros and cons of short-term contracting compared with long-term contracting, which was used as the chief institution in traditional public administration, bureaux constituting one of the most important kinds of hierarchy. When is the one, long-term contracting, more appropriate than the other, short-term contracting, and under what conditions?

Contracting under alternative regimes

Organisations may provide goods and services using either inhouse production or contracting out. Inhouse production tends to rely heavily upon long-term contracting creating hierarchies whereas contracting out relies upon tendering/bidding processes taking place in market forms and resulting in short-term contracts. Whether organisations use inhouse or outhouse production, they engage massively in contracting, a contract being a legally binding agreement.

When organisations employ numerous people, they tend to use the long-term contract which regulates only in a broad fashion what the agent is going to do for the principal against compensation in the form of a salary. The 'usual employment contract' is 'a relational contract', which specifies 'broad terms and objectives and putting in place some mechanisms for decision making' (Milgrom and Roberts, 1992: 330), providing the employer or his/her managers with authority to order the employee to do anything that is not outside of the scope of the contract.

The long-term relational contract has been typical of public organisations, especially the bureaux but also of the traditional public enterprises. Employment was basically life time, and the employees were instructed what to do by means of administrative law. The Weberian ideal type of a rational bureaucracy emphasises the positive consequences of long-term contracting for the evolution of expertise, agency independence and the Rule of Law. New public management breaks with this mode of organisation, replacing long-term contracts with short-term contracts.

Organisations may wish to enter the marketplace and buy the services they need for their provision of goods and services – outhouse production. Conventional markets operate with so-called spot market contracts, as they 'govern goods and services that are to be exchanged "on the spot"' (Milgrom and Roberts, 1992: 131). However, short-term contracting includes many other forms of contracting which has a limited time duration: procurement, contracting out, leasing, franchising and public–private partnerships. New public management is the theory that argues that these forms of contracting may provide government with better tools of governance than the traditional form of relational contracting, i.e. long-term contracting. Not all forms of relational contracting are long-term though, as several forms of principal–agent interaction have a short-term duration, but never as short as in spot market contracting.

Governments face the task of providing their citizens with goods and services. In traditional public administration governments employ the bureau or the public enterprise, i.e. inhouse production, to a high extent. In new public management there is a preference for outhouse production. This shift from one governance regime to another can be analysed by examining the pros and cons of long-term and short-term contracting, respectively.

Long-term public contracts

The theory of contracts has been developed in private sector settings where the buying and selling of objects is at stake (Shavall, 1998), as contract law and its derivatives constitute the basis of private law (Atiyah, 1996). However, it requires little imagination to approach public sector provision of goods and services as attempts at resolving contractual matters. Generally speaking, government may employ either a vast set of short-term contracts or a set of long-term contracts in order to contract for the provision of goods and services.

After all, the notion of a contract has figured now and then in political science and public administration. One of the main cores of historical political theory was the contractarian school, lasting from Grotius to Kant, i.e. over two hundred years. One may interpret not only constitutions as contracts, but also elections, although it is an open question whether speaking of elections as the making of a contract and the next election as an evaluation of the contract involves a reality or is only a metaphor. It is no doubt possible to stretch the contractual language very far. Here, we concentrate upon public contracts in a substantial sense, i.e. the making of an agreement about quantities, prices or costs between government and an agent, following negotiations about the terms of the contract.

Contracting, whether in the public or the private sectors, is always a form of exchange. Thus, state legislation falls in principle outside of contracting, as it expresses authority or command. Much state activity involves authority in the form of the making and implementation of rules of various kinds, for both the private and the public sectors. However, contracting is far from absent from the public sector. Government engages in contracting on a vast scale in order to solve allocative and regulative tasks. Thus arises the key question: which form should government choose for these contracts: long-term or short-term?

Traditionally, it has chosen the first type, but governments all over the world are now moving towards the use of the second kind. Why? Long-term contracting is at the heart of the two classical mechanisms for delivering services in the public sector, namely the bureau in the soft sector and the public enterprise in the business sector. More and more, the evaluation studies of the efficacy of the bureau and the public enterprise have indicated that they perform worse than private sector institutions when a comparison is possible (Boyne, 1998).

Allocative contracts

A considerable portion of the public sector consists of government providing services to citizens free or nearly so in the soft part of the public sector. Basically, the provision of these services is paid for by means of taxation. Here, we have not only the traditional public goods, but also the typical welfare state goods: education, health care and social care. In order to arrange a supply of these services government needs people that work for it, organising the supply. The traditional solution is to construct a bureau or an agency and hire people on long-term contracts.

Long-term contracting in public resource allocation has been seen as a positive solution to contractual problems between government as the principal on the one hand and bureaucrats and professionals as agents on the other hand. As governments tend to deal in services that have long time-limits, they face all the difficulties involved in writing complete contingencies contracts. Long-term contracting in the public sector, combining a broad based employment contract with instructions given in administrative law, offers a solution to contractual incompleteness. It identifies the contract under which a person accepts an obligation for a set of broadly defined duties against compensation in the form of tenure or life-long employment.

By using a long-term contract government accomplishes a form of stability that may be conducive not only to predictability and safety, but also to expertise among the employees. The latter would accept lower salaries than under short-term contracting, acknowledging the favour of having tenure in the form of demanding a lower salary. The standard image of public sector employment is that it is less lucrative than private sector employment, but it is safe and long lasting – so it was often stated at least.

Long-term contracting in public resource allocation employs the budgetary process, through which the agencies become funded out of taxation, to complement the direction given in administrative law. Although the budgetary process tends to result in yearly appropriations, it is still the case that the agencies funded tend to become almost immortal (Kaufman, 1976). They may be amalgamated but then they live on as sections within larger agencies. Budgeting tends to be marginalistic or incremental, except in periods of major reshuffling. The yearly budgetary process may be interpreted as a bargaining process about contractual terms concerning quantities, prices or costs (Wildavsky, 1988a), but what is typical of short-term contracting is missing, namely competition. Now, what are the chief problems in long-term contracting as used within bureaux?

Long-term contracting for agencies results in the monitoring problem, as government cannot simply trust the agency to live up to all the contractual expectations, especially when many of these remain implicit and the environment is unpredictable. What has actually been agreed upon? This is the moral hazard problem typical of contracting in a world of uncertainties. Thus, long-term contracting results not only in all the institutions that define the appropriations process funding agencies, but it requires also the setting up of institutions for monitoring. The literature in public administration is replete with various models of monitoring, centralised or decentralised, dealing with the problem of how shirking is to be minimised under a regime of long-term contracts. Monitoring costs can rapidly skyrocket. Another possibility is reputation, surrounding the agencies with a special aura, conferring prestige upon managers that uphold the reputation.

Yet, it is not the crew problem in itself that makes moral hazard so difficult in long-term contracting. How to use the personnel in an optimal fashion is a problem in both public and private organisations, i.e. metering in the analysis of so-called teams, where opportunism results in shirking strategies (Alchian, 1977). In the classical Niskanen analysis, public budgeting entails inefficient outcomes, as all agencies tend to become twice as large as their optimal size. This is a very exaggerated model about asymmetric knowledge. The key difficulty is the occurrence of X-inefficiencies as well as Y-inefficiencies.

In the budgetary process, government interacts with the agency in order to arrive at a decision about the quantity of services supplied and their cost, where government has accepted to put a grant that covers the expenses of the agency. Niskanen predicts that supply will be twice as large as optimal supply, but this outcome is only possible if government has no knowledge whatsoever about marginal costs and marginal value. In addition, it is a very cumbersome method for agencies to use private information in order to get advantages. The agency will run slack instead of maximising size – i.e. we have the problem of X-inefficiency (Frantz, 1997).

In long-term contracting between the government and its agency, there is bound to be massive moral hazard, i.e. problems of hidden action, aggravated by the severe problem of validating the contract. From a legal point of view, the agency belongs to the state and government does not take action against its own agencies by means of ordinary courts except when it is a question of the dismissal of individuals. The verification of the contract has to be done through monitoring and the use of special tribunals.

In long-term contracting, public contracts between government and the agencies are different from private contracts between parties, because the agencies are not legally independent bodies. In theory, they follow the commands of the authority of government, but in practice it is a bargaining interaction with asymmetric information, i.e. a principal–agent relationship, characterised by post-contractual opportunism meaning hidden action and private information.

In private sector principal–agent contracting, the focus is upon devising a contract that takes into account imperfect information on the part of the principal about the effort of the agent. Private principal–agent contracts involve profit sharing as well as risk sharing and compensation (Hillier, 1997). In public long-term contracts entirely different mechanisms have been used to compensate for imperfect information: planning and ex ante control, evaluation and ex post control including both auditing and performance analysis.

The special nature of the relationship between government and its agencies presents the former with a rather open contract with numerous possibilities for imposing checks upon the agency. These checks could be made by a special auditing agency on a continuous basis, or they could be done on a discrete basis as a one shot intervention. As a result of the disbelief in ex ante control, ex post surveillance techniques have become more and more frequent, involving often an obligation by each agency to evaluate itself on a continuous basis. However, long-term contracting in the public sector seemed to benefit the agent at the expense of the principal.

Despite all the innovations made in mechanism design to strengthen the position of government in relation to its allocative agencies, most of the evidence from performance analyses points to the existence of X-inefficiencies (Mueller, 1989; Boyne, 1998). The continued expansion of the public sector aggravates the inefficiency problem of the Leibenstein type, undoing whatever gains mechanism design such as the move from ex ante to ex post control may have brought about over the years. One could very well argue that a Leibenstein strategy is much more likely than a Niskanen strategy, if the agents behave opportunistically. This type of rent is much more easily captured than the maximisation strategy of Niskanen, which involves excessive supply. It is after all much more easy to hide slack than too large a supply.

Allocative long-term contracts were offered by government to either bureaux or public enterprises. Public enterprises of the traditional type had a legal status placing them in-between the bureau and the firm. Thus, they were part of government but possessed a limited degree of budgetary autonomy. However, major investment decisions and decisions on charges or rates had to be made by the ministry of finance or industry. The traditional public enterprise tended to constitute a drag on the budget, because these firms often required subventions to cover losses, especially when they were instructed to set charges low. The real cost of these firms, or the level where costs would be minimised, were not easily discovered due to the abundance of people employed as part of distribution concerns.

Yet, public enterprises were at one time considered an appropriate institutional mechanism for handling the risk of monopoly in infrastructure. Firms operating in situations of so-called natural monopolies were to be nationalised, because then government could be absolutely sure that the supplier would operate in the best interests of the country. Sometimes this is called the European solution to the problem of monopoly in infrastructure, because in the United States another institutional mechanism was put into place – the public utility, or the public regulation of a private firm. The traditional public enterprise was thus employed in public regulation, the aim of which was to enhance socially efficient solutions by means of long-term regulative contracts, stating a barrier to entry and thus creating a regulated legal monopoly (Spulber, 1989).

Regulative contracts

When taxation is not employed to pay for most of the costs in the provision of goods or services, then it is no longer a matter of bureau allocation. Instead the mechanism is the firm, which covers most of its costs by means of user fees, as in the business part of the public sector. These firms may have private or public owners. In order to curb their monopoly power government has written regulative contracts, stipulating quantity and price. These contracts used to take the form of long-term agreements, covering entry, quantities, service quality, customer remedies as well as prices.

Traditional economic regulation covered vast sectors of the economy where public enterprises or public utilities used to be active, but they have been undone in many countries (Vickers and Wright, 1988; Wright, 1994). Traditional economic regulation does not work, not even when the firm is owned by government (Stigler, 1988). The inefficiency of long-term contracting appears again in the form of hidden action on the part of the regulated industry *vis-à-vis* the regulator, i.e. government. And it takes the form of X-inefficiency, meaning that costs are not minimised. This time the higher prices allow for either excess profits, which end up with the owners as an economic rent, or it goes to the employees in the form of excess costs.

The long-term character of contracts in traditional economic regulation may not be easily detected, as such regimes used to involve yearly agreements about prices and quantities. Yet, the long-term nature of economic regulation appears from the entry restrictions that accompany agreements upon prices and quantities. Once a private or public firm had achieved entry regulation, then post-contractual opportunism became very lucrative. Again, the problem is moral hazard resulting in X-inefficiency or too high unit costs, aggravated by the difficulty of implementing the contract through monitoring devices.

It has been argued that the capture problem in public regulation – the tendency for producers to get the regulation that they basically want – can be solved by making the regulators highly credible. In order to steer away from government unconsciously choosing the regulation that maximises the interests of those concerned, especially the producers, one has suggested that regulation is handed over to independent regulatory boards with executive, legislative and judicial competencies (Majone, 1996). Yet, why would regulators have an incentive to find the optimal allocative solution and implement it, i.e. why could they still not be captured sooner or later by the producers? Because of reputation, it is argued, but is the reputation mechanism really the key to the problem of finding and implementing first-best allocative solutions?

If regulators want to build up reputation among the public, then perhaps they should care more about visibility and toughness resulting in spectacular decisions which attract mass media attention rather than display an interest in finding and implementing the optimal solution to an allocative problem. Why could not post-contractual opportunism occur among regulators, even if they focus upon reputation, in order to enhance credibility? The new theory that public regulation is feasible, reputation securing first-best solutions in allocation, bypasses entirely the strategic and tactical aspects around reputation building.

Perhaps creating contestability among competitors is more important for government relying upon the credibility of the regulators, if it wants to enhance economic efficiency in the provision of public services? The analysis of the difficulties with public enterprises as well as with public regulation point in the same direction as the analysis of the bureau, namely that government could well use another mechanism of governance than long-term contracts of various kinds.

Governments all over the world have dismantled many of the public enterprises, incorporating them into joint-stock companies, as this private firm institutional structure is more suitable both for the enterprise itself and for the governments (Rao, 1988; Clarke, 1995; Spulber, 1997). If public joint-stock companies are simply firms like any other private enterprise, then government is just an owner of equity. Public regulation cannot interfere in the specific details of a firm or put up barriers to entry, as all firms, public or private, demand the levelling of the playing field. There is little room for regulators whatever their reputation may be.

Whether one looks upon traditional public regulation as capture effort and rent-seeking or as the equilibrium outcome of legislative markets where the demand for and supply of regulation is allowed to interact (Stevens, 1993), it still seems to hold good that government could with success try another kind of governance mechanism, trusting that competition in supply is forthcoming naturally, and buy the services it wishes to provide or let the consumers buy them directly from the set of firms, be these private or public.

Summing up

The two basic institutional mechanisms in the public sector used to be the bureau and the public enterprise. They were both structured according to the logic of long-term contracting. Ongoing public sector reform activities express a profound disbelief in such contracts, which has led to a movement towards the employment of short-term contracting in both allocation and regulation. Moving away from long-term contracts towards short-term contracts involves vast institutional changes and new strategies for mechanism design. Table 7.1 depicts the four possibilities.

Table 7.1   Contracting, the soft sector and the business sector

	Contracting	
	Short-term	*Long-term*
Soft sector	Tournaments	Bureau supply
Business sector	Auctions	Entry regulation for the public enterprise

If moral hazard or post-contractual opportunism resulting in X-inefficiencies is the key to understanding the move away from long-term contracting, then are there no principal–agent difficulties in the new regimes based upon the employment of short-term contracting in the public sector? I will argue that adverse selection now surfaces, i.e. pre-contractual opportunism.

Short-term contracting regimes

Governments have started to use short-term contracting for allocative tasks in both the business sector and the soft sector. The resort to short-term contracts has been accompanied by rather dramatic institutional changes in the legal position of the providers of public services. Governments seem to prefer that they as principals interact with agents who possess a higher degree of independence than what is characteristic under long-term contracting. What matters crucially is competition among agents for the contracts with government.

Thus, there is now a clear preference for joint-stock companies as the legal form for the agent in the business sector. Often the joint-stock company remains public after the institutional reform with government as the owner of equity, partially or in total. The relation between government and the public joint-stock company is a very different one compared with the interaction between government and the traditional public enterprise. Instead of engaging in supervision and control, government may resort to market concepts like 'shareholder value' and 'return on equity'. The joint-stock company institution may also be employed in the soft sector, for instance in the provision of health care.

In order to engage in short-term contracting government looks upon the providing agents in a more neutral fashion than when doing long-term contracting. The crux of the matter in short-term contracting is competition between agents, real or potential. Thus, some agents will lose out and others will win, a relationship that may be reversed in the next round of negotiations. Agents would be drawn from a potentially large pool, including traditional public agencies, public joint-stock companies, private firms and entrepreneurs, as well as various hybrid forms.

Short-term contracting may be used for allocative purposes in both the business sector and the soft sector. What is common in both sectors is the use of tendering/bidding instead of appropriation/legislation. Although there exists a variety of mechanisms to be used in a process of tendering/bidding, tournaments may be employed in the soft sector and auctions in the business sector. Let us look in more detail at what is entailed in such short-term contracting schemes.

Tournaments

Under the internal markets regime or the purchaser/provider split mechanism, government tries to insert tendering/bidding into the provision of services in the soft sector. It involves abandoning long-term contracts and installing short-term contracts. Often agencies are reformed from public bureaux into semi-independent production units or straightforward joint-stock companies, although with considerable public ownership of equity (Thynne, 1994). Another mechanism used is the executive agency with a set of clearly specified tasks where a tendering process is used to hire a chief executive officer (CEO) on a short-term contract basis (Smith, 1999).

Moving towards tendering/bidding as the basis for making allocative contracts amounts to an immense change in government practices. It will only work if there is a pool of agents forthcoming and if government is capable of selecting the good agents rather than bad agents – the adverse selection problem. If the adverse selection problem cannot be resolved, then government will find its situation will have deteriorated compared with long-term contracting. What are the main difficulties with using short-term contracting for the supply of services in the soft sector?

Allocative functions taking place in the so-called soft sector of the public sector tend to be based upon professional expertise acquired by means of long-term training. Will a pool of competing agents always be forthcoming in relation to short-term contracts by government when agents need a long period to develop expertise? It should be pointed out that tendering/bidding has always been used by governments, but not on the scale envisaged in the new short-term contracting regimes. Thus, standard functions were often handed over to subcontractors. Can it really work on such a huge scale as entailed in the tendering/bidding schemes under new public management?

If all agents are not credible, if some agents only engage in pre-contractual opportunism hiding their real capacities – the so-called 'lemons' problem (Ackerloff, 1988), then how can government negotiate and make short-term contracts that limit both the risk of and the disruptive consequences of contractual failures in the soft sector? One can conceive of different instruments that a principal can employ to restrict the consequences of pre-contractual opportunism.

Yet, the experience with short-term allocative contracts is not entirely convincing as long-term contracting features tend to creep back in (Montin and Persson, 1996). The principal is often too eager to bind a well performing agent beyond the duration of the short-term contract agreed upon, when government has found a credible agent with specific performance qualities. In such a situation, short-term contracting will simply not work, as explained in the general model about the consequences about asset specific knowledge for the use of hierarchies versus markets (Williamson, 1986).

It is vital that one develops an understanding of the limits of short-term contracting in relation to its use within the public sector. Tendering/bidding may be achieved by means of alternative institutions such as different forms of tournaments for the provision of services in the soft sector. The impact of these institutions upon the interaction between the principal and the agent is basically negative in the sense that it helps solve the basic moral hazard problem of hidden action at the post-contractual stage, giving government an instrument to curb the opportunism of the agent. What tendering/bidding accomplishes is a reduction in asymmetrical knowledge on the part of an established agent, bound by a long-term contract. But how can government be sure that alternative bids are serious or capable of being implemented – the adverse selection question?

Tournaments involve pitting the agents off against each other asking them to deliver bids for allocating goods or services. If the bids specify not only the costs of the agents but also quantities and qualities in service provision, then one may employ yardstick or benchmark competition. Tournaments need to be organised in terms of detailed rules about tendering, the respect for which may increase the credibility of alternative bids. But contractual observation is a different matter. Short-term contracts are always, legally speaking, private law contracts between two independent parties whose validity is to be decided upon by ordinary courts, never public law or administrative courts. Adequately handled tournaments in no way guarantee that post-contractual opportunism will not occur in the form of contractual reneging.

When reneging occurs in contracts for the provision of soft sector services, then government may find little comfort in scoring a victory against an agent after a litigation procedure. Whatever compensation government may squeeze out of a reneging agent will most often have to be spent upon finding a new agent that can take over the supply quickly – the so-called switching costs. Government may of course lose against an agent in litigation simply because it signed a bad contract with a bad agent.

Auctions

Although auctions adhere to the same type of mechanism – bidding/tendering – their logic is somewhat different, making them more appropriate in the business sector (Smith, 1989). In auctions, one auctions away something to an agent who delivers the highest bid (English auction) or the agent who first accepts the requested price (Dutch auction). Thus, in tournaments the agents deliver alternative cost schemes whereas in auctions the agents offer various prices. What government may auction away is access to or use of infrastructure typically owned by government. It may also auction out property rights, thus divesting itself of infrastructure once and for all.

The classical question in traditional economic regulation concerned what to do with sunk costs and irreversible investments that were characteristic of the huge capital investments in infrastructure. Tendering/bidding schemes seem only to be viable if one disconnects ownership of the physical capital from its employment. Thus, competition between alternative agents in the delivery of infrastructure is only feasible if the owners of the assets auction them out for hiring during a specific period of time. Such leasing schemes may also involve other rights, such as the right to decide user fees, or they may be strictly limited to use of the connections.

Yet, arranging auctions may be a relatively simple task if one knows the future income streams from the operations that use the connections. But, alas, the problem of pre-contractual opportunism surfaces again. How is government to distinguish between credible bids and non-credible bids in auctions? Failure to fulfil a contract received in an auction may cause the principal as many difficulties as the agent. There are not only transaction costs involved in contractual disputes and legal action in court, as the switching costs could become considerable in relation to infrastructure.

Moving to a scheme with recurrent auctions presupposes massive deregulation of the entire sector of infrastructure. A condition is the well-known level playing field, which means that competition must be open to private firms and entrepreneurs as well as to various public producers, preferably organised in the form of public joint-stock companies. In a number of parts of the business sector, deregulation has gone hand in hand with the development of competition between several providers, such as in telecommunications, air transportation and the supply of energy.

It has been argued that the strong deregulation that took place in the 1980s and 1990s now should give room for a period of strong reregulation (Majone, 1996). However, if traditional regulation did not work, then what is the reason to belief that the new reregulation will work? Many parts of the business sector seem to have benefited from the move towards the use of auctions at least if one looks at how prices have come down and output has been expanded.

Outcomes: the trade-off between production costs and transaction costs

There now exists a wealth of studies about the effects of tendering/bidding and contracting out. The evidence for or against an outcome differs often from one study to another, as there is as yet no clear picture about the impact of the new governance models. However, we will underline one recurrent theme, namely the inverse relationship between production costs and transaction costs.

Most analyses of the outcomes of the introduction of NPM hint at the reduction in costs for government. The cost reduction seems to be at about 20 per cent or more, at least in the short run. The cost reduction has occurred in all the sectors at the regional and local government levels where NPM has been introduced, from garbage collection to health care provision. This is quite a substantial outcome, which when it takes place in a large county or metropolitan area like Stockholm means a lot (Jonsson, 1996).

However, most outcome analyses state that the direct and large cost-saving is to some extent dissipated into considerable transaction costs, i.e. into the effort to negotiate, execute and monitor a lot of contracts. Transaction costs differ from production costs in one crucial aspect, i.e. they are not strictly measurable. This makes it impossible to specify empirically the exact nature of the trade-off between transaction costs and production costs. One would like to know to how much of the cost-saving has to be foregone by mounting transaction costs. No evidence has been published that suggests that all the cost advantages are dissipated as transaction costs.

If costs are on the whole down, then how about service quality? Any gain from a strong economic outcome of reduced overall costs could be undone by low performance on the quality indicators of public service provision. The evidence is mixed concerning the outcomes. One finds examples of all three possible quality results: (1) quality deterioration; (2) quality improvements; and (3) no quality change. It seems as if outcome (2) is much more probable than outcome (1) at the same time as outcome (3) is the most probable one.

If the economics of NPM work well, then how about the impact of NPM upon democratic politics? It has been argued that NPM may accomplish economic objectives such as productivity or effectiveness, but NPM will in general have a negative impact upon democracy and its values. The capacity of politicians to govern is reduced by the NPM – this is the basic argument about the political outcome. The evidence points clearly at a major new or strengthened role for managers, but faced with a set of CEOs politicians develop new tools of management (Montin, 1998). NPM seems to strengthen the power of politicians to direct and change the public sector, but the successful implementation of tendering/bidding and contracting out requires a reliance upon managers, whose position becomes very strong. The stakeholders of public services adapt fairly quickly to the governance regime, finding out how to increase their capacity to safeguard their interests. Thus, trade unions do not uniformly reject NPM, but look for opportunities to prevail under such quasi-market regimes (Harden, 1992).

Finally, the evidence concerning the employment of NPM at the central government level, i.e. the use of chief executive agencies in the core executive, indicates, again, mixed results. On the positive side, government appears to be able better to clarify goals and tasks in relation to the central bureaucracy. On the negative side, the clear-cut separation between politics and administration aimed at seems difficult to accomplish. A key difficulty is risk and the allocation of responsibility. When things go well, government stays at arms' length from the executive agency. However, when things go wrong, politicians find it very difficult to stay far away from things (Rhodes and Dunleavy, 1995).

Promoting short-term contracting

Short-term contracting regimes are based upon the assumption that competition is naturally forthcoming. What needs to be done is to create a situation where agents may compete. The move from long-term contracting to short-term contracting presupposes massive deregulation, opening up both the public sector and the regulated sector of the private economy to competition. This is negative regulation, or the removal of constraints to competition. But should government also do positive regulation, i.e. engage itself or a set of powerful regulators in anti-trust policy-making in order to stimulate competition, as there may be a need for a uniform competition regime covering not only the public sector but also the private sector?

We are here referring to anti-trust regulation, the efficiency of which is a contested matter. Competition in the form of contestability exists always as long as government does not restrict entry by means of long-term regulative contracts (Demsetz, 1991). Government cannot create competition by fiat. The experience from vast deregulation suggests another answer. When long-term contracts have been removed, there is uncertainty among the agents about the rules, stating who can compete and under what conditions. It is difficult not to call for the creation of a uniform competition regime, governed by an umpire. To rely only upon contract disputes settlements in ordinary courts, as recommended by Posner (1992), seems inadequate. But how much reregulation is adequate?

Short-term contracting when employed throughout the public sector will require a transparent set of institutions, regulating matters both ex ante and ex post the tendering/bidding process. Questions are bound to arise about which agent can compete in which tournament/auction – ex ante – as well as about what behaviour is appropriate after an agent has received a contract – ex post. It would seem naïve to believe that all contractual problems – ex ante or ex post – could be handled by case law in ordinary courts. Some common regulatory framework appears unavoidable, which calls for the installation of a tribunal supervising the observation of the rules of competition. Thus, there would be case for reregulation, creating a uniform framework for short-term contracting in the public sector.

But the adherents of reregulation want more. They argue for the reintroduction of regulations concerning prices, quantities and quality. And such regulatory frameworks are to be handled by a set of powerful regulators, removed from democratic political control, enjoying more a status of societal trust than being the agents of the body politic as the principal (Majone, 1998). Such regulatory schemes could, however, seriously limit the scope of competition and thus reduce the applicability of short-term contracting.

There is thus a danger that a process of deregulation will be followed by a process of reregulation so extensive that it undoes what has been accomplished by the move towards deregulation. One may note this tendency in the British experience with denationalisation leading successively to the introduction of massive regulation, some of which is of the old public utilities' type, focusing upon the setting of prices and quantities (Thatcher, 1998). A new massive reregulation along the lines of the recent British developments could actually involve a step back towards long-term contracting.

It has also been argued that the European Union should develop into a regulatory state, consisting of a web of independent regulatory boards, including the new European Central Bank (Majone, 1999). However, a monetary authority is different from a regulatory board, as it is at the same time a productive entity, creating the money coins and bills besides regulating its use. European Union regulation, including the activities of the ECB, seems more in tune with the theory of negative regulation, underlining the removal of barriers to competition, than with the positive one, emphasising again state intervention.

Conclusion

Ongoing public sector reforms may be interpreted as an institutional change from long-term contracts to short-term contracts, both within the soft sector and the business sector. The recent experimentation with short-term contracting in the form of internal markets and compulsory competitive tendering as well as with the introduction of international rules for public procurement may be interpreted as a reaction to difficulties with traditional long-term contracting in the public sector. These difficulties stem from moral hazard problems. Hidden action problems characterise much of the budgetary process for the soft sector and they occur as well in the business sector under the traditional economic regulation regime focusing upon entry regulation.

The move towards short-term contracting requires that government must learn how to manage tendering/bidding processes from the start to the end of such a process. In particular, it must learn how to handle the adverse selection problem or ex ante contractual opportunism, as providers may decide to sue the government for contractual violation rather than correct the supply when faced with criticism by government. They may even both renege and sue, if government has written sloppy contracts. Hidden information is the problem.

The short-term contracting regime applies as well to the hiring of the CEOs who will be responsible for the incorporated public enterprises. They will have to be appointed on the basis of tendering/bidding, having a few years' contract. The same may apply to the core executive, as when a government puts in place a system of executive agencies. When sections of departments or ministries have clear functions, then they can be governed by means of CEOs appointed on the basis of short-term contracts.

Without a transparent set of competition rules administered by some tribunals at the national level, short-term contracting regimes may not operate smoothly. Thus, the British experience is that the shift towards all aspects of the use of short-term contracts – contracting out, market testing, outside suppliers – has been attended by a strong increase in public regulation. However, the risk is that the reregulation movement has become so extensive that one may slip back into the sin of traditional regulation, namely entry and price regulation.

8 Contractualism in the public sector

The basic approach

Introduction

New public management (NPM) is the theory that makes contracting the medium of communication in the public sector. NPM puts in place a contracting state, where personnel and other resources are to be managed by means of a series of contracts. These contracts will cover not only the employment relation but also be used for the clarification of objectives and tasks for service delivery. Government will rely heavily upon chief senior officials (CEOs) to write and handle these contracts, at the same time as the CEOs will relate to government through contracts.

To a considerable extent, then, contracting would replace public law or public administration as the coordination mechanism in the public sector. The reason that this is done is the basic belief that contracting enhances efficiency. What one needs to discuss is whether contracting is suitable for all kinds of public sector activities as well as under what conditions contracting indeed promotes efficiency. Public contracting will always have to be done under certain restrictions, deriving from the justice basis of the constitutional state. This means that one may face efficiency–equity trade-offs when service delivery in certain parts of the public sector is organised under a contracting regime. Let us first discuss what a contract is and second enquire into when contracting promotes efficiency.

Contracts and private law

Using contracts as a coordination mechanism in the public sector is in principle nothing new. But what is extraordinary in NPM is the comprehensiveness of its employment. It is as if contracting in NPM has become more important than the traditional tools of government when coordinating the public sector, i.e. law, regulations and budgets. This raises a few interesting and perplexing questions about the distinction between private and public law, as public policy directing service delivery will be contained in contracts, enforceable in ordinary courts. The critical problem in NPM is whether contracting generally is such a powerful tool for government to reach its objectives.

It must be emphasised that administrative law will still exist in the contracting state. The basic framework of a constitutional democracy will not be undone though government contract making. Citizens still have rights and the basic public competencies remain constitutional practice. Thus, when government or its departments/agencies/crown entities contract, then they must respect both the basic equity rules and the continued existence of a political agenda. Perhaps there has been a tendency to downplay the implications of justice as constraints upon NPM.

What is a contract? When government or its agencies allocate goods and services by means of contracting, they employ the contract in its basic private law context. 'Contract' has a wide sense in terms of ordinary usage, but a precise sense in law: 'an agreement which is legally enforceable or legally recognised as creating a duty' (Atiyah, 1996: 37). This is not the place to discuss various definitions of the word 'contract', but to emphasise three things that are very relevant for NPM and the contracting state.

The basic characteristics of a contract in the precise meaning of the word are: (1) a promise or agreement; (2) an obligation not to renege; (3) a compensation for good or service exchanged (Osborne and Waterson, 1994). An agreement is not enough. To be a contract, agreements must be much more specific, involving a consideration or (3) the payment for a benefit received as well as (2) enforceability, and including the duty to pay compensation for contractual failure. Contracts with characteristics (1)–(3) are typically defined in the private law of a country, involving a complex of rules concerning a wide range of applications of contract law. Contract law is always private law as part of the law of obligations, and it is never public law.

The public sector, by contrast, has of tradition been governed through the bulk of public law, which is administrative law. What are the implications when the allocation of goods and services are to be coordinated not so much by means of administrative law and budget appropriations but by means of contracting, i.e. private law? The following legal consequences for government and its CEOs are almost self-evident:

1   Government as a contractor can do no better than what is contained in the contract. If the contract is deficient or incomplete, then government cannot fill in by using its public law authority.
2   Government is as bound by the terms of the contract as any private person who contracts. If there is a problem of contractual fulfilment, then government is as likely to be sued as a private person.
3   Government can be no more powerful in contractual relationships than what a litigation can bring government in terms of compensation for contractual reneging.
4   Disputes about public contracts are to be settled in the last resort by ordinary law courts, not administrative courts or tribunals, meaning that government must acquire expertise in contract failures.

5   Enforcement of a contract can only be done by taking action in an ordinary court, i.e. litigation.

6   Government is responsible for all contractual damages that a court may inflict upon contractual failures caused by people acting on behalf of government.

7   Ownership relations become critical in government, as contractual interaction takes place between two equal parties, acting as owners of rights that are transacted.

8   Ownership relations also surface when the gains from contracting are to be distributed, meaning that government could act as residual claimant.

By moving to the employment of private law contracts, it could seem as if government were weakening itself. By using its public law capacities, government could – at least in theory – order by law or by regulations its own employees to deliver what it wants them to do. Why, then, start using private law contracts in allocation?

Variety of public contracts

Government under a governance structure like the NPM may find it useful to employ different kinds of private law contracts. It may wish to contract with a group of agents – the so-called CEOs – in order to instruct them to handle the contracting procedure resulting in the purchase of services. In so far as government operates public organisations, it may put in place CEOs to operate the organisations, i.e. be responsible for its contracts resulting in its provision of services. Thus, the allocative part of the public sector becomes a nexus of contracts. In theory, these contracts are private law contracts, governed by the standard principles of common law or civil law concerning how contracts are to be respected and enforced between two or more parties.

In so far as the public sector becomes a nexus of contracts connecting ministers with CEOs in the ministries, the ministries with CEOs in agencies, the agencies with provider units, and so on, one and the same contracting logic would apply right through the public sector as a system of contracts. Notice though that public organisations in themselves cannot be contracted into existence. They must be based upon public law instruments. Thus, even purchaser bodies, whether in central or local government, are not founded by contracts between ministries and CEOs, but derive their existence and resources from public law including budgetary acts. However, the CEOs in various public bodies may be instructed by means of private law contracts.

What has been said above applies to that part of the public sector that has not been incorporated. Incorporation of a public organisation immediately makes it a private one, introducing ownership and private law contracting (Thynne, 1994). Public enterprises have been massively moved out of the public sector through incorporation or privatisation in the last decade. Incorporation, or the use of the joint-stock company form, has often turned out to be the first step in a strategy which ends up in full-scale privatisation. Governments have been eager to transform traditional public ownership into equity ownership, but they have sometimes hesitated in selling out all or a major part of this equity to private owners.

When government incorporates, then it automatically becomes the private owner of the firm, holding the equity in that firm, acting as a shareholder. When incorporated, public firms become financially independent corporations, acting under the laws regulating limited liability companies. Contracting in an incorporated company presents no difficulties in principle, as government when contracting with the CEOs of the public firms that have been incorporated has to face up to all the problems that shareholders confront in relation to the managers of the enterprise – so-called principal–agent problems (Vickers and Yarrow, 1989).

In a contracting state, what kinds of private law contracts would government or its agents, the CEOs, wish to negotiate and sign? Basically, private law contracts for allocative purposes come in two versions:

1   Transactions: spot market contracts (TC) (e.g. buying and selling something instantaneously)
2   Agency: relational contracts (AC) (e.g. the employment contract)

The distinction between transaction contracts and relation contracts may be difficult to draw exactly, but it has to do with (1) duration; (2) completeness; and (3) good faith. There are several contractual types in-between an instant transaction contract and a tenured employment contract, including employment during a limited time period, franchise, rental or leasing arrangements. The variety of different types of contracts under private law is large, but they are governed by the same regime linking them to the law of obligations (Shavall, 1998).

NPM employs both transaction and agency contracts. The typical form of transaction contract in government would be contracting out, whereas the typical form of agency contracting would be the employment of CEOs and other public employees. In a contracting state where the nexus of contracts runs from government to the service providers, one would arrive at the following simple structure combining relational contracting with contracting out (Figure 8.1).

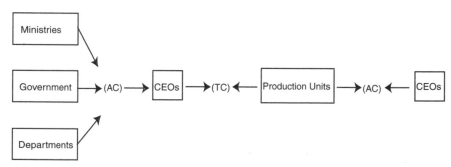

Figure 8.1   Structure of contracts in NPM.
Note: TC = transactional contracting.

Whereas relational contracting between principals and agents is basically a transaction cost-saving device, the gist of NPM lies in contracting out, or the creation of competition for public service delivery. Putting CEOs into place saves the government from the immense task of running a tendering-bidding process in each and every sector where public provision is forthcoming, which saves energy and time (transaction costs) so that government may concentrate upon overall policy-making. However, the basic purpose of NPM is to employ competition in order to reduce production costs, i.e. the money remuneration to the provider of goods and services.

The exact institutional version of Figure 8.1 that a country adhering to NPM will put in place will reflect its history or administrative legacies, but NPM requires a combined employment of agency contracts and transaction contracts. Government would use relational contracting to put CEOs into place, who would be responsible for the contracting out of service delivery to a production unit, public or private, on the basis of negotiations with the CEOs representing these production units.

NPM deviates from public administration in two ways. First, the frequency of transaction contracts is sharply up, as contracting out, internal markets or the purchaser–provider split is introduced on a major scale. Second, agency contracts tend to be short term instead of long term, especially in relation to the CEOs. When public employees are employed on a long-term contract, then the employment contract tends to be supplemented by a performance contract, which is short term. A performance contract under NPM is an individual agreement which specifies the job instruction. It can run into 100–200 pages and contain government policy when it is a CEO contract.

Whether a performance contract carries the same legal obligations as an employment contract is not clear, as the performance contract sometimes contains agreements that speak more of intentions than obligations. However, if the performance contract is seen as an extension of the employment contract, then it is also a strict private law contract. Failure to fulfil the performance contract would then entail that the employment contract has also been invalidated. Thus, short-term contracting replaces long-term contracting.

What is truly complicating matters is that NPM tends to use both contractual forms at the same time in relation to one and the same provider. Thus, a public hospital may have a large workforce employed as public employees, for whom government is in the last resort the employer. Alternatively, the hospital may be an incorporated entity, where government owns the shares, thus being the private law owner of the organisation. But at the same time, the services that the hospital provides are being purchased by a separate entity, to which government provides funds for contracting with hospitals. If no money is available or no contract is arrived at, then redundancy regulations imply that public employees have no secure employment. Or, in the incorporated case, a hospital downsizing its operations due to a loss of contracts from government as the purchaser could result in the organisational decline of that entity, hurting government as owner of that very same entity.

Now, what is the rationale in shifting from a public law governance mechanism to a private law or contracting governance regime?

Advantages

Why would it be more advantageous to allocate public goods and services by means of managerial contracting than by means of the traditional tools of coordination, i.e. administrative law and budgetary instructions? The philosophy of NPM focuses almost exclusively upon efficiency in allocation. The argument is then that transactional contracting or contracting out is superior to administrative coordination in getting the job done, i.e. arranging for the efficient provision of services. Is this true?

Contracting out or making private law agreements about what is to be done appears at first analysis to have most of the elements that enhance efficiency. It is mutually: (1) voluntary; (2) goal-orientated; (3) incentives based; (4) concrete and specific; and (5) of a limited time horizon. Contracting involves stipulating clear conditions about what has been agreed to – what is to be delivered? who is to pay? what additional obligations have been consented to? Although properties (1)–(5) are all efficiency enhancing, they do not secure efficiency. Let us spell out why.

It is conceivable that contracts that fulfil (1)–(5) may be poor contracts, either from the purchaser's point of view or the provider's point of view, or even both. They may not even be implementable, requiring third party intervention or court action to sort out what has been assented to. Contracts even made in good faith may be so incomplete that they cannot be put into effect. But why could not contracts in the public sector be made in bad faith? As a matter of fact, contractual failure is a typical feature of private sector contracting. Surely, reneging is an alternative also when government contracts. Contractual incompleteness, asymmetric information, corruption are just a few of the factors that may make it difficult for government, contracting under the NPM governance regime, to reach efficient agreements.

Suppose that government contracts with a hospital for a certain number of treatments during a certain period. Suppose that the hospital performs the specified number during a much shorter time period. Then what? Can the hospital refuse to take patients who urgently need this kind of treatment? Can government accept a refusal on the part of the hospital to accept new patients with the argument that there is no contractual violation? Or can government try to argue that the hospital did not perform the specified number of treatments because it proved that treatments could be done more quickly or efficiently than stated in the contract?

Thus, contracting out is not *per se* efficiency enhancing, as contracting can be attended by all kinds of opportunistic manoeuvres, all the way from misunderstandings at the time of signing the contract to reneging after the signing of the contract. Contracting out could suffer from both pre-contractual opportunism and post-contractual opportunism, as discussed below.

Yet, let us now suppose that public contracts are complete as well as fully enforceable in ordinary courts. Making transactional contracts as in contracting out would then be efficiency enhancing. This implication would follow from the existence of core solutions in bargaining. The buyer and the seller know that they can enforce the agreement. Thus, they would negotiate an efficient deal and honour the deal, since no other strategy would result in a better outcome from the point of view of individual rationality. Contracting is rational choice and rationality leads to Pareto-optimal outcomes, given that contracts are strictly enforceable. If contracts were not Pareto-optimal, there would be incentives to continue the negotiations until one arrives at an outcome which cannot be improved upon for one party holding the benefits of the other party constant. Thus, contracting out or transactional contracting would imply a Pareto-optimal outcome, because the purchasers and the providers have incentives to strike the best deals possible for both parties. Given full competition, the core of bargaining games tends towards the unique competitive solution, which is an equilibrium from the point of view of individual rationality (Hargreaves Heap *et al.*, 1992: 302–303).

It should be emphasised that arriving a Pareto-optimal solution in contracting may well mean that one party takes most of the benefit at the other party's expense, as one moves along the contract curve in the Edgeworth box model, showing the set of all Pareto-efficient points in exchange between two parties (Varian, 1987: 480–486) Purchasers and providers will struggle about how much the first is to pay and what the second is to deliver, where the first wants more for less and the second wishes to give less and receive more. This is basically a distributional conflict where the outcome will reflect bargaining strength, threat capacity and patience.

In order to arrive at transactional contracts that are not only Pareto-optimal but also acceptable from a distributional point of view, the people who do the contracting must have strong incentives to further their own interests and divide all the potential gains. Thus, efficiency in transactional contracting as well as acceptable distributional outcomes will at the end of the day depend upon the CEOs, sitting at each end of the bargaining table. How can contracts with managers be written in such a form that they genuinely attempt to promote the interests of their principals? This is the Achilles' heel of NPM.

Disadvantages

Contracting out implies efficient contracting, but only if the contracting parties have the incentives to really pursue bargaining to its end. As emphasised above, many different Pareto-efficient outcomes are conceivable involving alternative distributions of the mutual gain from contracting. The actual outcome arrived at will reflect the bargaining strength of the parties involved. Now, we must ask: why would all CEOs be equally motivated to keep on bargaining until their best situation has been reached? Why not accept a bid and get it over with? Why would CEOs try hard to get the best possible deal from the point of view of their principals, for instance government?

The advantages with public contracting regimes is that they highlight questions about supply and costs. However, whether supply will be maximised, given certain costs, or costs minimised, given a certain supply, depends upon agency relationships (i.e. relational contracting). How are managers to be contracted to do their job? Why would they have the incentive to find and implement efficient contracts, or contracts that involve a distributional gain for their principal? Here, we come to the crux of the matter: what would make CEOs sitting on either side of the bargaining table negotiate until the interests of principals have been served and there is not more to gain?

Suppose we assume that the public sector has been organised transparently and systematically into purchasing and provider units with the exception of the ministries. No matter what legal form these units have been given, they will be operated by CEOs. Thus, we have the structure as shown in Figure 8.2 where CEOs are responsible for the purchasing of services and also direct the organisations which provide the services.

We have shown above that efficiency in transactional contracting between CEOs in new public management will only be forthcoming if CEOs know what they do and try hard. This raises the fundamental question in a contracting state: how is government going to find and instruct managers who make good contracts? This is a principal–agent problem that receives a very special twist in NPM, as government may both be the principal of the purchasing agent as well as the principal of the providing agent. Take the example of public hospitals under a purchaser–provider scheme, where a purchasing agency contracts with several public hospitals as the potential providers of health care. Government would be the principal of the CEOs handling the purchasing and at the same time government would be the principal of the hospitals that provide services.

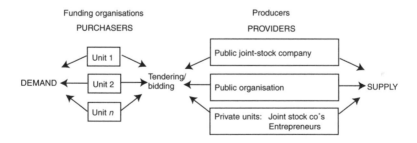

Figure 8.2   The contracting state.

As purchaser, government is assumed to maximise two objectives, namely minimise cost and maximise quantity and quality of services purchased. Thus, it wishes to hire CEOs who can implement these two goals. The purchasing CEOs are assumed to maximise their salary and reputation. But how can government make sure that the CEOs do not shirk? The general impression is that by offering very high salaries for CEOs, government could solve the principal–agent problem of making sure that the agent tries hard for the principal, i.e. by helping to bring forward an effort on the part of the agent which would result in lower overall costs in purchasing. We wish to argue, however, that this is a too naïve a model of principal–agent interaction under NPM for the following reasons.

Relational contracts with CEOs are based upon the following conditions: first, such contracts tend to be short-term ones, lasting between one and five years. Second, salaries tend to be substantially higher than what used to be paid administrators in positions corresponding to those of CEOs. Third, the principal has to rely upon the agent, because the effort that the agent puts in is not observable or verifiable. What is, fourth, observable are the outputs and the outcomes, but they may depend upon team effort and luck. Fifth, principal–agent contracts include rules about the firing of the agent as well as agent compensation against premature termination of a contract. The agent may wish to prolong a contract but the principal has, of course, made no such commitment. To conclude as in all contracting, the two parties have something to gain by working together, but there is also a conflict about how the mutual gain is to be divided between the two contractors. What is the likely outcome of an interaction with these five characteristics? We argue that the risk of a Prisoners' Dilemma is imminent (Hargreaves Heap *et al.*, 1992: 144–154).

The stakes are typically high in principal–agent contracting with CEOs. Outcomes will be closely monitored by the principal in order to find evidence about whether the CEO is successful or not. What the principal wants to avoid is the worst outcome, namely to pay a high salary to an agent who shirks. If the outcomes are not up to expectations, then there will be pressure exerted upon the CEO to explain what is going on. Bad performance may be due to CEOs delivering inefficient outputs or due to circumstances beyond their control, which question is often a matter of different interpretations where differences of opinion are difficult to verify. What the agent wants to avoid is the worst outcome, namely trying hard but getting fired due to bad circumstances which could not have been foreseen or prevented. Although being fired may not hurt the agent financially, his reputation could take such a serious blow that their career would start to go downhill.

The best outcome is that government is pleased with the outcomes and that the CEO trying hard remains in place during the entire period, enhancing their reputation. This is the Pareto-optimal outcome which maximises benefits. But is it the equilibrium that rational players will find? Not necessarily. A number of factors may induce both government and the CEO to choose another strategy pair than 'trust/try hard', which is discussed below.

The interaction between principal and agent is basically a short-term one, limited by the length of time of the contract between the two. There is no guarantee whatsoever that the contract will be prolonged or renewed. This is conducive to a spirit of cooperation where both parties focus more upon the formal terms of the contract than upon what the situation requires. Opportunism will sooner or later play a role.

1   Government's opportunism: it may wish to give an impression of determination when outcomes do not match expectations, whether the CEO really did wrong or not. By blaming the CEO, government rids itself of responsibility and gives an impression of firmness and control. Choosing the strategy 'terminate or not renew' may be a viable option whatever effort the agent puts in.

2   CEOs opportunism: they may engage in the strategy 'shirk' for the simple reason that they believe that it will pay off handsomely. Either government will not find out or it can be successfully denied. Another reason to engage in shirking could be that what the CEO does or does not do matters little in the situation. The CEO could be lucky and correct outputs are forthcoming in the situation. Or the CEO could be unfortunate, being unable to correct outcomes or facing an adverse situation. Why, then, not simply cash in on the remuneration and not try hard?

Is the talk about opportunism – self-interest seeking with guile – merely another form of Machiavellism, or just an invitation to speculate about human motivation? Whether the assumption about opportunism is realistic at all is one of those philosophical questions that mankind has been fascinated by ever since ideas about human nature emerged, but which only seem to give rise to eternal dissent (Etzioni, 1988). Yet, I fail to find any reason why opportunism could not be a viable consideration also in NPM. Agency relationships in the private sector must handle both adverse selection and moral hazard – why could these phenomena not occur in NPM?

Now, add uncertainty to the interaction between government and its CEOs. What would a CEO do if they fear that government will either terminate the contract in time, i.e. not renew, or prematurely, i.e. fire the CEO? Avoiding the worst outcome for the CEO – 'terminate/try hard' – the agent will shirk. What would a government do if it fears that the agent will shirk? Avoiding the worst outcome, government will terminate in time or even fire prematurely.

As far as I can see, there is no method that either government or CEOs can communicate in order to remove these two detrimental forms of uncertainty. If government communicates 'trust', then the agent would do better by shirking. If the agent communicates 'try hard', then would it be credible the moment government reciprocates, communicating 'trust'? Government may even have reasons to fire an agent who really tries hard, simply for opportunistic reasons. The only method for government is to communicate a conditional Trust, meaning that a revelation about shirking would call for immediate use of the other strategy 'terminate-fire'.

What we arrive at is a true Prisoners' Dilemma situation, where both would start out cooperating but defection is going to become more and more attractive to the agent as the contractual period goes by. The only credible response from government would be the 'grim strategy', i.e. first cooperate, but after defection never cooperate again (Rasmusen, 1994). Such a strategy is only credible if government now and then terminates the interaction with an agent or fires the agent. Thus, in order merely to keep the pressure upon the agent, the government may need to use the strategy 'terminate/not renew' now and then, independently of whether the agent tries hard or not.

A number of mechanisms have been suggested to the principal in order to increase their capacity to minimise the possibility of CEOs shirking including signing contracts based upon: (1) reputation; (2) risk-sharing; (3) boiling-in-oil; and (4) excessive wages. Yet, the agent's reputation in the past is no sure signal that the agent will not find shirking rewarding in the future. Whether government can at all write contracts involving risk-sharing is far from clear, as government is solely responsible for the public sector in the last resort. Agents seem to have been very successful in avoiding signing boiling-in-oil contracts, as seen from the frequent occurrence of very lucrative compensation schemes when agents are in fact fired. Finally, setting wages higher than the necessary market wage may make the agent more vulnerable to the threat of firing, but it also increases the attraction of shirking if the agent is lukewarm about a repetition of the contract.

If these pre-contractual strategies (1)–(4) do not work, then government may wish to invest resources in monitoring the agent as a post-contractual strategy. By such a device, government could assure itself that outcomes really depend upon the CEO's effort, whether performance results when poor despite output could be blamed or not upon the CEOs. However, monitoring is basically a public administration technique, which is not easily reconcilable with private contracting. In any case, it is costly. Would, then, government not be tempted to use 'terminate/fire', whether the CEOs try hard or not? If so, would not the CEOs use 'shirk'? We seem by an inexorable analysis of the logic of the interaction to arrive at a Nash equilibrium that is not the Pareto-optimal outcome, namely 'terminate/shirk', thus individual rationality contradicting collective rationality (Hargreaves Heap *et al.*, 1992: 101).

Soft sector and hard sector contracts

The empirical research on public sector reform will, I predict, result in one general finding about NPM and the contracting approach, namely that contracting schemes operate less well in the soft sector than in the business sector. The public sector used to consist of bureaux and public enterprises, both types being public law organisations, although of a slightly different nature from a legal point of view. Incorporation has changed all this, so that public enterprises are now almost always public joint-stock companies, if they have not been privatised. Incorporation goes well with the contracting approach, when it is a matter of business activities, i.e. the production of goods and services that can be fully priced and paid for under market conditions. But what about soft sector goods and services?

Public resource allocation in education, health and social care consists of that part of the public sector where goods and services are provided free or almost free. The basic mechanism of payment is taxation, as user fees may be used but not to cover all the costs. The reason for public resource allocation involves considerations about market failures. It used to be argued that public resource allocation must take the form of budget allocation by means of bureaucracy. However, the contracting state changes this, but will contracting in the soft sector be efficient when natural markets are not forthcoming?

Constructing a quasi-market for the allocation of soft sector goods and services by means of the purchaser-provider split may be just as artificial as bureaucracy. If bureaucracy is problematic because the board of a bureaucracy is both on the demand and supply side, then perhaps government in the new contracting state is again sitting on two chairs: (1) funding the purchasers; (2) running many of the provider units. Since contracting involves much distributional conflict about how the cake is to be split, once it has been baked, government through its principal–agent relations with the CEOs would in reality be negotiating with itself.

Suppose that the purchasing agents of government get the upper hand against a number of provider organisations, including some public organisations or organisations where government is the owner of equity. The resulting contracts will then be favourable for government as purchaser but hardly so for government as provider. In NPM, there is an in-built conflict between the two roles of government, as purchaser and as provider. Government as owner of public organisations or as owner of public joint-stock companies may wish to have contracts that are favourable to the provider side, and not the purchaser side.

In any case, the soft sector part of the public sector has certain special qualities that any coordination mechanism must take into account. Thus, the supply of goods and services within the police and the legal system, within education and health care as well as social care involves (1) a strong dose of professionalism; (2) a considerable consideration of rights or entitlements; (3) a mixture of quantity and quality that often defies definition; and (4) an urgency in need. These supply characteristics do not make the application of NPM tools run smoothly in the organisations of the soft sector, one may predict.

Variety of governance mechanisms

Public management needs to be aware of the separation of the business sector from the soft sector and develop methods of governance which take into account how radically different these two sectors tend to be. Whereas NPM methods seem appropriate in the business sector, they may fail in the soft sector. Thus, government needs to expand or enlarge its repertoire of governance methods by adding to NPM not only the old bureaucracy mechanism but also start designing mechanisms based upon trust, which may be a better governance medium in relation to professionals than tendering/bidding.

To us, NPM is only one theory about the governance mechanism to be employed in the public sector. It should be complemented by other theories as well. Public management would then include both the theory of tendering/bidding and its challengers, namely a revised theory of bureaucracy and the theory of trust as alternative governance regimes in the allocative sector. It is urgent that one states the pros and cons of alternative institutions for public service delivery.

Conclusion

New public management harbours a strong theory about the overall blessings of using contracting as the coordination mechanism in the public sector. By 'contracting' is here meant the writing and enforcing of private law agreements (Atiyah, 1996). NPM focuses upon contracting out in purchaser-provider interaction as well as relational contracting in principal–agent interaction with CEOs.

NPM replaces traditional public administration or policy networks in the public policy school with a long chain of contracts, transactional contracts as well as relational contracts. The objective is to enhance efficiency in allocation. In order to reach this objective of efficiency in bargaining, it is necessary that the so-called Coase conditions are fulfilled: (1) transactions costs must not start running high; (2) the ownership rights must be transparent (Cooter, 1991). But will these conditions really be fulfilled under NPM?

Much depends upon the behaviour of the CEOs. The CEOs must have strong motivation to write and implement first-best contractual solutions to allocative problems. One may ask where that motivation is going to come from, as the CEOs are after all not the owners of these contracts and cannot present residual claims on the gains made in contracting. In addition, government could have two sets of CEOs, one active on the purchasing side and the other responsible for the provider side. The gain for the purchaser is the loss for the provider, once one has reached the set of Pareto-optimal solutions. Government would thus basically be squeezing itself, when its purchasing agents manage to reduce the costs of its providing organisations, when these belong to government.

I wish to argue for a broadening of the concerns of NPM. It needs to realise not only the advantages of contracting in the public sector, as in the business sector, but also develop an understanding of the limitations of contracting regimes. Contracting is not always efficiency enhancing in the soft sector. It may actually happen that the rational strategies that players engage in lead to a Pareto-inferior outcome. NPM needs to incorporate the lessons from the study of other forms of contracting than contracting out, including not only long-term contracting but also other mechanisms such as trust and mutual understanding.

9 Variety of roles of government in contracting regimes

Introduction

A number of painstaking changes have been undertaken in countries that have conducted public sector reforms. Under new public management, the various roles of government are reconceptualised in a radical manner. One major change is the identification of government as a contractor. From being the source of authority, i.e. government as identical with legal authority, government is approached as the maker of contracts. Chapters 7 and 8 dealt with this role of government as contractor in alternative contracting regimes, in relation to agents or in relation to players in the economy.

However, there are other changes besides contracting under NPM. Recent public sector reforms involve the use of private ownership forms on a massive scale: privatisation as well as incorporation and the introduction of private capital accounting methods for all assets in government ownership – the so-called policy of activation of state assets. The remaking of public enterprises into joint-stock companies – incorporation – has as a matter of fact not only been employed in relation to traditional public enterprises in the business sector but also *vis-à-vis* public organisations in the soft sector such as hospitals and schools, meaning the remaking of bureaux into incorporated productions units.

Finally, not only has the role of government as owner changed but also government as regulator. Traditional public regulation focusing upon entry conditions and the issuing of licences has been abandoned, but it is not clear what the new regulatory role of government is or how interventionist it should be, nor how it should be put into practice.

This chapter will discuss these role changes in ownership and regulation accompanying the emphasis upon government as contractor. What is the rationale behind the search for an activation of public ownership and what are the advantages and disadvantages connected with this strategy? One would want to know who is the owner of the public assets in whatever form they are held and why such public assets would be better managed under private law regimes than under public law forms.

One also needs to reflect upon the implications of public sector reforms concerning contracting and ownership for public regulation. Government as contractor and government as active owner of huge physical or financial assets is only meaningful after vast deregulatory reforms, but perhaps re-regulation is necessary after deregulation? We will discuss the position of NPM on the issue of positive versus negative regulation and debate the risk of over-regulation.

Government as umpire

Under the contracting regimes suggested by NPM, the government negotiates and signs contracts for the provision of services. However, government cannot only be regarded as just another contractual partner, simply for the reason that the state is also the guarantor of all contracts, private or public, at the end of the day. Government plays a vital role regarding the stability of contracting regimes all over the economy, public or private, by being the umpire, interpreting in the last resort the nature of a contract.

It seems crystal clear that there are two different roles involved here, i.e. when the state is contracting and when the state acts as the umpire. Do we have to conclude that there is also necessarily a conflict between these roles? The answer is yes, but there is not a fatal contradiction between the two roles. What the state must see to is that these roles are conducted by different actors following different institutions.

Contracting between contractors without an umpire – that is not workable whether it is a matter of private players or public contractors. The difficulty is the immense consequences of contractual reneging. Reneging is the same as contractual failure. Within societies adhering to the Rule of Law, contractual failures are never left unresolved, because reneging is counterproductive to efficiency in economic life. In municipal law, the occurrence of reneging is counteracted by a number of mechanisms.

The logic of reneging is best modelled in terms of the Prisoner's dilemma game. It involves two sides of the same coin: how is the probability of reneging to be reduced? This is the ex ante aspect. And how is reneging to be handled once it has occurred? This is the ex post aspect of the problem. There would be massive contractual failures, if there were not an umpire to handle these two problems, reducing the ex ante probability of reneging and punishing the ex post occurrence of reneging.

All forms of contracts pass through two or three stages. First, there is the signing of the contract or the making of the agreement. Contracts by their very nature are voluntary, as they would not be signed unless they are in the interest of the signing parties. One can be forced to sign a contract, but even under such circumstances there is the possibility of not signing the contract, given of course that it is not combined with the consequence of retaliation like, e.g. premature death. Slave contracts are not voluntary contracts. The signing of contracts is thus based on a mutual understanding that contracts are efficient, if indeed they are intended to be kept or honoured. Why otherwise sign them?

However, contracts necessarily involve a second stage when it becomes relevant to ask whether the signatories will honour what they have signed. This is the testing stage of contract making, as it will then become apparent whether the contract will be carried through or not. It is impossible to bypass this distinction between signing a contract and honouring a contract, although the time elapsing between them may be absolutely minimal. In many situations, there is actually quite a time distance between signing and respecting a contract, which opens up the possibility of various forms of reneging.

One may distinguish between sincere and insincere behaviour when a contract is signed as well as behaviour honouring and not honouring a contract. These two distinctions would give four logical possibilities, which are relevant when one theorises why people such as governments, CEOs or private firms enter into contracts and why they respect the contracts they have made (Table 9.1).

Reneging need not be limited to case IV, but it could very well occur in case III. Perhaps case II is more of a theoretical possibility, but of course with a large enough time distance between signing and respecting a contract, then case II is not completely improbable.

One may wish to enter a third stage in the process of handling a contract, namely the implementation of the contract by a third party, usually a court of some kind or an arbitration mechanism. When the third stage is reached, which is far from always the case, then the contract in question is no longer self-enforceable, as it is enforced by an outside person in relation to the contracting parties. Not all contracts that fail are handed over to third parties for enforcement. The result of contractual reneging may simply be that a signed contract is not executed. When a contract is respected by the contracting parties, honouring the deal that they have struck, without the intervention of a third party, then we speak of self-enforcement.

In ordinary life, there is an immense amount of contracting between persons either in written form or orally. And one finds all the variety of contracting situations identified above. When it comes to government contracting, then as a contractor government is bound by the same logic of contractual behaviour of signing and honouring its agreements, first in relation to its agents and second in relation to contracts with service providers, often made by its CEOs. If government reneges, then it is likely to face litigation. Faced with reneging, government can only resort to litigation.

However, reneging is not a universal phenomenon, as there exists self-

Table 9.1 The signing (ex ante) and honouring (ex post) of contracts

	Signing	
	Sincere	Not sincere
Do honour	I	II
Do not honour	III	IV

enforcement under ordinary municipal law. As a matter of fact, self-enforcement is quite common.

Self-enforcement and reneging

Contracting would be meaningless without a considerable probability of self-enforcement. Why make commitments if the intention is to renege upon them? Although contracting always involves two stages, and thus opens up for the possibility of reneging, many contracts are made with the intention of respecting them and they are so honoured after they have been signed. The reason is self-enforcement, or that the contracting parties judge that it is in their interest to respect the contract. Contracting is after all the principal tool by which individuals interact in an efficient manner from which both stand to gain. Consenting to an agreement is usually interpreted as signifying that the contract involves a Pareto-improvement.

Self-enforcement implies that the signing parties to an agreement respect the contract by themselves without third party intervention. The reason for honouring a contract can however be different. The most simple case is that both parties gain more from respecting the contract than from reneging, as no one would gain more from unilaterally reneging. In the short run, one party could always gain by reneging, but they fear the consequences of not respecting the agreement with regard to the direct actions of the other party against them, in the short-term or long-run perspective (Axelrod, 1984, 1997).

Not underestimating the place of self-enforcement, we must still point out the many possibilities or opportunities for reneging, which means that the state or government as umpire plays a crucial role. Reneging may occur from the very beginning. Contractors may sign agreements but without any real intention of respecting them. In advanced countries, almost all types of reneging have been made difficult by means of the operation of enforcement institutions.

Signing insincerely may be a strategy for any contractor, because they may be under pressure, such as competition from other bidders, but they may have no intention other than to pay lip service to the terms of the contract. As the contract binds both parties, one party could always renege after the signing of the contract. The intention when signing may be that this type of reneging will be hidden or it may be the case that one party reneges openly in blunt violation of the contract signed, if they consider themselves forced to that or find it beneficial. Thus, examining the impact of signing a contract, contractors could always say: 'Well, one can always renege, if the worst comes to the worst or if an opportunity arises.'

Yet, signing insincerely would only be possible if reneging on any contract or agreement, old or new, is easy to get away with. Thus, the effective measure to take against the insincere signing of treaties is to make any form of reneging very costly. The basic problem is not insincere intentions, but the levying of punishments against any failure to live up to contractual obligations. Since this may occur all too easily, it is small wonder that government looks upon its role as umpire as of utmost importance.

The opposition between umpire and contractor

The basic point here which needs to be underlined is that government as the maker of a massive amount of contracts is bound by the same logic concerning reneging and the ultimate enforcement of contracts in the ordinary courts through litigation. Thus, the role of government as the umpire takes precedence over government as the contractor.

When government acts as a contractor, then it cannot at the same time frame the rules of contracting between itself and any partner with whom it contracts. The rules of contracting must be decided ex ante as well as be interpreted by government acting in an entirely different role. One need not refer to the necessity of the Rule of Law, as it is enough to argue that any contracting regime requires rules that are exeogeneous and that are interpreted impartially. If not, the players would succumb to the temptation of framing the rules in accordance with their own interests, or interpreting them in a partial manner. This danger is such a real one that the volume of transactions would suffer substantially, meaning that all contracting partners lose.

The institutionalisation of the distinction between the executive and judicial branches of government may be seen as a response to the necessity of separating between contractor and umpire. In the executive branch of government, there would be lots of contracting handled by the agents of government, the CEOs under a NPM regime. At the same time, government would be active as umpire but in a different branch of government, namely the judiciary. The judges would also be the agents of government, but they would be more regulatory agents than purchasing or providing agents. They could not receive instruction about how to interpret the rules of a general contracting regime, or how to handle contract law in specific cases where government happens to be a partner, for instance in litigation.

The same urgency applies also to the separation between government as legislator and government as umpire. In the former role, only general rules can be laid down concerning how parties may contract with each other, independently of whether the contractors are public or private acting subjects. Thus, the requirement of facilitating transactions implies that many of the rules employed in a contract are generalisable, meaning that they can be applied to any contract. Legislation with a retrospective import concerning the rules of contracting is generally considered extremely harmful to economic activity.

The legal theory about the rules of contracting regimes underlines either equity concerns or efficiency considerations. The well-known position of Calabresi and Posner propagating the so-called economic approach to law is that efficiency concerns weigh very heavy when basic rules about economic life are interpreted by judges in ordinary courts. The Calabresi–Posner idea encompasses such elements of law as torts, contracts, restitution and property. Let us quote from Posner stating that his theory about law:

> is that the common law is best (not perfectly explained) as a system for maximising the wealth of society. Statutory or constitutional as distinct from common law fields are less likely to promote efficiency, yet even they … are permeated by economic concerns and illuminated by economic analysis.
>
> (Posner, 1992: 23)

The conditions for arriving at a neutral and impartial umpire may be motivated by efficiency deliberations following the Calabresi–Posner approach to law. Or one may argue on the basis of equity considerations, entailing that umpires have to be neutral and impartial in order to satisfy the requirement of justice.

In any case, given the priority of the umpire role over the contractor role, it has been concluded that government needs to be very active in the former role, creating a regulatory state (Majone, 1996). Let us discuss this argument more closely, but first we wish to emphasise that government or the state is not only a contractor or an umpire. Government is also a most substantial owner of assets, e.g. property of various types.

Nature of public ownership

Recently, the importance of proper management of public ownership has been underlined to such an extent that one has looked for new principles of asset management. It is required that state assets be managed in accordance with private management criteria. No one would deny that proper management of ownership is rational, for the owners as well as for society. One only has to take a look at what happened in the Soviet Union in order to understand the entire ramifications of mismanagement of public property. However, much more is involved in the theory about active public ownership than is now advocated.

Public sector reforms have searched for an active management of public property. Basically, there are two questions involved: what is involved in the requirement that the management of state and local government assets be 'active'? What are the pros and cons of an active management of state assets?

Government or the state is a huge owner of property. Since it has a wide range of assets, it faces the need to manage these properly. This is the crux of the matter: what does 'proper' mean in the requirement of the proper management of state assets? Before we go into that question we must, however, discuss the general nature of public ownership.

Public ownership is a much more difficult concept than that of private ownership. Public ownership is different not only from private ownership but also from common ownership. When the state or government is the owner of assets, then it is not entirely easy to answer simple questions about who the owners are or who are the stakeholders, i.e. who is concerned with how government manages state assets. Presumably, the state itself is the owner and the most important stake-holder, but who is the state?

Public ownership of assets is a complex matter comprising three elements – the public, ownership, asset – which are difficult to conceptualise in a clear manner when they are taken separately. When these three elements are combined, then things become even more mind boggling.

First, who is the public behind public property? Sometimes public ownership is confused with common ownership, as when it is stated that state assets in reality belong to everyone. Common ownership of land or the various uses of land occurs in many countries, although the institutions differ somewhat from one country to another. It means either that land is not owned by anyone or that it belongs to a community (Ostrom, 1990). Common ownership of an asset is either in the form of *terra nullius* or in the form of a commons. Public property does not have the characteristics of these two types of ownership.

Public property is a specific legal institution under which a legal person or a corporation is the owner of an asset in the same sense as a private person is the owner of an asset. This legal person may be any kind of government or the state: the central or federal government, regional governments or local governments. Such a legal person is the full owner of its assets, meaning that they do not belong to anyone else but this legal person. Government or state assets may be of very different kinds, as is the case with private ownership.

It should be pointed out that public ownership is always exercised by people, i.e. real people not fictional people such as a legal person. The people handling public ownership are the persons in government or the persons whom the government hires to do the job. However, public property is never the property of these people, as they act on behalf of the owner of public property. Whatever profit public ownership may result in, it is still the case that it cannot be appropriated by the persons in government or the people managing the public assets. It is like a trust (McLoughlin and Rendell, 1992).

Public property is managed by real people, not juridical persons. However, they act on behalf of that legal entity, called sometimes 'government' and sometimes 'state'. Thus, the relationship between the people in government and government as a legal entity has been described as either a principal–agent relationship or as the management of a trust. In reality, it is neither the one nor the other. A principal–agent model or a trust model presupposes that one can identify two sets of people between whom the interaction is to take place. However, in public ownership there is only one real set of actors, the government people or the people it has hired to do the job of managing public property.

In reality, it is always the present government who defines what are the objectives of the management of public property. They are not the agents of any principal, nor do they act in trust for someone else. They can protect public property, increasing its value or at least not decreasing it, or they can mismanage the property of the state, diminishing its value or even destroy it completely.

Perhaps one could argue that the public is the principal of all state assets, or that the government people act in the best interests of the public meaning that they hold the property of the state as a trust in relation to the public. But the following question immediately arises: who is the public? Or, to pose the question a little bit differently: is the public an actor who may act like a principal or is the public a set of people whose property may be handled by another set of people, the government? We are inclined to answer 'no' to these two interpretations.

The crux of the matter is that the concept of the public, meaning all people in a country, is not identical with the concept of public in the words 'public property'. 'Public' in public ownership stands for the body politic or the public organisation of society, i.e. the legal person denoted by expressions such as 'the state', or 'the federal government' or 'the local government'. One can claim that the people occupying positions in public organisations are agents of the general public – the people as it were – as the principal of all public organisations. Yet, that is a matter of mere interpretation which reflects the adherence to a democratic political theory. To sum up: public property, or the assets of governments or states, are not the real property of each and everyone.

Activation of state assets

Since public property is different from common property, government may decide to activate its assets, i.e. require a yearly income from the employment of these assets. In fact, why could not government require that all its property, both physical capital and financial assets as well as land holdings, return a stable income equal to that of the average return on private investments? Such a rate of return requirement would, if effectuated, give government a considerable source of income, which may be crucial when budgets are to be balanced at the same time as taxation is not to be changed much. Typically, government is the owner of vast public property that could give a sizeable yearly return, if this property were put to practical and lucrative employment.

However, such an aggressive rate-of-return policy could backfire, as one would like to know: who gains by it? If public property is regarded as the assets of the people, which is often the case in a democracy, then the people may object to such a policy by arguing that charges on the use of public property ought to be determined without any profit motive. If government is the agent of the population as the principal, or if public property is held as a trust by the government in relation to the true owners, the people, then an aggressive rate-of-return policy implies that government is trying to make a profit on the use of public property on behalf of its 'true' owners. Why would the 'true' owners of a property wish to pay a higher user fee than that involved in covering only the cost of its use?

The 'proper' rate-of-return policy on public property has been much discussed. In so far as cost plus prices are defended by means of the theory that public assets are in reality common property, then this theory is wrong. Government may decide to employ public property as a source of income, as the owner of public property is the legal corporation, called variously 'the state', 'the province' or 'the commun', whose rights are exercised by the people in government.

Second, what is ownership in public ownership? In the theory about private ownership, legal scholars and economists agree that private ownership takes many forms, but they tend to disagree about what is the common core of all these various forms. In jurisprudence, there has been a long debate about whether ownership is about rights concerning objects or whether it concerns the objects themselves. In economics, one has discussed whether ownership is intimately connected with the economic functions of objects, i.e. to use them and to acquire and dispose of them. To have ownership is sometimes defined as fulfilling certain legal requirements about having come into possession of the object in a correct manner (inheritance or purchase), but sometimes ownership is regarded as a residual claim or interest in an object.

Since legal persons can exercise the functions of ownership to the same extent as private persons can, and since the state or the government is such a legal person with all rights and duties that are characteristic of legal persons, it follows that public ownership is ownership in the full sense of that word. It is up to the persons in government to decide how public property is to be managed and to instruct managers to put these principles into effect.

A government may decide to acknowledge restrictions upon the management of public property, such as for instance the use of cost plus prices in infrastructure. However, it need not do so, as it may argue that it has the right to the same rate of return on its property as private owners have on their assets. This is at heart a political question concerning the choice of alternative fiscal regimes and not a matter inherent in the interpretation of the nature of public ownership.

Third, what then constitute public assets? Private ownership accepts many different forms of assets. Assets can be owned directly by single individuals or by a legal entity such as a corporation. Assets can be owned in the form of equity. Ownership may cover a variety of different kinds of objects including intellectual property, e.g. patents. Two or more people may form partnerships that can own assets, which then belong to the partners in proportion to their stakes in the partnership. Yet, the most often discussed form of ownership is the limited liability company, which presents a number of advantages in terms of management and economic activity (Williamson, 1985).

The limited liability form of organising economic activity together with equity as its ownership correlate is what NPM has in mind as the ideal model for restructuring public assets and their handling. The public ownership of various assets under the traditional governance form were managed as elements of the public budget, either directly by the ministry of finance or indirectly through the control of this ministry of key parameters in the running of public enterprises.

Although the institutional recognition of public ownership has varied from one country to another, the traditional form of administering public property emphasised centralisation and uniformity. Thus, the property that bureaux used in the soft sector, e.g. their premises, was considered as state property to be handled by one separate bureau for such assets. Or the property that the public enterprises managed entered directly into the capital budget of the state, where major changes such as the making of new acquisitions or the taking of loans had to be accepted by the minister of finance.

The policy of asset activation entails an entirely different regime, underlining decentralisation and the retrieval of a high rate of return on the capital. Thus, public property may be managed by autonomous organisations as they deem appropriate within rules laid down by the government. Such rules of proper management would trade discretion for the organisation off against a rather substantial rate of return to the government, including not only interest payments but also dividends. In the new management philosophy of public property profit is considered a legitimate goal.

Moreover, the change from a centralised uniform asset management strategy, focusing upon the ministry of finance, to a decentralised or discretionary policy targeting the rate of return on invested capital is often accompanied by the incorporation strategy. Incorporation, or the shift from a public law regime for the organisation of production units in the public sector to a private law regime of organising the very same units, is considered as conducive towards the achievement of new or modern management of public property. Incorporated units, or public joint-stock companies in this case, possess typically many degrees of discretion against the owners of the firm. But their managers are controlled by means of measures of goal attainment against general principles such as the chosen rate of return on the capital invested or the consolidation of the capital assets of the firm.

Thus, one observes from one country to another, the combination of incorporation with the introduction of a new management philosophy for public enterprises. Governments are attracted by this dual strategy because it relieves them of the day-to-day responsibility of governing huge organisations at the same time as they may well receive a nice payment at the end of the fiscal year from interest payments and dividends. Governments are also in favour of this strategy pair for the simple reason that joint-stock companies are under the obligation to maintain their capital, meaning that incorporated firms will cut losses and cover the costs of capital maintenance without government interference.

One would be inclined to assume that governments would wish to keep the public assets in shape because like any owner they wish to maximise the future income stream of their capital. Although the people in government are never in the position of being themselves the residual claimers of income from public property, they may act as if they were in that capacity as long as that residual income ends up in the state coffers.

State ownership under the contracting regime: a conflict between two roles?

How is the manager of property to be combined with the role as contractor? Here arises one of the major limitations, it appears, in NPM, as NPM has not clearly realised the conflict that may arise between these two roles.

Government is not only a contractor or an umpire. Government is also a most substantial owner of assets, e.g. property of various types. We must ask whether the role of government as manager of property can be combined with the role as contractor without much difficulty. Many believe that this is indeed the case, but this is not so, for reasons to be spelled out below. In reality, there may be a contradiction between the role of government as contractor and the role as owner of public property, because government could end up sitting at both ends of the table meaning that it, as contractor, on one end of the table negotiates with itself, as owner of the capital of an organisation, at the other end of the table.

One should point out that it is never the people in government – the politicians – who act directly as contractors or as the representatives of for instance an incorporated organisation whose equity is government property. The direct interaction under a purchasing–provider schema is done by means of the CEOs, one part of which acts as the purchasing agents of the government whereas the other part acts as the agents of the provider organisation, which happens to be a public joint-stock company in this case. Thus, government does not talk to itself.

However, the conflict between these two sets of CEOs is not thereby removed and the risk of an internal contradiction in government still remains. One agent of the government, i.e. the CEOs who act as purchaser of services, confronts another agent of government, the CEOs who provide services. To some extent the interaction between these two agents involve a zero sum game, where the gain of one party is the loss of another party. Thus, what government may win as a successful contractor, it may lose as an owner of the organisation which receives a meagre contract.

It is often stated that organisations accumulate slack, or redundant resources that may be used for future or unexpected needs. Organisations wish to position themselves so that they have flexibility meaning that they can meet unpredicted challenges by adaptation. The implication of the slack argument is that organisations seek lucrative contracts that provide them with extra resources to meet future contingencies. However, when generating slack they will necessarily come into opposition with the CEOs who run tournaments in order to get bids which contain low cost offers.

As owner of organisations, government wants their bureaux, enterprises or joint-stock companies to grow financially strong and be capable of not only maintaining themselves in a competitive environment but perhaps also expanding when facing future challenges. However, participating in fierce competitive rounds in various tournaments or auctions these organisations, where government is the principal, may have to accept meagre contracts just to stay alive. Thus, what government gains from running schemes of tendering/bidding it may lose in the viability of its own organisations.

The contradiction between these two roles, government as contractor and government as owner, is hardly fatal to the workabilty of NPM, but it is an opposition that requires attention. Government may use this opposition between its two teams, the CEOs who contract for the public provision of services and the CEOs who take care of government property, to its advantage under certain conditions. First, it is vital that effort is forthcoming from both sets of agents meaning that they attempt to arrive at Pareto-optimal outcomes after successive rounds of negotiation. Second, only if these outcomes of tendering/bidding processes strike a balance between the purchaser and the provider can government gain at both ends of the negotiating table. The conflict between these two roles of government becomes acute when the CEOs give a contract to another party than the government provider, causing it to leave the market, i.e. to be dissolved. Re-creating a public organisation after a defeat in a tournament may be difficult and costly for government.

One danger is that the provider organisation gets squeezed too brutally and that its capacity to act in the future is hampered by winning tournaments with meagre contracts. Another danger is that the purchasing agents strike deals that involve too much slack for the provider organisations, which may merely result in X-inefficiency. A 'balanced' outcome would perhaps be that both parties share equally the mutual gain from negotiating a Pareto-optimal outcome – the so-called Nash solution to a cooperative game (Riker and Ordeshook, 1973).

Now, government under NPM is contractor, owner as well as umpire. It has been argued that government needs to be very active in the last mentioned role, creating a regulatory state. In a regulatory state the most important government role is that of umpire. Actually, if there is a strong regulatory state, then government could diminish its presence in the other roles, as contractor and as owner (Majone, 1996). What, then, is the logic of public regulation under new public management?

Is there a regulatory state?

Regulatory reform has been initiated and completed in many countries. It has been a cornerstone in public sector reform in all countries with an advanced economy, as reregulation has been accomplished in a number of sectors of the economy.

Based upon the analysis of public regulation within the Chicago School of Economics (Stigler, 1988), there has been widespread agreement that traditional public regulation was counter-productive. It focused upon so-called entry regulation, which creates a legal monopoly through the mechanism of the licence. Deregulation has targeted the enhancement of contestability in various sectors of the economy, especially in the infrastructure part where traditional public regulation loomed large earlier.

Deregulation is to be seen as a practical response to the challenges from globalisation. When national boundaries are taken away, and the playing field is levelled between public and private players regionally or globally, then traditional public regulation has no rationale. The key question then becomes: what is to replace traditional public regulation?

The concept of deregulation entails only that rules that frame economic activity are eliminated. Although few doubt the positive contribution of deregulation for economic growth and world trade, many point out that no economy can operate without rules or regulations. Thus, deregulation can never be one hundred per cent. Even a deregulated economy with open borders and with equal conditions for public and private firms must have some sort of basic regime, laying down the rules of fair competition and the regulations concerning contractual honesty and fulfilment.

Since deregulation is only the abolition of rules but every economy needs a regulatory framework of some sort, many have concluded that deregulation is only a first step and not the end result. After deregulation comes reregulation, it is argued. After negative regulation there must come positive regulation. If deregulation is closely connected with reregulation, then perhaps the choice is never: 'deregulation versus regulation', but it is a matter of alternative regulatory regimes: 'weak regulation versus strong regulation'.

New public management is clearly linked up with regulatory reform, as it accepts the critique of traditional public regulation set out in Chapter 4. NPM endorses the basic principles of a deregulated economy: (1) denationalisation of the economy; (2) levelling the playing field between public and private players; (3) regional competition mechanisms; and (4) world regulation of public procurement. What is contested, however, is the extent to which the implementation of these principles requires more than deregulation or negative regulation. Could NPM endorse also reregulation or positive regulation?

Thus, when it comes to replacing old style entry regulation with a new form of regulation, the consensus breaks down, some arguing that deregulation is enough but others looking for a new kind of regulation. What would positive regulation amount to? If traditional regulation did not work, then one may argue that there are limits to reregulation as strong state intervention will not work. Or is reregulation to be done taking into account the lessons from the failure of traditional public regulation?

The adherents of reregulation or strong positive regulation often envisage a need for competition regulation, i.e. the making and implementation of so-called anti-trust policy. We must ask: is there really a need for reregulation after deregulation? Can anti-trust policy-making work? At other times, the adherents of reregulation focus upon welfare state provisions, stating that the denationalisation of the economies together with the establishment of regional market and trading regimes create a need for the harmonisation of not only basic economic regulations but also welfare state provisions (Scharpf, 1997).

The risk of over-regulation

The introduction of NPM has in a few countries been attended by a rather considerable increase in the number of regulatory bodies as well as in regulatory activities. Such evidence suggests that the number of regulators and the costs of regulation have gone up sharply in the UK for instance (*Financial Times* 12 August 1999). This is the reregulation argument in effect, which claims that after deregulation must come reregulation. Without resources for active regulation, a competitive regime like NPM cannot operate efficiently.

There are two sides to this argument. On the one hand, it is true that NPM presupposes that a regime for competition is in place and operates with reasonable efficacy. Such a competition regime will be a complex mechanism responding to a complex world where the distinction between private and public players in the economy has been undone and where national boundaries have come down. A competition regime requires not only consistent state legislation creating the bulk of legal norms but also consistency in the application of the norms by an implementation mechanism.

On the other hand, the creation of an economy-wide competition mechanism which is also in harmony with such regimes in other countries or in agreement with a regulatory framework for the world economy could become the starting-point for increasing state intervention, resulting in excessive over-regulation. Reregulation may involve not only enforcement of rules about competition but also the inspection of market structure and firm behaviour. There is no limit to the number of inspectors that government can create, especially if various parts of government will each have their own inspections. Thus, reregulation may run into the problems connected with Parkinson's disease, meaning a rapid rise in the number and size of regulatory bodies.

The real possibility of reregulation resulting in over-regulation is evident in recent UK developments. Thus, we read:

> Since Labour took office two years ago, it has created almost a dozen inspectorates: one for housing; one for health service; a benefits fraud inspectorate; a youth justice board; a training standards council to inspect publicly funded training; a 'best value' inspectorate that will cover the whole of local government.
>
> (*Financial Times* 12 August 1999)

When the soft sector is opened for competition, then it is believed that securing a high quality level requires regulation and inspection. However, at heart this is a contractual problem under an NPM regime, the solution to which could be found in the use of the ordinary court system (Posner, 1992). In the business sector the drive for reregulation has been strong since deregulation was initiated. Thus, we also read:

> In the private sector, there has been some rationalisation of regulation. The Financial Services authority now embraces nine former regulations – a process that in theory should not extend regulation but in practice is beginning to. Electricity and gas have been merged into a single energy regulator, although a bus regulator may yet be added.
>
> (*Financial Times* 12 August 1999)

The reregulation of the business sector often extends far beyond that necessary for the achievement of a competition regime. The goal of reregulation is often to directly control the products that are forthcoming in order to ensure that quality is high and prices reasonable. Reregulation is thus never only the maintenance of a competition regime but involves other and additional tasks; again, we read that the British government:

> wants to see a testable, measurable outcome from every extra pound of public spending it produces, and it sees the inspectorates as providing that kind of guarantee.
>
> (*Financial Times* 12 August 1999)

Yet, the so-called inspectorates come with a considerable cost, involving both the direct costs for all the inspectors and the inspections as well as the indirect cost for the compliance with the complaints from inspections and the anticipated reactions to inspection. Running the inspectorates could involve increasing rent-seeking costs or the money that providers would be prepared to spend in order to soften the impact of future inspections.

If one argues that reregulation is essential to any deregulated economy, then one must reflect upon the costs of reregulation, especially inspection. Again we face the problem of finding the optimal amount of inspection which involves setting the marginal value of another inspection equal to the marginal cost of that inspection. Any deliberations about the size of the regulatory effort cannot avoid reflecting upon the two basic alternatives for accomplishing reregulation. Either one employs a plethora of special public regulatory bodies, each for every special sector of the economy. Or one relies upon regulation by means of the ordinary courts, expressed in a set of decisions with long-term effects (precedents). Whereas the first method tends to be interventionist and result in detailed regulations, the second method tends towards general rules, although with effective implementation.

Now it is argued that NPM requires a massive regulatory effort, especially of the first kind including besides a competition regime also lots of inspections by a set of inspectorates. This is the argument that we wish to rebut. NPM does not entail the first method of regulation but it requires the second method discussed above.

Creating lots of inspectorates will only in the beginning improve the relation between benefits and cost, producing value for money. The marginal value of inspections is large when it is conducted parsimoniously, but it declines rapidly when inspections become frequent. At the same time the costs increase when inspectorates grow larger and their activities expand. At the end of the day, it is competition itself that is the most effective tool for checking quality, especially if combined with litigation and strict liability (Posner, 1992).

Reregulation and anti-trust

Let us now return to the argument that traditional regulation is irrelevant but that the economy would need a substitute in the form of strong reregulation. Majone develops this argument in relation to the European Union, stating that the EU is basically a new regulatory state along the American model of public utilities regulation.

A number of EU institutions could be seen in the light of public regulation. Such a perspective could embrace not only the Court of Justice and the European Central Bank but also the Commission with its twenty commissioners. Often one focuses upon the competition regime, contained in the EU constitution (Goyder, 1992). But if entry regulation fails, then maybe competition regulation or anti-trust policy-making also is questionable?

Economic activity needs institutions, but how far should the institutionalisation of the economy proceed? What Majone has in mind as a model for European regulation is actually the old American combination of public utilities regulation and anti-trust policy-making. When European governments dismantle their public enterprises and move towards levelling the playing field in various sectors of the economy, then one could claim that they should also start regulating prices and quantities or conduct anti-trust policies. One must, however, ask whether or not the regulators in such new schemes of regulation could become captured by special interest groups.

Majone replies that reputation will guarantee that public regulation is honest and efficient. This is basically again a principal–agent problem, where the agents – the regulators – may choose from different types of rewards from the principal, the government, one of which is reputation. There is no guarantee that reputation will be the most important consideration of the agent or that it constitutes a strategy proof mechanism.

Against the Majone argument, one may state the Demsetz conclusion that anti-trust policy-making does not work. Governments appear very hesitant in stopping firm mergers due to firm pressures. But the key point is that it is not worth doing it, because there are no natural monopolies. Contestation is always forthcoming in an economy with open entry. Government need not stimulate competition by forcing efficient companies to brake up (Demsetz, 1991).

If anti-trust regulation is not necessary, then perhaps also most kinds of regulation of prices and quantities are superfluous? What is important is that there is a basic framework of institutions that safeguard honest market operations with few limitations on the free movement of goods, services, labour and capital. This has been accomplished in Western Europe through negative regulation by the EU. The erection of a new and strong regulatory state in excess of that seems, strictly speaking, not a well-founded proposal.

The quest for reregulation appears unfounded to a large extent. What has happened in many European countries is that the traditional public enterprises have been transformed into public joint-stock companies and in some cases privatised. At the same time, these new players have become the target of new regulation, aiming at the traditional American system of sector boards with strong independent regulators. But if the critique of public utilities regulation is correct, then it should not be tried in the European context.

Is the EU a super regulator?

If one asks the question: what is the EU?, then there are so many alternatives: 'cooperative federalism without a state', 'specific Community Method', 'decision-making with variable geometry', 'convergence in public policy or on a European political model', 'mutual recognition versus harmonisation', 'European public sphere', 'partnership', 'common sphere of mediation at the European level' and a 'regulatory state' (Mèny *et al.* 1996: 1–22). If one describes both the Union itself and its interaction with member countries as characterised by 'uncertainty', 'openness' and 'opacity', then there may not exist any single label to be employed as an overall description. Perhaps it is more fruitful to focus upon what the Union does – the pragmatic approach. The EU is a regulatory mechanism.

What stands out is that the Union is firm as regards for example the rules of the common market and its adjacent legal orders. But the EU is also a loose institution as in the interaction leading up to policy-making either in the form of norms or the allocation of money. This very double nature of the Union – transparency versus complexity – cannot probably be eradicated by any realistic institutional reform.

The European Union has been seen as involving a conflict between legal integration and policy-making integration, which could be coupled with the distinction between negative and positive regulation (Scharpf 1997). If one takes the position that there is too little positive integration in the Union framework, then that is seen as a resultant of this conflict between the legal order and the political institutions. European integration in terms of the existing institutions implies that negative integration at the Union level blocks national policy-making at the same time as the intergovernmental nature of the Union restricts positive integration at the Union level.

Does European integration really need more positive regulation to tame 'capitalism'? One should not underestimate what has been achieved by means of negative regulation in counteracting market deviating behaviour. The call for more public intervention at the Union level contradicts the lesson why positive regulation has been so difficult to achieve within the EU. If positive regulation is so difficult to arrive at, especially when capitalism is international and trade unions national, then maybe the whole idea of extensive positive regulation is not worth it? One seldom speaks about the consumers, who may actually be the real winners from extensive negative regulation.

The Union is very much about regulation. Much has been achieved in terms of regulatory reform by the Union despite its implementation deficit. There is a logic to EU regulation in that European integration has been done thoroughly with regard to basic regulatory tasks. However, one must not underestimate both the amount of income redistribution that has taken place by means of the regional funds and the macro-economic convergence that is apparent already when the monetary union has been put into place.

The Union focus on regulation far ahead of other kinds of government intervention is to be understood as a rational adaptation to the situation. Given the vast legal resources of the Union and its systemic lack of other kinds of state attributes than law and money as well as the needs of the member states to create common rules without free rider problems, the EU concentration upon regulation is understandable.

In fact, European integration has proceeded where and in a manner that makes sense. It is when one confuses regulation with welfare policy that the risk of policy failure increases. Social regulation includes the many directives of the Union targeting the environment, consumer protection, product safety, health and safety in the workplace as well as equal rights of men and women. Welfare policies would be much more demanding.

How would positive regulation be done in the Union? Following the theme of rent-seeking, one could examine the decision-making process from the point of view of the influence of organised interests. The informal status of much EU lobbying by Euro-groups and national organisations is a fact, but many would have liked to see some kind of corporatist regime for the Union (Streeck and Schmitter, 1996). At the same time the attempts at EU corporatism were defeated by the marketers.

The risk of rent-seeking appears from the discussions about the role of interest organisations within EU policy-making. There is talk about a gigantic number of so-called Euro-associations as well as of consultative committees, connected with primarily EU policy-making. However, certain decision rules – standard operating procedures – tend to emerge which express an internal logic corresponding to the power relationships within the EU institutions. The Union is basically about negative regulation.

The European Union is both exchange and domination, from which constellation arises the paradoxes described as the 'joint decision trap' or the 'two-level game'. The players – public and private – involved in the 'multi-level game' in Brussels, Strasbourg and Luxembourg may engage in all kinds of coalitions, ad hoc and temporary, but once the game has been played and the decision been identified, then authority prevails.

EU regulation has strongly reinforced the Europeanisation of economic rules in a broad sense. Standardisation, harmonisation, mutual recognition as well as a levelled playing field all over Europe constitute elements in a legal order that applies with state force (Craig and De Burca, 1997).

European integration is more order than chaos, and modelling the emergence of this order by resorting to speaking of 'policy networks' or 'policy community', is much too vague. Only in relation to the EU projects funded with the structural funds money does the term 'network' seem appropriate. The EU makes policy by a small professional bureaucracy (the Commission) developing ever closer relations with a complex *mélange* of other policy actors.

By employing the distinction between competition and industrial policy one may identify a characteristic feature of European governance, that is the priority given to the first policy kind and the more or less lukewarm action in the latter kind of policy. The explanation is that the Union is doing what it is best at – the introduction of common market regulation – and abstaining from what it does worse – discretionary public intervention.

The institutions of the Union are capable of resolving collective action problems by putting into place public goods such as the common framework for an integrated European economy whereas they do not seem to be able to carry through huge-scale single projects in the form of an industrial policy. Industrial policy-making, if feasible, is seldom successful but often very costly.

The EU regulating orders are chiefly negative regulations as with the unification harmonisation and mutual recognition of the rules of markets. The EU is hardly a super regulator, engaging in massive reregulation.

Conclusion

New public management places a huge responsibility for public sector operations with politicians and managers, contracting between each other about the provision of goods and services. Whereas traditional public governance created order by means of huge bulks of public law, administered by bureaucrats and professionals, new public management employs contracting, because it is conducive to efficiency. While the public policy school either relied upon top-down implementation – steering or bottom-up implementation – discretion, NPM adheres to a different theory of efficiency, as efficiency is forthcoming from contracting in a deregulated economy where all players – public or private – play by the same institutions with a minimum of government intervention.

What we need to examine in relation to new public management is the connection between rationality in behaviour and efficiency in outcomes. If that tie is not as tight as new public management claims, then rationality may not be the great promoter of efficiency. What we face here is the problem of motivation in the contracting state, whether rational politicians and managers will find and implement first-best contracts, or Pareto-optimal contracts. Thus, we ask: are efficient contracts always forthcoming in new public management and are they self-enforceable? This way of posing the question takes us into the logic of contracting, where basic concepts in game theory are relevant such as Pareto-efficiency, the Nash equilibrium and rational outcomes that are not desirable.

In the next chapter motivation in the public sector will be analysed, focusing upon the major role of chief executive officers and regulators under NPM. Thereafter in Chapter 11, the question of contradictions in NPM is raised, which allows a statement of the limits of NPM in the concluding chapter.

10 Public policy, contracting and the CEOs

Introduction

New public management (NPM) is a theory that is broad enough to compete with other existing approaches. It has emerged as a serious competitor to public administration and public policy. New public management looks upon government and the public sector as a nexus of contracts, a stream of reciprocal commitments that binds participants because they have agreed to these contracts.

In public administration, government decides what is to be done and authorises bureaucrats and professionals to go ahead doing it. In public policy, the policies government decides centrally are to be implemented either by means of central bureaux steering public employees at lower levels or through wide discretion on the part of policy networks. In the contracting state, there are basically two categories of people contracting with service providers: politicians and their managers, especially the CEOs.

How about public policy-making in public management? Government is typically engaged in the making and implementation of public policies. We must discuss how public policies enter the writing and monitoring of contracts in NPM. Public policy results in something that is very public: laws and budgets, but contracting is something private, a concern between two contracting parties only. How, then, can public management employing contractualism take into account the concerns of public administration for legality and publicness?

We need to discuss how politicians relate to the CEOs as well as how contracts can be written so that they satisfy public criteria.

The legality dimension

In traditional public administration as well as in the public policy approach, questions concerning legality are given a very prominent role, as it is regarded as a high risk that public authority could be misused. 'Legality' refers basically to the notion that public power must be exercised in accordance with rules, which define what is to be done and how it is to be done. It is a simple idea, but it can be developed in a very complex way, containing a number of provisions.

First: the legal permission. Legality implies that no action can be taken by the agents of the state without the existence of rules which admit the action or obligate the action. State activities must have a foundation in a legal system, which entails that activities that are not permitted are in principle ruled out. Since what is a duty must be a permission, all state activities need a permission in law.

Second, the legal entailment. Lots of minor activities in the public sector are conducted in accordance with instructions issued by public officials. Legality implies that all such instructions are entailed by a law which permits or obligates the public official to issue instructions. If activities lack instruction, then that is a violation of the legality norm. If instructions are issued without the backing of a law, then that is also a violation of legality.

Third, the lex superior requirement. The hierarchy of rules for the conduct of public activities goes all the way from the minor workplace instructions at the bottom to the fundamental laws of the state, enshrined in a constitution at the top. All the time, higher norms make lower norms possible, as the lower norms are issued in accordance with a competence stated in higher norms. At the end of the legal hierarchy of norms, higher norms are introduced because the constitution allows that (Kelsen, 1967). The constitution is thus the highest possible norm or the basic norm, which is a law of a special kind, having more protection than other laws in the form of severe rules about constitutional change or inertia.

To maintain legality in the public sector has been considered as a major goal of public activities, especially in public administration. Legality is alternatively described as the restrictions upon another major goal of public activities, namely productivity or effectiveness. The relationships between legality and efficiency have been much discussed also in the public policy approach, whereas in the management framework efficiency considerations tend to take precedence before legality concerns.

Legality may be interpreted as a means to containing public authority as with Max Weber, but it may also be seen as a value in itself, constituting an aspect of justice, giving each one what is due to him/her. Legality enhances predictability, as officials may calculate what they are expected to do and citizens may likewise make predictions about how they will treated by the officials. Legality and predictability do not ensure the Rule of Law, however, because the Rule of Law requires more in the form of protection of human rights. No doubt, these concepts are closely related, as legality in an authoritarian regime tends to degenerate into arbitrariness sooner or later.

The case for an emphasis upon legality would be strengthened if it could be shown that legality supports and does not reduce efficiency. Yet, the standard analysis of legality has been to consider it as reducing efficiency, i.e. as inflicting a cost upon efficiency. In itself, this may not be problematic, because legality could be seen as offering something inherently valuable, namely justice under the laws. Thus, one arrives at the conventional model of a trade-off between economic efficiency meaning reducing costs and justice in the sense of predictability under the laws.

However, besides economic efficiency there is also administrative efficiency. Rules when considered as restrictions upon action do not have only one impact, i.e. increasing costs, but rules may also stabilise the situation, meaning they could decrease costs. When legality is in place, then standard operating procedures emerge, which could economise upon the costs of searching for information and reduce transaction costs in the making of decisions. Legality may also help reduce the dissipation of rents through illegal activities, especially various types of corruption.

Administrative routines are not always the source of red tape and rigidity. They may structure a situation channelling effort in certain directions, enhancing the achievement of organisational goals. The rules governing public sector activities may be looked upon as rationally devised mechanisms for channelling individual effort and ambition towards the accomplishment of objectives.

One may find in both incrementalism and rational choice theory arguments for the rationality of legality in the public sector. According to the first theory, legality presents the public sector with rules that may develop into standard operating procedures, whereas according to the second theory rules that establish so-called equilibria in decision-making tend to evolve.

Yet, the most profound explanation of the role of legality is to be found in the theory of the state suggested by Hans Kelsen. Government cannot operate in a stable fashion without a system of norms that is backed by sanctions (Kelsen, 1961). It is of the essence of the state to function with norms of various generality, which are linked in a logical fashion, where lower norms entail higher norms, which sanction the lower norms. Kelsen focused much upon the hierarchical nature of rules in the public sector which is the essence of validity in his conception of a pure theory of law. One may also enter another criterion, namely publicness in Kant's conception.

Publicness

Legality is not the same as publicness, although legality tends to enhance publicness. It is conceivable that laws may give governments the right to put in place secret activities. Yet, on the whole legality supports publicness, as legality tends to be accomplished through laws and instructions which are available to all, in principle. Thus, a state which scores high on legality tend to score high on publicness. The opposite also holds, because publicness requires legality, or the request for rules.

Publicness seems to be a highly relevant requirement upon the public sector. Public decisions concern a community of people, who would justifiably wish to know why such a decision was taken and not another one. If the grounds of public decisions cannot be stated publicly, then it is likely that these decisions lack proper justification.

Public officials and citizens may endorse the Kant criterion basically for two reasons. One the one hand, they would wish to know for their own sake what rules apply so that they can act rationally. Thus, public officials must be correctly informed about the competencies that they exercise and in terms of which they relate to other officials as well as to citizens. Citizens would wish to know about their rights as well as their obligations, not the least because they may wish to take action against an official who in their opinion does not respect their rights.

On the other hand, people take a positive view as to the Kantian argument in favour of the inherently just nature of the criterion of publicness, especially in relation to matters in the public sector. If public decisions and their reasons cannot be stated openly, then one would either believe something wrong is taking place or one would accept that state security or some such special reason requires an exception from an almost universally valid rule of publicness.

Both legality and publicness constitute basic requirements upon a democratic state and its public sector. In the 1990s, they have been extended also to the private sector to some extent. However, NPM does not endorse these two requirements, focusing instead upon getting the job done as effectively as possible by means of contracting, i.e. in terms of a chain of agreements between government and managers and managers and service providers.

Thus arises the question about how public sector management can strike a middle-way between the strong emphasis upon legality and publicness in public administration and public policy on the one hand and the heavy commitment to managerialism on the other hand with NPM. Resolving this problem involves discussing how people are motivated to do the job in the public sector.

In traditional public administration government employs a huge number of people and instructs them with public law documents and budgetary instruction. In NPM, government hires public managers who contract for service provision by means of processes of tendering/bidding. The key group in NPM is the set of CEOs. We must ask how they are to be instructed and what motivates them to try hard. Especially we wish to enquire into how the nexus of contracts can satisfy publicness.

Public managers or the chief executive officers

NPM suggests that public policy enters the contracts with public managers, the so-called chief executive officers or the CEOs. How can that be done, given that contracts are incomplete and are to be subjected to ordinary court disputes? Public policies used to be confirmed in public law documents or in budgetary instructions. If they are to be entered into employment contracts, then how can their public nature be maintained and respected?

Public policy-making as contracting raises a number of questions about the limits of the use of contracting for allocation in the public sector, especially with regard to the soft sector. There are two things involved: (1) Can contracts really be specified as completely as is desirable from considerations about the Rule of Law or the requirements that follow from the need to surround public authority with restrictions? – the legality issue. (2) Can contracts containing public policy be regarded as open to the public? – the publicity issue.

We wish to argue that although efficiency in contracting would be enhanced, if contracts are properly negotiated and self-enforced, it is far from easy to satisfy the legality requirement and the publicity requirement, when employment contracts are extended considerably to contain also lots of public policy. This leads us to the question of how to handle managerial motivation with the contract institution.

As a result of NPM, the CEOs are rapidly replacing bureaucrats and professionals. Are the CEOs in the public sector – the public managers – more managers than public servants? The question that the contracting state raises is whether there is anything left of public administration, bureaucracy and public law. Can there really be public sector management without the Rule of Law framework?

Why NPM cannot do without public law

Getting things done by mainly public law instructions as in public administration or exclusively by private law contracting as with NPM – this way of posing the question implies that one could choose either one or the other governance model. However, public sector management may strike a balance between these two governance techniques, mixing public law and budgetary instructions with private law contracting. How, then, can private law contracting be used in a public law environment?

Under various schemes of public management using contracting on a major scale there will always be a need for public law arrangements. However, the score and range of administrative law will diminish, as contracting expands. That which is to be done is stipulated in contracts. At the same time one must emphasise that contracts cannot entirely replace administrative law.

In NPM, there has been a tendency to put everything into the contract. Thus, a contract between government and the CEOs could run into hundreds of pages. And besides the employment contract a performance contract in a public organisation could contain an immense detailed specification of what the employee is expected to do. However, the limits to replacing administrative law with specifications in contract law must be pointed out.

First, contracting suffers from the problem of systemic incompleteness (Milgrom and Roberts, 1992). Except for simple transactions, contracting often fails to specify all the conditions and circumstances that impinge upon contractual fulfilment. Attempting to write complete contracts covering all contingencies is impossible. General and simple public law frameworks may complement contracting where contracting becomes incomplete or too complicated.

Second, some things are too important to be handed over to the contracting mechanism. People claim rights against the state which they would not want to become the target of negotiations in contracts of a private law kind. Officials exercise competencies, which again cannot be hidden in private law contracts.

Third, rights and competencies need to be stated publicly – this is part of the requirement of legality in the public sector. When the employment contract in the public sector starts to contain lots of legal matters relating to rights and competencies, then one runs the risk of losing the public nature of a state to be run in accordance with the Rule of Law. Thus, detailed contracting may endanger legality.

Looking at the public sector by means of the public administration framework, one may claim that contracting in the public sector must respect an institutional setting, which goes beyond merely the institutions that are necessary for the respect of contracts, or contractual validity and enforcement. Public law contains numerous regulations about public sector activities, which cannot be negotiated in the contractual process. Administrative law hands down restrictions upon contractualism.

Seen from the looking glass of the public policy school, the public sector is governed by objectives which cannot be communicated merely in the form of contracts with the CEOs or in the performance contracts of public employees. The policy objectives belong to public discourse, which entails that they are not merely an element in a contract between two parties.

If there are limits to how far contracts can be employed to govern public sector activities, then it is also the case that contracts remain necessary and desirable for motivating people to get things done in the public sector. Contracts are very suitable for agreements about who is to pay what for receiving which services. How, then, is motivation forthcoming among the people who handle the provision of services in the public sector?

Motivation: politicians, managers and the professionals

What is motivation in the public sector and why is it problematic to come to an agreement about work effort and compensation in the public sector? Traditional public governance focused upon tenure and vocation as the motivational mechanisms for accomplishing the quid pro quo or reciprocity between politicians and the public officials, remunerating public officials and at the same time eliciting their interest in their work.

The idea about motivation in traditional public governance has long ago been abandoned. The various stakeholders in traditional public governance – politicians, bureaucrats and professionals – are not modelled as motivated by vocation, as in the Weberian approach. Instead, each group is modelled as maximising their self-interests, especially in the public choice approach.

Replacing the assumption about vocation with the assumption about self-interest maximisation opens up entirely new ways of looking at motivation in the public sector. If people active in the provision of services in the public sector are driven by self-interests, then what stops them from pursuing strategies which reduce public interests such as productivity and effectiveness?

When it is recognised that self-interests may be pursued with guile, then arriving at a *quid pro quo* in motivation between remuneration and work effort becomes far more difficult than realised within traditional public governance.

The new insights into incentives and the economics of information focus upon the occurrence of opportunistic behaviour in various forms, with e.g. politicians, bureaucrats and professionals.

When it is assumed that the key groups of actors in the public sector are driven by self-interests, then one begins to understand not only why contractual fulfilment may be problematic but also why it may be tempting to engage more or less in cheating. A number of concepts for cheating or reneging have been suggested, all referring to the motivation on the part of people to get something for nothing.

In the standard employment relation between the employer and the employee, the motivation to get something for free is described as various forms of shirking. With regard to the self-interest seeking behaviour of politicians, the opportunism of politicians is expressed e.g. in the political business cycle or in popularity functions. Incentives combine with information advantages to create strategies actors choose *vis-à-vis* each other (Campbell, 1995).

Whether one starts from traditional or modern public governance, one is bound to encounter interactions between people that may be analysed by a general model of principals contracting with agents, paying a remuneration to the agent as compensation for the effort that the agent is putting in for the achievement of the objectives of the principal.

Principal–agent theory was developed in economics in order to state the difficulties for two parties to arrive at an efficient contract in the private sector as soon as the interaction lasts longer than the elementary market interaction between buyers and sellers. The employment relationship is one kind of principal–agent interaction, and the relationship between a lawyer and his/her client is also a kind of principal–agent relationship. Agency relations occur often in economic life.

One may speak of principal–agent interaction in the public sector as well, at least in a figurative sense. Thus, politicians may be looked upon as the agents of their population. Bureaucrats, or the top officials in the bureaux, could be regarded as the agents of the politicians. And, finally, professionals could also be interpreted as agents when they are active in service delivery organisations. But to state who is their principal is far from clear cut, as besides government one could mention the bureaucrats, the population or the discipline to which a professional adheres by virtue of their training.

In modern governance, the problems in principal–agent interaction have received much attention, whereas in traditional public governance they were almost neglected. Following the framework stated in the introductory chapter, principal–agent problems arise both in the interaction between politicians and the key managers, the executive agencies or the regulators, as well as in the interaction between politicians as owners of enterprises and their CEOs. Which, then, are the key principal–agent problems?

Agency problems: moral hazard and adverse selection

In modern governance, government relies heavily upon chief executive officers, the CEOs. The CEOs will be at the head of the allocative and regulative agencies and they may also direct the provider organisations, especially when they have become incorporated. Then, how does government write contracts with the CEOs that motivate them to put in a great effort?

The crux of the matter is that government as the principal and the CEOs as the agents have common and conflicting interests at the same time. By collaborating, both principal and agent are better off than if nothing is done. However, the agent wants as large remuneration as possible for as little effort as possible whereas the principal has the opposite preference, i.e. low compensation and high effort.

Figure 10.1 displays the basic logic in principal–agent interaction. The outcome of the interaction is a contract which specifies remuneration w against services q. The principal's profit (π) depends on the quantity that the agent provides as well as his/her wage. The same factors determine the utility (U) of the agent in two different environments: easy and difficult. Contract C1 gives the agent too high a wage and the principal too low a profit, if the environment actually is difficult and not easy. A contract closer to C2 would be more efficient.

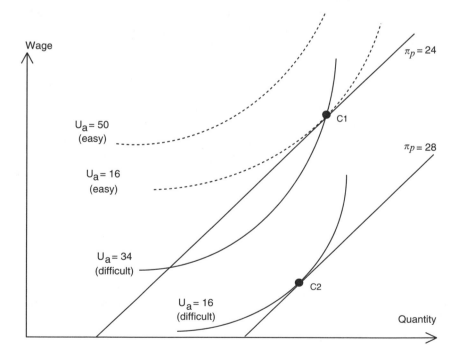

Figure 10.1   Interaction between principal p and agent a.

Principal–agent contracting or relational contracting involves making an agreement which binds two parties during a long time interval, which entails that the contract is bound to be either incomplete or simply based upon incorrect information about what is likely to happen after the contract has been signed. Contractual fulfilment is open to post-contractual opportunism. But the problem in writing an optimal contract between the principal and the agent is also vulnerable to pre-contractual opportunism (Rasmusen, 1994).

Moral hazard

The agents of government, the CEOs and the regulators, may not live up to the expectations of the principal after the contract has been signed. Post-contractual problems could arise due to many causes or reasons.

First, there is the ever-present fact of contractual incompleteness. It is impossible to foresee all circumstances that may become relevant for the fulfilment of a contract, due to both objective and subjective risk. Nature displays only probabilities due to randomness and people seldom know these probabilities exactly due to fundamental human cognitive limitations.

Second, contracts may contain numerous written clauses, but how they are to be interpreted may cause conflict that can only be resolved by action in court. At the end of the day, it is the judge who decides upon the content of a contract, and judge-made law changes with time and circumstances. It is impossible to predict in detail how a contract will be implemented in a court.

Third, one cannot assume that all parties are driven by an ambition to effectuate a contract in a complete and honest manner. Contractual opaqueness opens up the possibility of opportunistic behaviour and strategic possibilities of improving upon one's advantages, even if such behaviour would go against the spirit of a contract.

Finally, there is the employment of explicit contractual negligence or cheating and not complying with a contract. Contracts are made at one point in time but they are often effectuated much later on, which opens up for possibilities of negligence or criminal behaviour. Litigation is the answer to such tactics, but litigation takes time and is not without risk.

'Moral hazard' is the general concept for all kinds of post-contractual opportunism which hinder the smooth and frictionless implementation of a contract between a principal and an agent. Both the principal and the agent may find it advantageous to engage in moral hazard. There is no contract that can be written in such a manner that it entirely avoids moral hazard.

Adverse selection

If post-contractual opportunism is difficult to handle, not the least because of the considerable costs connected with litigation, then the dangers involved in pre-contractual opportunism should also be recognised. How is a principal to know whether an agent is credible or not when they present the conditions for a contract?

When government picks the managers of its public joint-stock companies, its purchasing agencies, its service providing organisations or its regulatory boards, then government as the principal must be able to make the distinction between serious people and so-called lemons. Managers as agents have strong incentives to present a rosy picture of what they can accomplish for the principal, simply in order to raise the stakes involved and receive a better compensation. But is credibility to be tested before the signing of the agreement, after which only litigation will work effectively?

The problem of credibility has received much attention, it being suggested that the uses of signalling or reputation are conducive to the making of a correct decision concerning 'good' and 'bad' managers. Signalling could enhance the detection skill of the principal, whereas reputation would make the agent less inclined to engage in pure opportunism, which is risky for contracts in the future.

Yet, there is no standard signalling device that government can use when selecting CEOs. And reputation only works if the situation of selecting the CEOs is repeated several times. In fact, there is no standard and safe method for handling the problems of adverse selection.

Principals' responses

Modern public governance results from an awareness that moral hazard and adverse selection occurred within traditional public governance. Actually, one may interpret the public choice school criticism of the bureau and the public enterprise with the arguments about budget maximisation or rent-seeking as basically principal–agent hypotheses where the mechanisms of traditional public governance work to the advantage of the agent (Mueller 1989; Stevens, 1993).

The principal has a number of mechanisms that they may use to counteract the opportunism of the agents. They all involve the principal giving up traditional public governance and using modern public governance, involving the use of CEOs but keeping them in check by means of market mechanisms. What is absolutely essential is the use by the principal of tendering/bidding in relation to the selection of agents. The skilful employment of tendering/bidding in the choice of all kinds of CEOs would enhance the position of the principal. But it does not remove moral hazard and adverse selection, which occur under any principal–agent interaction.

Under traditional public governance, principal–agent problems arise from the top all the way down to the level of street bureaucrats. Modern public governance cuts these long principal–agent relationships by putting CEOs in place who are responsible for the arrangement of tendering/bidding processes between the players in the economy, public or private. Sometimes governments move to modern public governance, but they forget to arrange a tendering/bidding process for the selection of the CEOs. This is a great mistake, resulting from the so-called 'lemons' problem (Ackerloff, 1988).

Now, how to minimise the risk of moral hazard and adverse selection in public management? How to instruct agents by means of contracts when the agent cannot be trusted and where effort by the agent is not automatically forthcoming? In relation to managers – the CEOs and the regulators – I suggest the use of the strategy of boiling in oil and in relation to the providers of services I would recommend the use of proper tournaments and auctions.

The CEOs: boiling in oil

In relation to the CEOs, wherever they may work, government should be checking credibility by continuous threat of contract termination: the strategy of firing when performance is not considered adequate will, however, only constitute a real threat if government is prepared to use it. Thus, government must fire a certain number of managers in order to show that it means business.

Paradoxically, it may even be necessary for government to fire managers who have not performed in a mediocre manner just to show who sits in the driver's seat. Talking about firing as a response to bad performance will not do, as managers will very soon find out that it is just empty talk.

In addition, government must all the time be prepared to change its CEOs, recruiting new ones and not prolonging the contract with the old ones. Only if government can instil in the agents the impression that nothing is certain, then government can stay up front in command. Once the agents get the impression that their contracts will be prolonged, then the temptation of shirking or opportunism becomes a real one. Yet, threatening the termination of a contract with a manager involves a strategy that is not costless, as we will see in the next chapter. Manager will demand high salaries as compensation.

The players: tournaments and auctions

In modern public governance, the provider of services will be any player who is forthcoming and gains a contract after a process of tendering/bidding, arranged by the CEOs of government and checked by the regulators of government. How to instruct in an optimal manner by means of private law contracting: what services are to be provided and what they should cost?

The service providers may interact with government as under the purchaser–provider scheme used in the soft sector or they may interact directly with the population as within the business sector. The service providers may be private or public players, all competing under the same logic. The regulators are the umpires monitoring the rules of the game. When government is a service provider, either as the principal of a public organisation or as the owner of a joint-stock company, then it is not only the ultimate umpire in the economy but constitutes also a player. Optimal contracts with service providers will be forthcoming when the process of tendering/bidding works. There are in principle two such processes: tournaments and auctions.

Tournaments are highly suitable in purchaser–provider schemes where the goods and services to be tendered are standardised ones and contestability is naturally forthcoming from various players, public and private ones. Tournaments used to be employed within traditional public administration for services like catering and cleaning, but modern public governance has extended their use to many other areas. In new public management, there is an ambition to arrange tournaments for practically all public services. However, there are limits to the employment of tournaments in the soft sector, which will be stated in the next chapter.

How can tournaments be arranged in the business sector where huge infrastructure often limits contestability, which is conducive to the occurrence of natural monopolies? With services like electricity, water, sewage, communications and telecommunications tournaments are basically impossible, because the net cannot be supplied by each provider. How, then, is a process of tendering/bidding to be arranged?

When governments are in the possession of the net, then auctions is the method employed. The use of the net may be auctioned out for a longer period of time as with railroad tracks or water and sewage nets. There have been many innovations in the techniques for auctioning out infrastructure components, including the establishment of bourses for electricity, by means of which transmission and distribution nets can be accessed momentarily – third party access.

When governments are not in the possession of the net but it is in the hands of private owners, then governments may legislate about Third Party Access. The principle of Third Party Access may be sanctioned in international regimes, set up by states in a region, as for instance the European Union with regard to the gas net in Western Europe.

In modern public governance, governments must not only improve their skill in writing and implementing contracts. Governments must also become specialists in handling processes of tendering/bidding, like the variety of tournaments and auctions.

Continued relevance of public law

In the two dominating approaches in the twentieth century, public administration and public policy, government would use public law to a very high extent in instructing civil servants what to do. The immense expansion in administrative law is ample proof of the belief in the possibility of governing the public sector through instructions, issued unilaterally by governments based upon the principle of legislative supremacy.

Yet, NPM has meant a decisive change in this development, as private law is preferred to public law. Services are to be provided in the public sector by means of contracting, and contracts constitute the core of private law. This basic break in the expansion of administrative law also involves a preference for using ordinary courts instead of public law courts.

Under NPM, contracts may be used not only between the service purchaser, the government agencies or the public, and the provider organisations, public or private. Contracts are also to be employed when government hires its chief managers, the CEOs and the regulators, not only to settle salary and working conditions but also to lay down what is to be accomplished.

Still however, the range of application of contracts or private law in government should not be exaggerated. There will still be public law in the future public sector. Public law fills very basic needs in a constitutional democracy, which cannot be met merely by contracting. A number of reasons point towards the continued employment of various kinds of public law. I mention here only a few reasons why public law cannot be reduced to a minimum in a constitutional democracy. Actually, public law is vital in a society where government operates under transparent restrictions stemming from a valid constitution and meeting the requirement of publicness.

First, public law contains the essential rules about human rights. These cannot be put into contracts. Instead they are to be considered as presuppositions for the making of contracts about public services. The requirement of publicness also requires that human rights be stated in a transparent and easily accessible manner.

Second, administrative law is still necessary to regulate how modern public governance operates, although it will be far less detailed than used to be the case under traditional public governance. The development in recent years of administrative law towards framework legislation is almost an anticipation of the transition from traditional to modern public governance.

Third, entitlements are considered by huge groups in the population so important that they cannot become objects of negotiation between government and its managers or be put into purchaser–provider agreements. Instead, entitlements are seen as given restrictions upon modern public governance, which must be respected in whatever contracts are made concerning the provision of public services.

Finally, although modern public governance is oriented towards efficiency, or 'getting the job done', administrative law is not always a hindrance to the efficient accomplishment of objectives. Adherence to strict procedures in public service provision or in the management of public organisations may enhance the accomplishment of objectives. This is often the case in service provision in the soft sector.

Conclusion

Public sector reform has now advanced so much in several countries that one can speak of a system or regime shift. Traditional public governance is being replaced by modern public governance. Although the new governance model is not yet in sight completely, some major elements may be pinned down, based upon the experiences in the UK, the United States, Australia and New Zealand as well as the Nordic countries.

Traditional public governance had certain characteristics: (1) it underlined the role of politics in directing the public sector, (2) it employed almost exclusively public law to direct the employees, (3) it made a sharp separation between the public and the private sector and (4) it separated the tasks of government in allocation from its tasks in regulation. The new emerging model of public governance does not involve a minor reform of these key features of traditional public governance, as it replaces them with an entirely different model of how the public sector should be governed.

Modern public governance is the governance by means of contracting, which requires a complicated web of different kinds of contracts. By means of contracting regimes, one wishes to: (1) get the job done; (2) to use private law; (3) to level the playing field; and (4) integrate allocation and integration. To put these features in place, modern public government conceives of government contracting with managers, the CEOs, and regulators, as well as managers contracting with players, public or private.

Are there no dangers with such public governance by means of contracting? We must ask if there are no weaknesses in contractualism. It is my belief that NPM underestimates the difficulties with a contractual state. Especially, I wish to emphasise the continued relevance of public law.

11 *The contracting state*: no risk for organisational failures?

Introduction

The new public management philosophy for the public sector makes contracting the central medium of interaction. The public sector will operate better if contracts are made explicitly, stating what is expected in terms of outputs and how accountability for outcomes can be exercised. Institutional reforms are needed in order to make more room for contracting, both at the central level and at the operating level.

Contracting will remove many of the inefficiencies of the public sector by clarifying what is expected by whom as well as who is responsible for what and by setting the incentives correctly, tying them down to the fulfilment of contractual obligations. Costs will be revealed at the contracting stage and deliberations about benefits will enter when contracts are made. Contracting as the major coordination mechanism will enhance efficiency and counteract opportunism, or so it is argued.

Contracting as the key coordination mechanism in the public sector is definitely a new idea. In public administration, the public sector is conceived of a system of authority, coordination taking place through rules stemming from but also regulating or taming the unique power of the state, sometimes referred to as 'sovereignty' or at other times as 'legislative supremacy'. Contracting involves bargaining and reciprocity, whereas authority is based upon domination. In the public policy approach, the making of policy is seen as a highly political process, involving gainers and losers, which is very different from private sector decision-making as exchange or mutual benefits. Public policy implementation, on the other hand, could involve considerable amounts of bargaining, if a decentralised model of implementation is preferred above a centralised one. Whereas contracting has always been the core of private sector operations, new public management amounts to a theory that massive contracting focusing upon managers in the public sector will increase allocative efficiency.

What we need to investigate is whether contracting with managers or contracting by managers always results in finding efficient solutions to allocative problems in the implementation of which there is enough private commitment. Efficient contracts may exist, but rational actors might not arrive at them.

Incentives and the chain of contracting

New public management as contracting does add a new dimension to earlier dominant approaches. Public resource allocation by means of exchange – this is a novel theoretical conception that governments all over the world are rushing to. What kinds of contracts are there? Who is making these contracts with whom and are these contracts both efficient ones and contracts that are self-enforced or ones that can be enforced? Evidently, managers are much involved on either side of contracting, but they are surely not the only group of actors.

'Contract' may stand for a legally valid agreement between two or more parties, which can be implemented by means of court action. 'Contract' may also mean any form of agreement, explicit or implicit, between two or more parties, which contains promises – unilateral or reciprocal ones – but nothing more. Such agreements are not typically enforceable at all, as they state intentions and not binding commitments. Typically, contracting in public management focuses upon the provision of goods and services, i.e. allocative contracts. One could see the entire system for the public provision of goods and services as a nexus of real contracts, running from top politicians through managers to service providers, right through all kinds of public organisations playing a role in the provision of goods and services.

Changing the coordination mechanism may be interpreted as the attempt by government in relation to a set of production units of different types – departments, bureaus, boards, authorities, quangos, crown entities – to economise on the costs that government will have to pick up in order to provide for goods and services in the public sector. Can government as the principal arrange for an efficient supply without staggering coordination costs? The problem concerns how the agent is to be committed to an efficient supply, which raises the question about how motivation costs can be kept low.

Government, one would assume, is interested in finding the governance mechanism that minimises the combined coordination and motivation costs. Table 11.1 lists the three governance mechanisms and the two types of costs involved, stating a hypothesis about high (H) or low (L) costs involved in each mechanism.

There may be an inverse relationship between coordination costs and motivation costs, as the principal would either have to face large costs for instructing, monitoring and evaluating the agent in order to have the agent do the job or the

Table 11.1   Governance mechanism and costs for public provision (high, low)

	Coordination costs	*Motivation costs*	*Outcome*
Central coordination	H	L	Inefficiency
Decentralised coordination	L	L	Inefficiency
Contracting	L	H	Efficiency

principal would have to incur considerable motivation costs in order to work with agents who have a high commitment to the job. Central coordination as well as decentralised coordination implies huge coordination costs, whereas public contracting entails large commitment costs.

Contracting between principals and agents

In theory, new public management changes the coordination mechanism in public resource allocation from authority or command to contracting or exchange. We must ask whether this can really be done without blurring the basic distinction between state and market. In economic organisation theory, the basic theory of contracting makes a distinction between spot market contracts and relational contracts, which two types of contracts resolve the basic fact that complete contracts are impossible to write. Spot market contracts are inflexible contracts, which minimise the ex post uncertainty about what behaviour is required on the part of the contractors. Relational contracts settle for an agreement that only frames the relationship between the contracting parties (Milgrom and Roberts, 1992).

Principal–agent interaction typically takes place through relational contracts whereas simple exchange occurs in spot market contracts. Public sector employment has often been analysed as a principal–agent relationship, as it used to be based upon relational contracts, the employee accepting a broad mandate for the employer to direct work against job security and a pension. Government would, however, not primarily act on the basis of its power as employer but use its public authority to direct the work of its employees. One must not confuse the public law authority of the state and the private law power of employers.

The contracts in the new contracting state using a giant nexus of contracts from the top to the bottom in the state hierarchy, including governments at various levels, whether there is a unitary or federal state format, will be different from the contracts used earlier. On the one hand, spot market contracts would be much more in use in regimes like internal markets or purchaser–provider separation. But, on the other hand, there would still be relational types of contracts, although never of the duration that was characteristic of earlier regimes, except in certain special jobs, i.e. for people with asset specificity, the new economics of organisation predicts (Williamson, 1975, 1986).

In the new contracting state, there would thus still be short-term principal–agent relationships, but there will also be spot market contracts – the use of both reflecting the drive towards tendering/bidding. Table 11.2 shows some possible ways of contracting including two parties, A and B.

The distinction between A and B in Table 11.2 covers a number of possible actors. Thus, managers acting upon a relational contract with government could in themselves take on the role as principals in relation to other managers or employees. However, we do not wish to analyse complexity here which can arise both when governments on various occasions constitute a principal or when managers engage in long series of relational contracting.

Table 11.2　Relational contracting and spot market contracting

		B	
		Relational contracting	Spot market contracting
A	Relational contracting	I	II
	Spot market contracting	III	IV

Government (A) would basically do relational contracting *vis-à-vis* the top managers who direct the departments of the state or the joint-stock companies which the state owns. Government could also engage in spot market contracts, for example when it runs auctions on its infrastructure assets that it wishes others to rent and operate. Managers (B) in their turn would have a definitely much larger choice between relational contracting and spot market contracting.

What is critical in new public management is type II, the combination of relational contracting between government as the principal and its departmental heads or executives of public firms as agents on the hand with spot market contracting by the managers themselves on the other hand. It is this very combination that is going to do the trick, i.e. deliver contracts that implement solutions that increase allocative efficiency, decrease technological inefficiencies, remove waste or X-inefficiencies and yet afford enforceable contracts with reasonable motivation costs.

Now, let us try to spell out what more precisely this kind of contracting state – type II in Table 11.2 – involves. Can it identify efficiency in allocation? Is it proof against any invasion from opportunistic behaviour of the participants, the principal or the purchasing or regulating managers or the service providers? The coordination mechanism between government as the principal and managers as the agents as well as with regard to the providers is to be contracting, not state authority. When, then, is a public contract?

Public contracts as metaphors

It should be pointed out that one can interpret lots of public sector activities as contracting. Contracting can be seen to occur not only in relation to allocation, or the provision of goods and services. Redistribution or income maintenance programmes may be designated 'contracts' between politicians on the one hand and the population on the other hand. One could make a distinction between true contracts and figurative contracts here, as talking about some things as 'contracts' is merely using a metaphor. Contracts as fiction are typically indeterminate, as it is far from clear who the contracting parties are, when the contract was actually made and how it is being observed or monitored. Fictional contracts can not be implemented by a third party.

Similarly, election results can be called 'contracts' but who are the signing parties – government or the state? Do such electoral contracts include not only the winners but also the losers? When politicians renege on their electoral promises, then one may wish to speak about a break of contract, but the only way to retaliate is to choose another cabinet or president, which is far more difficult than to take someone to court. Similarly, constitutions may be called 'contracts', but this is only again using a metaphor, because who are the contracting parties? Perhaps the generation that actually wrote and enacted the constitution or the presently living population who lives up to the constitution, or some new interpretation of it.

One may wish to remember of the so-called contractual school in political theory from Grotius to Rousseau that interpreted politics as stemming from a grand contract between rulers and the ruled or among people, legitimating the use of state authority. The rejection of the contractual school by Hume was basically the empiricist objection: where is the contract, concretely speaking? How can I see it or verify its existence? If public contracts are merely contracts as fictions or *als ob* in Kant's interpretation, then there is hardly any limit to what may be interpreted as public contracts. Budgets would be a reasonable candidate, regulation would be another, whether one focuses upon the regulator or those regulated. Clearly, the entire welfare state could be seen as a contract, or an agreement between the state and the population about future rights and duties.

Although one may find this metaphorical use of 'contract' or contracting in much moral political theory, new public management is about real contracts. Contracting actually occurs and contracts are monitored, if not implemented through third party action, ultimately through litigation. In public management, one of the contracting parties is always a manager. Thus, public management is a theory about writing and implementing efficient contracts with managers. This focus upon managers and real contracts makes new public management different from public administration as well as public policy or policy implementation. To get things done, new public management gives much discretion to public managers and contracting is the mechanism for efficient provision of goods and services.

Real contracts

When contracts are made in new public management, it is not only a question of a manner of talking. By a 'real' contract I mean an agreement between two or more parties which is either a contract in the private law or an agreement that is in all essential aspects similar to a private law contract, although it does not fall under civil law. Contracts in new public management would thus include the signing of an agreement between politicians and managers or between managers about what is to be done or what is to be delivered at what cost during what time and with what consequences if there is either contractual failure or disagreement about contractual fulfilment.

Since some of the contracting in new public management is the making and carrying through of private law agreements, the 'meaning' of contracting in the public sector is moving away from the metaphorical use of 'contract', in the sense of either merely promises or the one time creation of a superior law like the constitution. Yet, contracting in new public management also includes agreements between parties which are not contracts in the true private law sense, as they cannot be vindicated by means of court action.

Enforcement here rests with the contracting parties, but it is still the case that we have here quasi-real contracts, as these agreements would tend to contain the specifications that private law contracts include. When a contract is signed between a minister and one of his departments or bureaux about what he expects them to deliver during the next few years – creating so-called executive agencies – then this is not a private law contract. But it has some of the essential features of such an agreement, as long as there is a high probability that failure to comply with the contract will result in the firing of the managers of that department.

Public authority or policy and real contracting

Real contracts never figured prominently in earlier dominant approaches to the public sector. In public administration, contracts figure only in relation to the employment of personnel. Tasks were to be laid down in public law documents, including the statutes of a department and its follow-up instructions, or in the budget appropriations with its follow-up line-item specifications. Laws, instructions and budgets do not constitute real contracts. They lack the reciprocity that is the characteristic feature of true contracts because they are based not upon exchange but upon the authority of the state.

Governing the public sector by means of public law and tax financing through the appropriations process implies public administration but not public management This is Max Weber more than Chester Barnard, as the focus is upon formal organisation, rules and the Rule of Law – bureaucracy. Public administration needs employees, but the preference was clearly for long-term contracting, giving the employees the assurance of tenure against the opportunity to develop expertise through life-long learning. Departments or boards are to be sealed off from all kinds of competitive pressure in order to focus upon a very clearly defined set of tasks, where the department would be the sole provider searching for the best available technology at its disposal.

Bureaux tended to become immortal (Kaufman, 1976). In theory, bureau chiefs would really know what they are aiming at and they would care about their performance, the employees working in departments in a life-time career being willing to trade less relatively speaking in salary against high prestige, backed by the devotion of the employees towards the public interest (Kaufman, 1981). Public enterprises would be governed in a similar manner, as long-term contracting through the public law instrument of licences and regulatory acts created a safe heaven for these organisations, some of which were true dinosaurs whose financial viability – it was argued – could be secured through giving them the legal form of a public monopoly. This included entry protection and the setting of rates and subsidies in such a manner that operating losses would be covered by the public.

Real contracts were no less visibly absent from the public policy approach, if one does not want to speak about policies or implementation as contracts in the fictional sense. In the public policy framework, the basic interaction between government and its production units, the departments/bureaux or the public enterprises, is either authority as in top-down implementation or bargaining as in bottom-up implementation. Neither of these two implementation models, however different they may be, conceive of the public provision of goods and services as contracting in a more specific sense of that term.

In top-down implementation, the emphasis is upon control ex ante, steering and obedience towards directives laid down in public law documents. In bottom-up implementation, what is underlined is discretion, trust and evaluation ex post. Both techniques are basically long-term contracting methods in the figurative mode of 'contracts'. In top-down implementation, initiative rests with the central authority to monitor and correct whatever deficiencies it may discover in departments and public enterprises, using its general power to command its own organisations, where the employment contract is usually a very general one, allowing for wide supervision and extensive subordination. In bottom-up implementation, decision-making about the provision of goods and services is decentralised to the extent that any notion of accountability is virtually annihilated. If implementation is merely evolutionary learning, then departments and enterprises could be trusted to the extent that they become self-evaluating organisations (Pressman and Wildavsky, 1984). Nothing is ever contracted in either top-down or bottom-up implementation. Command is not contracting, nor is blind trust.

Thus, new public management enters a practically entirely new concept into the public sector, real contracts or quasi-real contracts. Real contracts carry a clear set of reciprocal commitments that must be checked after a short duration of time, calling for the observation of defined rights and duties with the threat of sanctions against contractual failure. The attraction of management by means of real contracts must be seen in relation to the difficulties inherent in the governance forms used earlier, where agreements that were in reality only contracts in a figurative sense were employed. What authority or trust is vulnerable to is post-contractual opportunism, or what is called the occurrence of moral hazard.

One may distinguish between two kinds of contracts in new public management. On the one hand, we have strictly private law contracts, fully implementable in ordinary courts by means of litigation. On the other hand, we have quasi-private law contracts, which are not implementable in ordinary courts but may be enforced by one of the contracting parties by e.g. termination of the contract. Let us discuss these two types of contracts and investigate whether they enhance efficiency in the public provision of goods and services.

Intentional contracts or quasi-contracts

The principal's contract with departmental managers could involve two different kinds of agreements. First, there is an agreement about what the department should do in terms of outputs. If the department is responsible for a policy area, then the agreement would outline what is to be provided in that area and what the objectives for the achievement of outcomes in that area are. Such agreements constitute intentional or quasi-contracts, which need to be backed by a genuine private law contract, or a second agreement specifying that under-performance of the department in relation to the objectives agreed upon would result in the termination of the employment contract between the principal and the agent either after the contract period or prematurely.

Intentional contracts may occur also between the principal and the executive manager of a public joint-stock company. Yet, without the backing of a private law contract which contains the provision that the manager can or will be fired if the intentions are not lived up to, such an agreement about goals is merely a façade. Thus, the force of the quasi-contracts as an instrument of management replacing the traditional power to command of government derives from the private law contracts that employ the managers or senior executives.

Private law contracts

Not only the contract hiring the executive managers of departments or public firms would be private law contracts in the strict sense, enforceable basically in the last resort through court action. The managers' contracts arranging for the supply of a good or service by a production unit would in the new contracting state have more resemblance to a strict private law contract than a public law contract as used to be characteristic of public administration or public policy.

The executive manager of a department or a public firm would face the choice of choosing a contractual regime for the provision of various goods and services. Most probably, the manager would chose some mix of relational contracting and market spot contracting, depending upon how far the purchaser–provider split had been institutionalised and depending upon the opportunity to arrange meaningful tournaments. If the manager chooses inhouse production, then relational contracting would be used, but if the manager contracts out, then there would probably be market spot contracting. Both types of contracts would be enforceable by means of litigation in ordinary courts.

The variety of contracts and contractors is increased with the advent of NPM. Apart from contracts to be won in public procurement, there will be lots of agency contracts. Agency contracts will occur in relation to the executive agencies, the regulating bonds and the service providing units, especially if they have been incorporated.

Public governance and contracting

Contracting as governance regime is a new answer to an old question about the public provision of goods and services: how to arrange a supply that is both efficient and incentive compatible, given the available information and the existing motivations of the participants in the allocative process? When evaluating coordination mechanisms, one may also wish to take distributional questions into account. Yet, the basic problem would be to find a coordination mechanism that employs the best available information in order to deliver an efficient provision of goods and services while at the same recognising the realistic motivational forces of the participants and minimising the impact of opportunism.

Competitive markets may be interpreted as a coordination mechanism that comes close to the above stated criteria. Competitive markets tend to deliver allocative solutions that are Pareto-optimal and at the same time incentive compatible, but the conditions for using competitive markets as the coordination mechanism are so strict that they are not applicable for several of the goods and services that figure in public provision (Varian, 1987).

The business sector

One solution to the problems of efficiency and opportunism in the public sector is to reduce the commitments of the state by moving the supply of certain goods and services out of the public sector completely. One may see the movement from the welfare state to the welfare society as a search for a relative change in the employment of coordination mechanisms, from public provision to private provision. But, not only do several countries seem hesitant about trusting markets to the extent to which marketers claim possible or desirable, it is also the case that market allocation of many goods and services seems unrealistic despite new theory that market failures can be avoided by institutional innovations (Coase, 1988).

In relation to the goods and services allocated by public enterprises, the possibility of using competitive markets has increased due to both technological and institutional changes. Coordinating the provision of infrastructure by means of entry regulation and legal monopolies is far less efficient than the use of competitive markets, which call for institutional reform of the public enterprises. In order to be able to compete on a domestic or international market, the governance regime of a joint-stock company is more appropriate than trading departments. Incorporation has been the reform strategy chosen by many governments to move trading departments out of the public sector and introduce them as firms in the market economy.

What is not clear is why governments would wish to remain the owners of the incorporated public enterprises, acting independently of government in a deregulated economy where government is not only the owner of these firms but also the umpire of the entire economy, searching to level the playing field. How can one treat all competitors equally when one at the same time has stakes in one group of the competitors?

With regard to the business sector, moving to contracting as the coordination scheme is in principle not problematic. Public enterprises used to be clustered in a very special part of the economy – infrastructure, where technological changes have made contestability much more easily forthcoming, especially in the immensely expanded international economy. The analysis of institutional effects in economics indicates that licences and public monopolies create inefficiencies of their own (Stigler, 1988). What could be discussed is how far governments in practice are prepared to go in order to implement contestable markets in infrastructure. It is not uncommon that deregulation is not carried through completely or that incorporation is attended by opportunistic strategies by stakeholders.

The soft sector

What, then, is the relevance of contracting as the coordination regime for the soft sector in the public sector? It is an open question whether it be employed in an efficient manner in relation to the allocation of public goods, environmental protection and merit goods and services. If the outcomes are efficient and forthcoming due to the incentives of the providers, then are the outcomes also acceptable from a distributional point of view? Efficiency and incentive compatibility would take precedence over distributional concerns, because government could after all always employ income maintenance policies to correct for distributional injustices.

Asking if the soft sector can be run only by means of quasi-contracts or private law contracts, one must remember that the soft sector involves questions about proper procedures and rights, individual rights but also increasingly group rights. These matters require public law regulation, without which accountable government as well as democratic government would be impossible. Also a contracting state will have a public law framework, within which managers will have to act, at least the managers who are active in the soft sector. Even managers in the business sector cannot ignore public law.

Private law regulation can never replace public law regulation within a constitutional democracy. In the contracting state, the principal and the executive managers can rely more on private law instruments of coordination than before. But the use of all new kinds of contracting under NPM must be done in such a manner that the restrictions emanating from fundamental public law are respected.

Let us ask why coordination as control or coordination as trust fails in relation to the two criteria of efficiency and incentive compatibility. The reason that contracting has come to be seen as the best available coordination mechanism involves the awareness that already tried coordination mechanisms failed in relation to these two criteria.

The inefficiency of control

A coordination mechanism must be able to use all existing relevant information in order to arrive at efficiency in allocation. This is a necessary condition, because without information about preferences and technologies, allocative results will not be Pareto-optimal. However, it is not sufficient to know which outcomes are allocatively efficient, as one must also be able to implement them. In the public sector, public resource allocation in whatever form it occurs involves principal–agent relationships, often of a rather complex nature. If the principal cannot motivate the agent to implement an efficient allocation, then it will not be forthcoming, although it may involve the correct solution to an allocative problem. The commitment problem is as severe as the information problem (Eatwell *et al.* 1989), e.g. in enforcement.

In the state, there are not only multiple level principal–agent relationships, where a principal interacts with an agent who in turn is the principal of other agents, and so forth, but there is also interaction between several principals. One may wish to speak of the state as *the* principal, and all actors as agents of the state, but this is only legal fiction. In reality, governments hire agents in their departments and public enterprises, who in their turn act as principals for other agents, and so forth. Much public resource allocation involves collaboration between the central government and regional or local governments – whether they be placed in a unitary or federal state format – which creates complex patterns of principal–agent relationships. Without agents, public resource allocation is not forthcoming. But agents will not work for free. At the very least they will demand their participation price, i.e. the price for their input that they could retrieve elsewhere, for instance in the private sector. At the very most, agents will look for a rent, i.e. a higher than necessary compensation for his/her input, if the agent can get away with it.

In public administration or in top-down implementation, it is assumed that the principal has the relevant knowledge about what to provide and how to provide it. When it is matter of multi-level government allocation, then it is assumed that the central government knows best. Since it still needs a set of agents to carry out its plan, it will simply hire the agents at the going participation price and then tell the agents what to do. Thus, the agents will receive a low salary but a lifetime one. Since it is too complicated to write a contract with such a time perspective that would stipulate what the agent should do in various circumstances, the agent will be hired by a most general relational contract, involving the right to command and supervise the work of the agent on the part of the principal.

This is the model of ex ante control that was used by many countries when setting up a modern welfare state in the wake of the Great Depression. The initiative, resources and power rest with the top echelons of the state, who employ central coordination techniques in order to tell the agents what to do, which frameworks of rules to follow or which policies to implement. The agent can resist the principal by means of their general right to tenure, but the upper hand is with the principal. At least so it was believed. Coordination costs were high, but motivation costs were low – this is the central coordination mechanism in theory. But in practice low motivation costs would mean low commitment, if incentive compatibility theory is correct.

Systems of central coordination founder upon the lack of information about allocative solutions. The key organisational failure is efficiency. One source of inefficiency is cognitive limitations, of people in general and of organisations. It is simply not feasible to consider all alternatives of action, know all outcomes and their probabilities as well as retrieve information and store it about the social utility(ies) of these outcomes. If the central government cannot handle the information requirement for knowing which allocative solutions are efficient, then perhaps allocation should be handled by the lower echelons of the state. Information may be more easily available further down in the state.

Another source of inefficiency is the behaviour of the agent in central coordination. If the central government does not know what is efficient, then it may rely upon the agent to go and find out. But now the principal becomes dependent upon the agent, who will immediately demand a rent for the knowledge that they possess. When the agent knows more about the efficiency conditions, then the agent will no longer accept the participation price, as it is not incentive compatible. Agents with asymmetric knowledge will play games with the principal using self-seeking strategies, even with a guile that will raise their remuneration (Rasmusen, 1994). Thus, there will be waste in public resource allocation.

The most grim version of agent opportunism is the Niskanen model of the budget maximising bureaucrat. The agent here uses his asymmetrical knowledge in order to contrive an output of goods and services that can be twice as large as the optimal size of a bureau, involving massive allocative inefficiency or losses that will be covered by the principal (Niskanen, 1971, 1976). A less cruel version of organisational failure in central coordination is the mere occurrence of X-inefficiency or the tendency of a bureau to run slack. Here the problem is again inefficiency, but it is a matter of technological inefficiency, the principal paying too high a unit price for the agent, who shirks (Leibenstein, 1966).

It may be pointed out that the analysis of traditional public regulation as rent-seeking points at the occurrence of organisational failure within the other main agent that the central government may employ, the public enterprise. Agents in a public enterprise will capture a rent by running slack, in principle corresponding to the excess profits that a private monopoly would be able to sustain, given its market power (Tollison, 1982).

If central coordination does not work, either because of inherent cognitive limitations or because of the impossibility of combining efficiency and incentive compatibility, then what about decentralisation or bottom-up implementation as the coordination mechanism?

Agency commitment in policy networks

Decentralisation as the coordination mechanism for the public provision of goods and services was an attempt to overcome the information weaknesses involved in central coordination. When there is intergovernmental collaboration, then principals placed lower down know better how public programmes can be made to run efficiently, as they know the actual workings and preconditions of policy. Decentralisation involves giving more discretion to agents when they possess knowledge that is relevant for policy implementation. Since agents at the lowest level are responsible for the day-to-day operations, they – if anyone at all – would know how a policy may be put into effect in a flexible manner in different situations.

Decentralisation was coupled with evaluation in order to check the drive towards shirking, as discretion would allow agents not only to get their participation price but also to engage in all kinds of strategies, based upon asymmetric knowledge, providing them with a rent. Since central government would still provide considerable amounts of the resources for policy implementation, it could not rely completely upon trust but needed a plethora of evaluation studies to find out what decentralised authorities or agents were actually doing with policies. In order to increase both the information available and the motivation of people participating in the implementation, it was suggested that policy networks be created as the coordination mechanism, involving all stakeholders in the public provision of goods and services (Jordan, 1990; Rhodes, 1990).

In theory, policy networks would reduce coordination costs and motivation costs compared with central coordination. By decentralising policy execution, the principal would economise on coordination costs. And by involving the agents with the stakeholders of a policy, the motivation costs would also be reduced, as commitment would be forthcoming without shirking. In practice, policy networks are just as likely as central coordination to result in waste and technological inefficiencies, because faced with a minimum of monitoring commitment will become a major problem in policy networks. Why try hard, if there is lots of discretion and trust.

Faced with waste or shirking, the principal would respond with the conduct of evaluations but these raise coordination costs without having much impact upon commitment, especially if the principal can take few actions in relation to the agent. Policy networks may become iron triangles where rent-seeking is the standard practice. There is no guarantee that policy networks would want to implement efficient solutions, even if they had the information necessary (Olson, 1982), resulting in distributional coalitions.

In both central and decentralised coordination, the agent gets the upper hand. They can react to the low motivation costs by strategies that present the agent with a rent, which entails that the provision will not be efficient. Perhaps the principal will become stronger in relation to the agent, if motivation costs would go up triggering a better commitment, while at the same time coordination costs go down, because the principal would be less interested in steering the agent. Yet, the principal must change to another agent within a relatively short time span. Thus, the principal could economise upon coordination costs but increase the motivation costs in order to elicit commitment and reduce the risk of rent-seeking, using e.g. tendering/bidding as the coordination mechanism.

Contracting: advantages

New public management employs an entirely different coordination mechanism from public administration or public policy. It employs short-term contracts, either quasi-real contracts or private law contracts, in order to regulate the inter-action between principals and agents. Here, we have relational contracts but not of a long duration. First, government or ministers enter into quasi-contracts with the managers of departments about what their output should be – the principal's contract. Then, managers in their turn enter private law contracts with suppliers as the final agents when that is possible or quasi-contracts with production units in order to make sure that provision is forthcoming – the managers' contracts.

The principal's contract

Whether it is a matter of quasi-contracts or private law contracts, the principal relies upon managers to arrange the provision of goods and services by means of contracting for transaction cost reasons. The role of managers, especially the CEOs, is absolutely essential in new public management. They are responsible to the minister for the output within a policy sector and they contract with production units within that policy area. The principal will not pay huge coordination costs in order to govern the manager, who acts with a large amount of discretion, but he will pay a high salary to the agent in order to elicit commitment and reduce rent-seeking. The principal will have several opportunities to review managerial efficiency, as the contract between the principal and the agent will come up for renewal quite often. If the salary is quite high, then reneging by an agent would be very costly to the agent and there would be little incentive for the agent to create waste in order to seek a rent. Thus, there would be low coordination costs but high motivation costs. Since the agent stands to lose much, they would try to effectuate an efficient allocation. But would there really be no danger of opportunism in the new management state and would allocative outcomes really tend to be efficient?

Writing intentional contracts specifying what governments really expect from a department or a public firm during a specified period, allowing for the monitoring of chief outputs and outcomes to an extent that would make possible conclusions about managerial effort, could increase transparency in public affairs, enhance accountability and also allocative efficiency. But more is needed than simply signing a number of contracts expressing intentions. The risk is that these contracts enter into opportunistic strategies or even become the vehicle of contractual opportunism, these contracts stating what is believed to be popular at the moment with the possibility of contractual reneging either on the part of the principal or on the part of the senior executives.

The managers' contracts

When managers resort to the establishment of internal market schemes, along the lines of the abolished CCT regime (Compulsory Competitive Tendering) in the UK or as envisaged in the new Best Value regime in the UK, then what kinds of contracts are involved? Arranging a tournament and giving the contract to the winner, scored according to efficiency criteria, would not necessarily mean that it is a question of spot market contracts. One can have tournaments ending in relational contracts.

This uncertainty in the new management state about the nature of the contracts that lead to the provision of goods and services stems partly from the fact that it is not quire clear who is on the other side of the managers' table in the provider–purchaser model. Theoretically, all providers are simple production units fighting for their survival in a competitive market, whether these units are departments, public joint-stock companies or private entrepreneurs. In reality, things are slightly different, because in so far as these production units consist of former government employees, then they are often still protected by public law regulations about job security. It frequently occurs that the manager who negotiates the contracts with production units is at the same time the manager who handles the negotiations with the trade unions about government's responsibility for their employees.

In so far as it is a question of relational contracting, the manager would then supplement the agency contract with intentional contracts or quasi-contracts in order to be more specific about what the agency relation involves in terms of provision and costs. The risk is that one uses spot market contracts and relational contracts at the same time in order to stabilise the situation in the long run, thus creating confusion about what 'contract' denotes. When a spot market contract has been signed with a hospital, but at the time there is a relational contract lasting longer than the spot market contract, then which one is to be tested in court if there is a contractual dispute? Making matters even more complex in the contracting state, intentional contracts signed with regard to the long-term development of the hospital may involve commitments on the part of the principal or their manager that are at odds with the spot market contracts, regulating day-to-day operations. Then what?

Contracting: disadvantages

Although there is too little empirical research available for a complete evaluation of the new contracting state, one could at the very least suggest a few drawbacks that may occur as the new public management picks up steam, not only in welfare societies but also in welfare states. Are there any signs of inefficiencies or rent-seeking behaviour in empirical studies?

The public choice school argued basically that governance regimes outlined in public administration and public policy or policy implementation had the outcome that agents would tend to be stronger than principals, asymmetrical knowledge causing a considerable increase in the costs for public provision, corresponding to an agency rent or reflecting allocative inefficiency or waste. Moving to competition in supply would be conducive to information symmetry and reduce rents or waste. Why, then, may one ask, is it the case that the salaries of public managers have skyrocketed at the same as the governance regime would make the principal have the upper hand? Coordination costs are down, but motivations costs go up.

The basic difficulty in new public management is that contracting does not necessarily result in Pareto-optimal outcomes in allocation. The contracts made may be the best ones possible, i.e. for the contracting parties. But since both the principal and the agent act for the general public, the contracts made may not be in the best interest of the public. Opportunism, or self-seeking with guile, is by no means ruled out in the contracting state. Contracts between principals and agents are not strategy-proof against rent-seeking. Quite the contrary, one may distinguish between several kinds of contractual opportunism. Let us briefly recapitulate.

Pre-contractual opportunism

Whether it is a matter of relational contracting or spot market contracts, both principals and managers may make bad deals. A minister may fail to pick the best manager and may sign a contract that is not the most cost efficient – contractual failures on the part of the principal, reflecting inadequate preparations for the signing of an agreement. Similarly, a manager may not be honest, signing deals that involve dissipation of rents.

How is one to test contractual credibility beforehand? An interesting example of opportunism in new public management is the demand by senior executives in public enterprises to receive the same salaries as senior executives in private firms at the very moment of incorporation. This is the so-called 'lemons' problem: why not run a tournament among many candidates, public and private, when the positions and their salaries are changed as a result of incorporation?

Only external pressures upon the principal and the manager can guarantee that they really try hard to run proper tournaments or auctions and that they examine the reputation of people who offer contracts. Tendering/bidding is a process of decision-making with several loopholes. Very strict rules about public procurement are necessary in order to make sure that tendering/bidding promotes efficiency. The mass media will play a most important role in looking into public contracting, disclosing favouritism or simply negligence. Another concept for pre-contractual opportunism is adverse selection in the economics of information and corruption in political science.

Post-contractual opportunism

A contract that at the time of signing appears to be adequate, the contracting parties coming to an agreement after a proper tendering/bidding process with sincere intentions to implement what has been agreed, can during the post-contractual phase turn out to be something very different. The great problem is opportunism in reneging, ranging from merely different interpretations about what has been agreed to straightforward negligence in carrying out the terms of agreement or even wilfully breaking a contract.

Moral hazard is the economists' concept for this type of contractual failure that is handled in new public management by court action ultimately. Contractual disputes will have to be resolved in the contracting state. If these contracts are private law contracts, then litigation in ordinary courts is the only remedy, but it is neither costless nor predictable. If the contracts are of the intentional kind – quasi-contracts – then the contractual differences can be resolved in the end when the employment contract is terminated. Both parties in the contracting state – government and managers – will have to consider the strategies to be used in order to handle post-contractual opportunism.

Playing the managers' game

Although pre- or post-contractual opportunism is likely to occur on both sides – government and managers – we will here just focus upon how government as the principal could handle opportunism on the part of managers. We are not sating that opportunism will occur all the time. We are only saying that it may occur in the contractual state. The question is whether opportunism, if it occurs, will hurt the basic objective, i.e. economic efficiency.

Opportunism may occur on both sides of a contractual relationship, since both may renege on the contract.

If government is playing games when it contracts with a manager, then they need to be aware. Government may wish to appoint a new manager just to give an impression that it is tackling the problems. In reality, the situation may be such that whatever the manager does, the cause is lost. However, let us assume that government is sincere. How can it protect itself against shirking on the part of a manager?

The principal would face two strategies against managers. Either government fires them, including not prolonging any short-term contract after it has expired, or government sticks to its CEOs keeping them even when outcomes are below expectations. Managers would have two strategies, either they try hard or they shirk. Effort is, as in all principal–agent models, not observable or difficult to observe and costly to verify by means of litigation. How will government and managers interact? Table 11.3 suggests an answer based upon a reasonable attribution of pay-offs.

The Pareto-optimal outcome would be when both parties are pleased,

Table 11.3   Principal–agent interaction

		Managers' strategy	
		Try hard	Shirk
Government's strategy	Not fire/terminate	5, 5	−10, 10
	Fire/terminate	10, −10	−2, −2

managers putting in a huge effort and government being reasonably comfortable with outcomes, or in any case pleased enough to keep the managers in their job (5, 5). Advertising for new managers all the time involves costs. What government would dislike the most is that it gives confidence to managers who fool their principal, i.e. managers shirk (−10, 10). What managers would hate is to end up being fired or not having their contracts renewed, even though managers had done as much as they could (10, −10). The best outcome for managers is to have the confidence of the principal but to get something for nothing, i.e. shirk, whereas the best outcome for government is first to elicit a true effort from managers, but second to look around for another agent in order to stay on top. Given these preferences of the players and the accompanying payoffs in Table 11.3, one would expect government and managers to find and implement the first best solution, i.e. 'not fire' and 'try hard'. However, it is not the equilibrium of the managers' game. The Nash equilibrium is 'fire' and 'shirk' (−2, −2).

How dangerous is such a tendency towards contractual failure in new public management? Government and managers would have profound difficulties in settling down to the Pareto-optimal strategy, each tempted to defect, because they cannot trust each other. Thus, one would arrive at a situation where government looks for managers and managers look for contracts, but cooperation would not be long lasting. For reasons of opportunism, both parties would not stick to the best outcome. If managers believe government will not 'fire', then they 'shirk'. But if government believes managers will shirk, then they 'fire'. And if managers believe government will 'fire', then they still 'shirk'. The management state will not always deliver efficient outcomes.

If the managers' game is played once, then it will result in contractual failure. In repeated play, the parties may settle on the Pareto-optimal outcome. Managers develop reputation in order to convince government that they will not shirk. And government may sign intentional or quasi-contracts in order to make managers confident that their contracts will be renewed. However, there is little stability in arriving at the Pareto-efficient outcome, as the parties could alternate between cooperation and defection, depending upon the other's response (Axelrod, 1997).

Conclusion

Is contracting superior to instructing and evaluating? NPM suggests that government is more firmly in the saddle if it signs numerous contracts about what is to be done and makes an assessment about whether a contract has been fulfilled, than if government orders its employees to do what it wants done. If steering is problematic, if control is out of date, if policy networks are too far away from government, then contracting with highly paid managers could lead to efficient deals that are incentive compatible and thus self-enforceable. Thus there is no need for lots of instructions and line-items budgeting, no huge investigations about policy alternatives and their consequences, no continuous evaluation – just sign an optimal contract, pay the manager their salary and wait until the output and the outcomes are forthcoming. Should they not do so, government makes a new contract with another agent, and starts litigation against the former, if possible.

It is not that easy. Contracting regimes may appear very attractive – optimality, commitment, self-enforceability. Yet, contractual failures do occur, as pre-contractual or post-contractual opportunism may pay handsomely. To run a contracting state requires skills in concluding contracts and in policing them. Coordination costs will go down but motivation costs will go up, compared with earlier governance regimes. Rationality in contracting does not ensure efficient contracts.

Making agreements about what to do and paying people what they say they want to do the job have the appearance of efficiency, because why consent to something which one does not want to fulfil? Contracting would achieve efficiency, because contracting implies exercising a veto, which is the essence of the concept of Pareto-optimality. However, stating what one does not want to do does not mean that one wants to achieve what is best for all parties concerned.

Two caveats must be pointed out: (1) Although the contracts between government and its CEOs or between the CEOs and other production units may be optimal to the contracting parties, there is no warrant whatsoever that they are optimal to society. Both government and CEOs may sign contracts that result in rents. (2) Contracts that are optimal for the contracting parties are not in themselves self-enforceable, as there is always the possibility of reneging. There is no organisational regime which excludes the negative consequences of opportunism.

Conclusion: the relevance and limit of contractualism in public governance

Introduction

Public sector reform has been a major endeavour for more than a decade, although it has been conducted with varying degrees of zest in different countries. It has brought the process of public sector expansion so characteristic of the twentieth century to a halt and deregulated the economies of many countries of the world. But perhaps the most interesting achievement is a new approach to or theory about public sector management: contractualism.

New public management (NPM) places the contract in the centre of public governance and not authority as with the traditional approach, public administration. And it would hardly be completely erroneous to state that the contract is a private sector mechanism, first and foremost. An agreement between two or parties becomes a contract when it is recognised as such by private law institutions.

It is now argued that NPM has seen its best days and that it is rapidly losing in relevance. However, we must not throw out the baby with the bath water. I do not believe that we have seen the beginning of the end of contractualism in the public sector. It remains to be clarified how far is it possible or desirable to use contractualism in government.

The purpose of this chapter is to discuss contractualism in order to state its pros and cons. It is essential that one identifies all the elements of a full-scale public sector contracting model. It involves not only tendering/bidding but also the use of chief executive officers, the CEOs. Thus, we must theorise both the relationship between the CEOs when they interact as purchasers and providers and the principal–agent relationship between government and its CEOs, in executive agencies, regulating boards and purchasing and producer organisations.

Traditional public sector governance

What were the truly key difficulties in traditional public sector governance which provoked the massive acceptance of NPM? In traditional governance models, government employs people, money and laws to get things done resulting in public resource allocation, income maintenance and public regulation. The chief governance mechanism in all three branches of government used to be state authority, as manifested in public law, especially administrative law.

If we here focus mainly upon the public sector as the provision of services to the population, then the key question concerns how to get things done. Let us concentrate upon the so-called allocative part of the public sector and only bring in income maintenance at the end of our deliberations.

Public regulation was never really part of public management, as it targets mainly economic activity in the private sector. However, the new requirement of the levelling of the playing field means that in the future regulatory schemes must cover both the private and public sectors. Thus, the new form of public regulation – deregulation and contestability – enters NPM as one major source of institutional restrictions upon contractualism in the public sector.

Many suggestions as to why traditional forms of public resource allocation fail have been made, claiming that the two mechanisms employed – the bureau in the soft sector and the public enterprise in the business sector – tend towards inefficiencies, either X-inefficiency or social inefficiency. These arguments include hypotheses about numerous deficiencies such as: lack of competition, rigidity and red tape, principal–agent difficulties such as asymmetric information, bureaucratisation, excessive professionalism, lack of evaluation or too little participation, the capture of regulators, etc.

Confronted with the organisational theories about public policy pathologies or the public choice school allegations about the occurrence of rent-seeking or fiscal illusions, one may ask: why trust government at all with any allocative tasks? The basic argument in Chicago School Economics is that if the public provision of goods and services is basically inefficient, then one should use private provision, i.e. market allocation. The best government is the Manchester liberal state, the guardian state that monitors contractual enforcement in the private sector.

It is true that many governments have argued somewhat along this line during the last decade and have proceeded to engage in much privatisation, hiving off activities into the private sector, especially selling off their traditional public enterprises. Yet, public resource allocation remains large in most societies. What is characteristic of the 1990s is not that the private sector has increased dramatically, but that the governance mechanism has been reformed in a public sector that stays at between 30 and 60 per cent of GDP in the OECD countries.

Evidently, there must be some advantages involved in the public provision of services because public sector expansion so typical of the post-war period has been merely halted. Few countries have massively rolled back their public sectors. It is actually the case that the costs for transfer payments keep increasing in many countries, cancelling out the public sector reductions that stem from privatisation.

The public provision of services today comprises two distinct parts, the soft sector comprising education, care and law and order and the business sector comprising infrastructure. Despite the many public sector reforms since 1980, these two sectors are still there but the institutional set-up has been radically changed.

The two traditional governance mechanisms in the public service provision, the bureau and the public enterprise, have been extensively reformed. Today, the soft sector often employs a contracting regime of some sort, whereas the business sector consists of public joint-stock companies, which is basically a private enterprise where the equity is owned by the state, completely or in collaboration with private sector players (Minogue *et al.*, 1999).

This is not the place to speculate about why governments and electorates seem reluctant to give up public resource allocation and endorse a Manchester liberal government. One may suggest a number of reasons why the public sector remains fairly large in the countries which adhere to the politico-economic regime of a market economy in a democratic state: market failures, redistribution and justice, or the behaviour of politicians in legislative markets.

In the set of OECD countries, some countries provide many services publicly – the welfare states – whereas other countries employ the market for several of these services – the welfare societies. But how is the public provision of services to be organised in a welfare state or a welfare society in order to avoid the difficulties of traditional public sector governance? The answer given is that one should adopt the key private sector mechanism (exchange) in so far at it is possible. This means contractualism in the governance of the public sector.

Ricardo: why markets are superior

Markets are based upon the fact that people find contracting mutually advantageous. A contract is the legal outcome of a process of negotiation or bargaining, which may terminate in an exchange between two parties. The contract as an institution is one of the key elements in private law, especially in the law of obligations and in tort law.

Contracting has one attractive property – it elicits voluntary acceptance. But it needs the state to guarantee that cheating is not an option. Enforcement is critical in any kind of contractual regime. If choice is real for people and they do not have to accept any deal offered (as with slavery) then contracting will reveal what things are worth to them, i.e. what they are willing to pay in order to get hold of something, or what they are willing to forsake in order to arrive at possession.

The value-revealing capacity of exchange is what makes the institution of the contract so valuable for society. Economists have focused upon various aspects of exchange in order to lay down additional conditions that will ensure that contracting really consummates all the potential value, i.e. achieves a so-called Pareto-optimal outcome, from Adam Smith focusing upon competition to Richard Coase underlining property rights.

Yet, no economist other than David Ricardo realised the essence of exchange as revealing value. His analysis of both functioning markets and perverse markets points to the contribution of exchange in stating what things are really worth. Since contracting is the legal form of exchange and since exchange takes place in a market environment, market contracting constitutes a most valuable mechanism for society. If things do not pass through the market, how then can their value be established?

Yet, many of the services that people wish to have are allocated by means of the public sector. For a number of reasons, countries with an advanced economy place a substantial portion of their service provision with government in the soft sector or the business sector. But how could value be revealed in traditional public governance? Perhaps this is the fundamental reason that traditional public governance in the form of administrative law and incremental budgeting has met with so much criticism. It shows the costs of public service provision in a most transparent way, but it cannot display the value of public service provision, at least not its marginal value which is after all the same as the willingness to pay.

Perhaps many of the difficulties in traditional public governance could be undone through the use of contracting regimes in the public sector? This is basically the reply of NPM. Above we have examined this argument seriously. In order to state the pros and cons of contractualism, I will use an ideal-type model of public contractualism. In a pure public contracting regime, government simply acquires through ordinary civil law contracts the services that it provides the population with. There is no bureaucracy, no public enterprises, because there exists only a set of contracts according to which the public provision of services is forthcoming and these contracts are enforceable by ordinary civil law courts.

Contractualism is no strange phenomenon in government, as it employs it massively in public procurement (Laffont and Tirole, 1993). When governments in the OECD area go to buy materials or construct buildings, they use tendering/bidding. There are institutions in place which punish governments that do not follow the international rules of public procurement, the rules of public procurement becoming not only Europeanised but also globalised under WTO. Why not use tendering/bidding throughout the public sector?

Public procurement used to be reserved for the purchase of materials to be used in running bureaux or the arrangement of repairs of public buildings. However, the principles of public procurement could now to be used throughout the public sector in order to get things done. What are the pre-conditions for a successful public sector contracting regime?

Public sector contracting: the ideal type

Contracting, which substitutes for authority on a major scale, requires a whole new set of institutions, what I call a 'public sector contracting regime'. It contains three elements (a–c). The basic tool of communication of what is to be done in the public sector as well as what it is to cost the tax-payer is (a) a contract, i.e. a private law agreement between (b) a purchaser and a provider, following (c) a process of tendering/bidding.

Now, governments cannot itself handle all the contracts necessary for simple transaction cost reasons. Writing and managing these agreements calls for a new group of people in government – the CEOs. The CEOs would manage the public contracting regime through the signing and monitoring of agreements based upon tendering/bidding, with the intervention of ordinary courts if enforcement so requires.

Under an ideal type of a public sector contracting regime, the agreement about the provision of services – quantity, quality and cost – would be a strict private law contract, and not merely a promise, a verbal commitment or a mutual understanding. Such an agreement would be a legally binding mutual promise about considerations and stipulations, enforceable in ordinary courts, taking action upon the filing of a suit against either one of the two contracting parties.

In an ideal-type public sector contracting regime, the key to pinning down what is to be done – the job as it were in the public sector – is to be found in a set of agreements, containing the specifications necessary to get things done. Managing the public sector is thus less legislation and budget-making – hierarchical instruments of authority – and more contract making, i.e. bargaining, reciprocities and mutual consent. The state would operate through contractual regimes, and in principle the state would employ private law to regulate the contracts made in a public procurement regime. The law of contracts would be the main substitute for administrative law.

An ideal-type public sector contracting regime as the general mode for arranging public services would replace not only bureaucracy but also considerable parts of public policy. What is absolutely essential is that there exist general rules for the making and monitoring of public contracts and that they are somehow enforceable.

The conditions for the use of a general public sector contracting regime would, I believe, include at least the three following ones. The relevant institutions must foster:

1 a clear identification and separation of the purchaser and the provider;
2 that both the purchaser and the provider have self-interests in finding and implementing optimal contracts;
3 that the purchaser and the provider have conflicting interests in how to divide the mutual gain from arriving at optimal contracts, which may be fully appropriated and internalised.

When these conditions are not fulfilled, then public sector contracting regimes start to degenerate. When the conditions for public service provisions are very different from the ideal type, especially when all the three condit ions are not met, then the old Weberian structure – the bureau – will surface again. Or one may employ policy networks.

The above three conditions can be described as the fundamental principles of an ideal-type contracting regime in the public sector, combining bargaining (1) optimality (2) and ownership (3). One would perhaps wish to describe them as a combination of the Edgeworth model with the Coase model.

Now, why are these three conditions sometimes difficult to implement in the public sector? Because, I would be inclined to answer, of the heavy reliance upon the CEOs, which is conducive to fundamental problems in the soft sector although it may work well in the business sector and in public regulation.

Government, i.e. the politicians, cannot do the contracting itself. They rely on a set of people who do the contracting for them, the chief executive officers. Thus, the CEOs will handle the public firms operating in the business sector, the purchasing bodies operating in the soft sector as well as the public provider organisations in the same sector and finally the regulatory agencies.

The employment of CEOs

Implicit in the model of the state as government engaged in massive contracting, i.e. the ideal-type public sector contracting model, is a sharp separation between decision-making and implementation, or policy-making and policy execution, to use the words of the policy approach. Politicians identify the objectives and they hire the CEOs to implement them by means of the management of contracts.

The separation between politics and management arises for transaction cost reasons. What else can government do other than searching for agents who will handle or manage the procurement process? What government must do, however, is to instruct the CEOs about the objectives that it wishes to achieve in the public provision of services as well as pay the CEOs for their work. The rest is a task for the managers. This amounts to a fundamental distinction between *politics* and *contracting*.

The CEOs do not negotiate upon objectives with government. They take the objectives as given. The key question in relation to the selection of CEOs is how government can find the CEOs who will be most effective in accomplishing government objectives, given a financial restriction as to their remuneration. This is again a contractual question between government and the CEOs, which concerns opposing strategies in a principal–agent game (Maor, 1999).

Government may either motivate the CEOs by means of huge salaries or government may attempt to monitor the CEOs. Neither strategy guarantees that CEOs will write and implement optimal contracts with service providers. Why could not CEOs be sloppy, negligent, corrupt or simply fools? However, what aggravates the difficulties is that the CEOs really do not have property rights as to what they negotiate about or accomplish.

The CEOs will be forthcoming by the use of the very same mechanism, i.e. under a process of tendering/bidding which results in a contract which is enforceable in ordinary courts. Sometimes government employs one central group of CEOs to handle all the contracts with the managers, as for instance in the New Zealand model with its Civil Service Commission. One can imagine the public sector consisting of a series of principal–agent relationships, which are all to be handled by the same institution of tendering/bidding and private law agreements.

The use of CEOs in NPM should be discussed in relation to the three different sectors: (1) the business sector; (2) the soft sector; and (3) public regulation. I believe government can handle the problem of finding and instructing CEOs in an efficient manner in the business sector and in public regulation, but I wish to argue that the interaction between CEOs in purchaser–provider relationships in the soft sector creates several difficulties. Here, we have the limit of the NPM.

Ownership under NPM

In the soft sector, providers must be forthcoming if public provision is to work in accordance with the tendering/bidding schema suggested by NPM. They need not be plenty, but they must at least provide for contestability between each other. In NPM, it is argued that the providers of public services could be anybody, whatever the form of the organisation within which they happen to act. Yet, this amounts to only a half truth, as it disguises the fact that the question of ownership of the organisation in question matters.

It is true that the providers could be public organisations, private ones or even mixtures, but what is not unimportant is the nature of the ownership interests behind a provider organisation. One must focalise upon the self-interests at work behind the provider organisations. What matters is not only the motivation of the employees in such organisations but also the interests of their owners.

In tendering/bidding, private providers seek contracts that give them a profit that is sufficient to motivate them to take on the task of providing a service. This profit somehow ends up with the owners of the provider organisation. But how about public owners of provider organisations?

When public organisations themselves engage in bidding processes, stating bids and competing in public procurement, then which interests are at stake? The self-interests of the employees are present no doubt. But what about the interests of the owners of public organisations such as hospitals, schools, universities or infrastructure capital?

In negotiations over private contracts, the buyer and the seller have rational interests in bargaining until they reach a Pareto-optimal solution. At the same time, buyers and sellers remain in opposition about how to divide the mutual gains from an optimal agreement, as they both wish to grab the lion's share of the gain. Then what is the logic of the interaction between purchasers and providers when public organisations as providers face public purchasers, where the contractual interaction is handled by CEOs?

Can the purchaser CEOs and the CEOs in the public provider organisations reach the Pareto-frontier? One must ask: what motivates them to do that and how are they to split the gain from having reached the set of Pareto-optimal outcomes? Since the state is the principal of both parties, the CEOs in the purchaser and the provider organisations, then how does government instruct these two sets of agents to behave in order to maximise the interests of the state as principal?

What is crucial is to realise that the state as the principal of the buyers, the CEOs, or the principal of the providers, the public organisations or the public joint-stock companies, is an abstract entity, a legal corporation. The state in action is always the government in power for the moment. If government as the purchaser is always represented by an agent, then so is government as the owner of the service provider organisation, whatever the legal form of that organisation. Now comes the puzzling question: why would these state agents at either ends of the bargaining table find it to their advantage to identify and implement Pareto-optimal contracts?

When there is a whole set of Pareto-optimal contracts, involving different divisions of the mutual gain, then these agents of the state – the purchaser CEOs and the provider CEOs – fight each other in order to arrive at their best outcomes. As contracting between agents may involve all kinds of forms of self-interest seeking with guile, we must raise the question of why these agents would find it in their best interests to (1) first reach the Pareto-optimal set of outcomes and then (2) really dispute which one solution each would finally favour out of their respective self-interests. This difficulty of government interacting with itself is endemic to the use of NPM in the soft sector, where the providers often are public organisations.

Sitting at both ends of the bargaining table

The major objection against NPM that follows from this analysis of public sector provision is that government may end up sitting at both ends of the table. Government would instruct its purchasing agents to be as determined as possible towards the provider organisations. At the same time, government as the owner of provider organisations would be most interested to see that they do not succumb to predatory tactics by the purchaser agents. What is the logic of such a game, which has clearly zero-sum properties? Another way to pose the same question is to ask what, if anything, the state maximises under NPM?

There is a risk here for a contradiction in NPM, as the mechanism of public procurement may involve government negotiating with itself. Government would be interested in 'cheap' deals when it acts as purchaser but it would favour 'expensive' deals when it comes to maintaining its organisation that acts as provider.

Thus, a general model of public sector contracting involving both principal–agent relationships and government acting in both the role of purchaser and the role of provider seems somewhat contradictory. Not only would there occur rather meaningless distributional conflicts between agents or CEOs who have the very same principal, but in addition there would be the risk that the CEOs would not extract all the gain that could be reaped, i.e. they would not move all along the Pareto-optimal frontier.

NPM is an explicit attempt to use contracts instead of authority. If a general model of public sector contracting is to work, then the ownership problem of public organisations must be resolved. In order to clearly separate between purchasers and providers, public organisations that compete for government contracts must be given a legal status making them fit for competition whereas government would focus upon its role as purchaser. In the business sector, incorporation of public enterprises goes a long way to clarify the purchaser-provider separation. However, in the soft sector this strategy of incorporation has limited application.

Manufacturing competition: the business sector

Much attention has been given to institutional change of the public organisations that are active in the provision of public services. Thus, public enterprises have been changed from semi-bureaucracies to public joint-stock companies. And even bureaux have been made into public joint-stock companies. The general transformation of incorporation has been carried far in most countries (Thynne, 1994). Will it resolve the problem of government sitting upon two chairs at the same time?

Incorporation moves the problem further away, meaning that it becomes less acute and visible. However, in principle it is still there. In order to arrive at a market where traders are truly independent of each other, one must privatise the public joint-stock companies. Many governments hesitate when confronted with this radical requirement. Governments should do more privatisation in the business sector, but in the soft sector it makes little sense.

In the business sector, government can if not completely at least to a large extent combine various roles: (1) owner of equity in public joint-stock companies: (2) donor of public contracts; and (3) umpire of the economy as regulator. It may be in the interest of government to give contracts to other providers than its own public joint-stock company, because in the long run government as owner is best served by a competitive company.

Governing a public joint-stock in a deregulated economy within a global setting has become institutionalised to a high extent, as common rules about tendering/bidding have been developed regionally and internationally in order to dissuade government from the short-run temptation of favouring its own enterprises. Thus, government may accept the creation of a competitive environment for its enterprises because it may in the long run maximise the value of its equity by such a strategy, in particular if all government agree to a common regime, punishing free riding.

But why manufacture markets in the soft sector when it creates many additional difficulties? If in the soft sector competition is not naturally forthcoming, then why attempt to manufacture it? The answer given is that competition reveals value. But competition comes with certain kinds of transaction costs.

Competition is short-term contracting. It involves the running of tournaments and auctions continuously. But often the provider organisations can hardly sustain such treatment. In the business sector, matters are different, as public joint-stock companies tend to be large enough to be able to compensate temporary losses of contracts with new contracts won elsewhere.

Fierce competition under tendering/bidding involves considerable risk for the destruction or degeneration of public institutions. If they lose in one competition, they may be out for ever. This is the crux of the matter. What matters for credible competition regimes is the capacity of competitors to survive a defeat or the possibility that newcomers will enter the race in the next round.

What matters in a general model of public sector contracting is that defeats do not carry the risk of extinction and that the potential set of contestors changes over time. If these two conditions are not met, then fierce competitions must be mitigated somehow. But do we have to go all the way back to bureaucracy?

Competition in the business sector is now universally accepted. But there must also be competition among the CEOs for the running of the firms of the government, the public joint-stock companies. Simply reforming the public enterprises by means of incorporation and not running a tournament among potential CEOs would be playing the lemons' game.

Bureaux and the soft sector

Theoretical arguments and empirical evidence point at the limited relevance of competition in the soft sector of the public sector. Education, health and social care are simply not the kinds of goods and services where competition, on the whole, results in decidedly more advantages than disadvantages. The danger is that one destroys public service organisations, which cannot be recreated or whose recreation incurs massive costs.

Getting the job done in the soft sector often involves reliance upon bureaucratic organisations with strong elements of professionalism. They cannot operate without a long-term perspective, including organisational survival and integrity. Parts and pieces of such organisations may use tendering/bidding to get things done, but they themselves cannot camp on the seesaws, if the environment is too turbulent.

In the soft sector, the providers are to a considerable extent made up of large-scale organisations like agencies, universities, schools, hospitals, courts and various care centres, which may well employ contractualism to some extent themselves but they cannot be completely left to the market.

A formal organisation that is not subject to the vagaries of the market such as the firm institution identifies what Max Weber had in mind when he made his recommendation of the bureau as the most effective institution for the exercise of political authority. The bureau to Weber is an organisation that operates according to a specific institutional logic that he took great care to spell out in terms of his ideal type of bureaucracy.

In order to develop its specific characteristics – hierarchy of competencies, division of labour, recruitment and promotion by means of professional criteria, remuneration by fixed salaries, tenure, disciplinary control under judicial procedures, devotion to the office – the bureau needs stability in relation to its environment, which can only be provided for through the use of taxation as the major source of funding. Bureaux may tend to be immortal, as they develop their expertise over time, standing firm against all the turbulence in the environment. Universities, hospitals, courts and agencies do not come and go like firms do as a result of creative destruction.

Weber was careful to point out that the bureaucratic mechanism needed masters to give it direction. The bureau is an institution which can be used for different purposes, handed over to it by the leaders of the organisations. Weber identified two types of masters, the politicians, which constitute elected officials in a democracy, and the collegial group of experts, the professionals (Mintzberg, 1983).

Thus, we have two kinds of bureaux: political bureaux like ministries or agencies on the one hand and collegial bureaux like universities and hospitals. They are not private sector firms. And their special nature requires another form of environment than the market situation. Having said this in favour of placing the political bureaux as well as the collegial bureaux in the public sector, we must point out that Weber played down the risk that bureaux develop pathologies.

Contracting with political bureaux: the executive agencies

Political bureaux or collegial bureaux need not obey the Weberian logic. It is true that bureaucracy tends to be more efficient than other historical forms of domination such as patrimonialism, feudalism and charismatism. Yet, the analysis of formal organisations during the twentieth century has revealed that bureaux could develop pathologically, despite the institutional web suggested by Weber and laid down in that part of public law that is administrative law.

The list of complaints against the bureaux is as a matter of fact long in organisational theory: goals displacement, means–end confusion, red tape, Parkinson's disease, garbage can process, budget or size maximisation, and rigidity. How, then, can one employ the bureau in public management and at the same time insulate it from the tendencies towards degeneration? The answer is that these can be achieved through contractualism.

Weber concluded his painstaking exposé of various forms of rulership claiming that public administration, or bureaucracy, is the most rational or efficient type of authority. Authority is very much a unilateral concept, meaning that one party orders and the other party obeys. It is a most Hobbesian concept, the will of the government being the law of the country, as Austin would have argued.

I take it that classical public administration was almost all about public authority, or the legitimate use of public power for the efficient achievement of state tasks. By using authority, government could achieve things that were in the public interest, such as public goods and infrastructure. Since public power could be misused, it had to be institutionalised in a transparent manner, involving a paraphernalia of legal devices stated in public law or administrative law.

However, the theoretical innovation made by NPM is that contracts may achieve more than authority. One may use contracts in government bureaux without moving to the full-scale model of tendering/bidding inherent in NPM. Contracting with CEOs is relevant not only for governmental agencies under the authority of ministries but also for independent regulatory bodies.

Again, there must be tendering/bidding or tournaments for the choice of the heads of the executive agencies, the CEOs. If not, there is the lemons' problem. Tournaments and short-term contracts with the CEOs for executive agencies increase the capacity of the principal, government, to run its ministries and agencies.

Contracting with professional bureaux: the use of trust

When the providers of public services are made up of schools, universities and hospitals, then the employment of the full-scale public contracting model seems an error. The government as the purchaser of the services of these organisations would be interested in contracting but the relevance of tendering/bidding is not always crystal clear.

Although competition may certainly occur in the soft sector in many ways, it is still the case that professional organisations operate in a manner and according to a logic that is different from the market, meaning that full-scale exchange must be tempered by the development of long-term relationships between the purchaser and the provider. The civil law contract is not the best instrument to define and stabilise trust, especially if used according to the tendering/bidding scheme (Coulson 1998).

Preferably, the choice of CEOs for professional bureaux can be made among professionals. However, there must be a tournament in order to reveal competence and make a connection between work load and claim to remuneration.

A model which could harbour trust is the policy network. It is often employed in the soft sector. Its main difficulty is how one may guarantee efficiency without excessive monitoring costs.

Contracting in public regulation: trust versus capture

In public regulation, government employs a regulator to achieve certain objectives in the economy, acting in the role of umpire, not as purchaser or provider of services or owner of capital. It has been argued that the European economy in Euroland requires strong and independent regulators. This is not the place to discuss alternative theories of public regulation, or the pros and cons of alternative regulatory schemes.

I only wish to emphasise that the CEOs appear with full force also in public regulation and the same problem of designing a contract between government and the CEOs resurfaces again. Whether one adheres to the theory about regulatory capture or to the theory about trust and reputation, one still must find a contract between government and the regulator which stipulates what the latter is to do against a certain remuneration by the former.

Using contract law instead of public law in regulation may enhance the achievement of government objectives, making it more probable that the regulator can be held responsible for his/her achievements. This may involve putting some administrative law into the performance contract linking government with a particular CEO, which may also occur in the other relationships between government and the CEOs, such as in allocation in either the soft sector or the business sector. Finally, there should be full-scale tournaments among the CEOs of regulatory boards.

NPM as practical theory

Perhaps it cannot be emphasised enough that NPM is a tool for governments to employ in the governance of the public sector. What it is not is a theory about how governance is done in various countries. NPM does not describe the various country models of public sector governance that have emerged in the 1990s: the New Zealand model, the Australian model, the CCT scheme under Thatcher or the Best Value scheme with Blair in the UK, the Reinventing Government scheme in the US, or the Swedish purchaser–provider model in its local and regional government. NPM is a normative theory about how government may use a new tool for getting things done, namely contracting.

Governments may wish to use NPM or it may decide to stay with public administration or employ the policy network. Governments may use NPM in certain sectors of the economy or it may decide to employ some features of NPM, not engaging in full-scale use of NPM. To analyse all the various versions of NPM as well as state all actual outcomes of the NPM reforms is a task that goes far beyond this book. Here, we shall attempt to pin down the basic concerns of NPM, as a pure model so to speak.

Sometimes NPM is equated with the Reinventing Government scheme in the US. However, this is hardly the case. Many of the reforms of the Reinventing Government programme more closely resemble various efforts at reforming traditional public governance from inside than the efforts of NPM to suggest a new mechanism for public sector governance. Reinventing Government deals more with cut-back policies as well with benchmaking and management by objectives than with contracting (Verheijen and Coombes, 1998).

Sometimes it is argued that NPM is merely a new name for contracting out. This is wrong, because the gist of NPM is not outsourcing or outhouse production, but contracting in itself. Provision can still be inhouse, but there will be contracts with the internal providers that govern the resource allocation.

Sometimes it is claimed that NPM is a theory about public sector reform in the countries with an advanced economy and a democratic polity. Such a theory would account for the variety of reform initiatives and the policy consequences. Yet. NPM is not a descriptive theory. It is a normative theory suggesting a mechanism for enhancing efficiency in the public provision of goods and services. This does not mean that it is not important or relevant to study how different countries have chosen various reform strategies as well as to enquire into the different country experiences with such policies.

Sometimes NPM is equated with the New Zealand model. This is not correct, because the New Zealand public sector reforms were driven by a special combination of supply side economics, public choice theory as well as law and economics approach with the definitive effort to roll back the state (Kelsey, 1995; Evans, 1996). NPM may be used also by welfare states with the aim of revitalising a large public sector. NPM is not the same as privatisation.

Finally, it may be added that just as it is important to pin down what the pure theory of NPM would amount to so it is vital to examine what the outcomes of the introduction of NPM are in different country settings. However, the outcomes cannot automatically be attributed to the pure model of NPM, as NPM may be put into practice by different policies in various settings. The variety of policy-making inspired by NPM as well as the variety of outcomes connected with NPM deserve their own study, from which it may appear how the pure model of NPM may be translated differently into policies as well as how the outcomes of NPM are affected by the country setting.

Conclusion

The theory of public sector management must integrate the positive ideas of new public management. Public contracting offers an alternative mechanism to state authority in order to get things done. Public contracting helps to reveal what services are worth, not only what they cost, when they are provided publicly, i.e. with the involvement somehow of government.

A public contracting regime must be based upon the use of chief executive officers, which makes public contracting a complicated process. How can the best CEOs be found and motivated? On the one hand, there is interaction among CEOs when they sit at both ends of the bargaining table as purchasers and providers. On the other hand, there is the interaction between government and its CEOs. How to make sure that in both kinds of interaction efficient contracts are arrived at?

The public contracting model seems highly applicable in the business sector and in the interaction between government and its political bureaux as well as between government and regulators. It seems less relevant for professional bureaux in the soft sector. Public contracting will depend upon the quality of the contracts that are forthcoming between CEOs as well upon the capacity of government to chose 'good' CEOs. What is essential is not only competition between providers of public services but also the running of tournaments among the CEOs.

References

Ackerloff, G.A. (1988) 'The Market for "Lemons": Quality Uncertainty and the Market Mechanism', in Barney, J.B. and Ouchi, W.G. (eds) *Organizational Economics*. San Francisco: Jossey-Bass, pp. 27–39.

Alchian, A. (1977) *Economic Forces at Work*. Washington: Liberty Fund.

Alford, J. and O'Neill, D. (1994) (eds) *The Contract State*. Deakin: Deakin University Press.

Appelby, P.H. (1949) *Policy and Administration*. Alabama: University of Alabama Press.

Atiyah, P.S. (1996) *An Introduction to the Law of Contract*. Oxford: Clarendon Press.

Axelrod, R. (1984) *The Evolution of Cooperation*. New York: Basic Books.

—— (1997) *The Complexity of Cooperation*. Princeton: Princeton University Press.

Barnard, C. (1968) *The Functions of the Executive*. Harvard: Harvard University Press.

Barro, R.J. (1990) *Macroeconomic Policy*. Cambridge, MA: Harvard University Press.

Barry, B. (1989) *Theories of Justice*. London: Harvester Wheatsheaf.

—— (1995) *Justice as Impartiality*. Oxford: Oxford University Press.

Barzelay, M. (2000) *The New Public Management: Improving Research and Policy Dialogue*. Berkeley, CA: University of California Press.

Baumol, W.J. (1965) *Welfare Economics and the Theory of the State*. London: Bell & Sons.

Blümle, E.B. and Schwarz, P. (1980) 'Öffentliche Betriebe in der Schweiz', in *Zeitschrift für öffentliche und gemeinwirtschaftliche Unternehmen*, vol. 3: 309–331.

Borcherding, T.E. (1977) *Budgets and Bureaucrats: The Sources of Governmental Growth*. Durham, NC: Duke University Press.

—— (1984). 'A Survey of Empirical Studies about Causes of the Growth of Government' (mimeo). Paper presented at the Nobel Symposium on the Growth of Government, Stockholm.

Borcherding, T.E., Pommerehene, W.W. and Schneider, F. (1982) 'Comparing the Efficiency of Private and Public Production: The Evidence from Five Countries', in Bîs, D., Musgrave, R.A. and Wiseman, J. (eds) *Public Production*. New York: Springer-Verlag.

Boston, J. (1995) (ed.) *The State Under Contract*. Wellington: Bridget Williams Books.

Boyne, G.A. (1998) *Public Choice Theory and Local Government*. London: Macmillan.

Brus, W. and Laski, K. (1990) *From Marx to the Market: Socialism in Search of An Economic System*. Oxford: Clarendon Press.

Buclaus, D. (1998) *New Public Management*. Berlin: De Gruyter.

Campbell, C. and Wilson, G.K. (1995) *The End of Whitehall*. Oxford: Blackwell.

Campbell, D.E. (1995) *Incentives. Motivation and the Economics of Information*. Cambridge: Cambridge University Press.

Cane, P. (1987) *An Introduction to Administrative Law*. Oxford: Clarendon.

Castles, F.G. (1998) *Comparative Public Policy: Patterns of Post-War Transformation*. Cheltenham: Edward Elgar.

Choi, Y-C. (1999) *The Dynamics of Public Service Contracting*. Bristol: The Policy Press.

Clarke, T. (1995) *The Political Economy of Privatization*. London: Routledge.

Coase, R.H. (1988) *The Firm, the Market and the Law*. Chicago, IL: University of Chicago Press.

Considine, M. and Painter, M. (1997) (eds) *Managerialism – The Great Debate*. Melbourne: Melbourne University Press.

Cooter, R.D. (1991) 'Coase Theorem', in Eatwell, J., Milgate, M. and Newman, P. *The World Of Economics*. London: Macmillan Press, pp. 51–57.

Coulson, A. (1998) (ed.) *Trust and Contracts: Relationships in Local Government, Health and Public Services*. Bristol: The Policy Press.

Craig, Paul and De Burca, G. (1997). *EC Law, Text, Cases and Materials*. Oxford: Clarendon Press.

Crozier, M. (1964) *The Bureaucratic Phenomenon*. Chicago, IL: University of Chicago Press.

Dahl, R.A. (1947) 'The Science of Public Administration: Three Problems', *Public Administration Review*, vol. 7: 1–11.

Deininger, K. and Squire, L. (1997) *The Deininger-Squire Date Set*. <http://www.worldbank/org/html/prdmg/grthweb/dddeisqu.htm>

Demsetz, H. (1991) *Efficiency, Competition and Policy*. Oxford: Blackwell.

Demsetz, H. and Jacquemin, A. (1994) *Anti-trust Economics – New Challenges for Competition Policy*. Lund: Lund University Press.

Domberger, S. (1998) *The Contracting Organization*. Oxford: Oxford University Press.

Dunleavy, P. (1991) *Politicians, Bureaucrats and Democracy*. Hemel Hempstead: Harvester Wheatsheaf.

Eatwell, J., Milgate, M. and Newman, P. (1989) (eds) *Allocation, Information and Markets*. London: Macmillan.

Eggertson, T. (1990) *Economic Behaviour and Institutions*. Cambridge: Cambridge University Press.

Esping-Andersen, G. (1990) *The Three Worlds of Welfare Capitalism*. Cambridge: Polity Press.

—— (1999) *Social Foundations of Post-Industrial Economies*. Oxford: Oxford University Press.

Etzioni, A. (1964) *Modern Organization*. Englewood Cliffs, NJ: Prentice-Hall.

—— (1988) *The Moral Dimension. Toward a New Economics*. New York: Macmillan, Inc.

Evans, L. (1996) 'Economic Reform in New Zealand 1984–95: The Pursuit of Efficiency', *Journal of Economic Literature*, vol. 34: 1,856–1,902.

Evans, P.M. (1995) (ed.) *Workfare: Does It Work? Is it Fair?* Montreal: Institute for Research on Public Policy.

Feld, L. and Kirchgässner, G. (1999) 'Direct Democracy, Political Culture, and the Outcome of Economic Policy: Some Swiss Experience' (unpublished paper, University of St Gallen).

Fenno, R.F. (1966) *The Power of the Purse*. Boston, MA: Little, Brown & Co.

Ferlie, E., Pettigrew, A., Ashburner, L. and Fitzgerald, L. (1996) *The New Public Management*. Oxford: Oxford University Press.

Flynn, N. (1997) *Public Sector Management*. Hemel Hempstead: Prentice-Hall.

Frantz, R.S. (1997) *X-efficiency: Theory, Evidence and Applications*. Dordrecht: Kluwer.

Fredrikson, G. (1996) 'Comparing the Reinventing Government Movement with the New Public Administration', *Public Administration Review*, vol. 56(3): 266.

Frey, B. and Bohnet, I. (1993) 'Democracy by Competition: Referenda and Federalism in Switzerland', *Publius, The Journal of Federalism*, vol. 23: 71–81.

Friedman, M. (1953) *Essays in Positive Economics*. Chicago: Chicago University Press.

—— (1964) *Capitalism and Freedom*. Chicago: University of Chicago Press.

Fry, B.R. (1989) *Mastering Public Administration: From Max Weber to Dwight Waldo*. Chatham, NJ: Chatham House Publishers.

Goyder, D.G. (1992) *EC Competition Law* (2nd edition). Oxford: Clarendon Press.

Graham, C. (1998) *Private Markets for Public Goods*. Washington: Brookings.

Gutmann, A. (1998) (ed.) *Work and Welfare*. Princeton: Princeton University Press.

Halligan, J. and Power, J. (1992) *Political Management in the 1990s*. Melbourne: Oxford University Press.

Harden, I. (1992) *The Contracting State*. Milton Keynes: Open University Press.

Hargreaves Heap, S., Hollis, M., Lyons, B., Sugden, R. and Weale, A. (1992) *The Theory of Choice*. Oxford: Blackwell.

Hayek, F. (1935) (ed.) *Collectivist Economic Planning*. London: Routledge and Kegan Paul.

Hill, L.B. (1992) *The State of Bureaucracy*. Armonk: Sharpe.

Hillier, B. (1997) *The Economics of Asymmetric Information*. London: Macmillan.

Hodge, G.A. (2000) *Privatization*. Boulder, CO: Westview Press.

Hogwood, B.W. and Gunn, L.A. (1992) *Policy Analysis for the Real World*. Oxford: Oxford University Press.

Holsey, C.M. and Borcherding, T.E. (1997) 'Why does government's share of national income grow?', in Mueller, D. (ed.) *Perspectives on Public Choice*. Cambridge: Cambridge University Press.

Hood, C. (1990) 'Public Administration: Lost an Empire, Not Yet Found a Role', in Leftwich, A. (ed.) *New Developments in Political Science*. Aldershot: Gower.

—— (1991) 'A Public Management for All Seasons', *Public Administration*, vol. 69: 3–19.

—— (1995) 'Contemporary Public Management: A New Global Paradigm', *Public Policy and Administration*, vol. 10: 104–117.

—— (1998) 'Individualized Contracts for Top Public Servants', *Governance*, vol. 11: 443–462.

ILO (1992) *The Cost of Social Security: Thirteenth International Inquiry, 1984–1986*. Geneva: ILO.

—— (1997) *World Labour Report, 1997–98: Industrial Relations, Democracy and Social Stability*. Geneva: ILO.

—— (1998) *The Cost of Social Security – Basic Tables 1990–1993*. <http://www.ilo.org/public/english/110secsco/css/cssindex.htm>

IMF (1984) *Government Finance Statistics Yearbook 1984*. Washington, DC: IMF.

—— (1994) *Government Finance Statistics Yearbook 1994*. Washington, DC: IMF.

Ingram, H.M. and Mann, E.E. (1980) (eds) *Why Policies Succeed or Fail*. Beverly Hills, CA: Sage.

Johnson, C. (1984) (ed.) *The Industrial Policy Debate*. San Francisco: Jossey-Bass.

Jakobsson, U. and Normann, G. (1974) *Inkomstbeskattningen i den ekonomiska politiken*. Stockholm: Almquist & Wicksell.

Jones, L.R. and Schedler, K. (1998) (eds) *Advances in International Comparative Management. Supplement 3: International Perspectives on the New Public Management*. Stamford, CT: JAI Press.

Jonsson, E. (1996) *Har betalning per patient givit mer vård för pengarna?* Stockholm: Spris förlag.

Jordan, G. (1990) 'Sub-governments, Policy Communities and Networks: Refilling Old Bottles', *Journal of Theoretical Politics*, vol. 2: 319–338.

Joyce, P. (1999) *Strategic Management for The Public Services*. Buckingham: Open University Press.

Kaufman, H. (1976) *Are Government Organizations Immortal?* Washington: Brookings.

—— (1977) *Red Tape: Its Origins, Uses and Abuses*. Washington: Brookings.

—— (1981) *The Administrative Behavior of Federal Bureau Chiefs*. Washington: Brookings.

Kelsen, H. (1961) *General Theory of Law and State*. New York: Russell and Russell.

—— (1967) *Reine Rechtslehre*. Wien: Franz Deuticke.

Kelsey, J. (1995) *Economic Fundamentalism*. London: Pluto Press.

Kettl, D.F. (1994) 'Reinventing Government? Appraising the National Performance Review', A Report of the Brookings Institution's Center for Public Management.

—— (1997) 'The Global Revolution in Public Management: Driving Themes, Missing Links', *Journal of Policy Analysis and Management*, vol. 16(3): 447–462.

Kickert, W.J.M., Klijn, E.H. and Koppenjan, J.F.M. (1997) (eds) *Managing Complex Networks: Strategics for the Public Sector*. London: Sage.

Kirchgässner, G. and Pommerehne, W.W. (1997) 'Public Spending in Federal States', in Capros, P. and Meuldus, D. (eds) *Budgetary Policy Modelling*. London: Routledge.

Klijn, E.-H. (1996) 'Analyzing and Managing Policy Processes in complex Networks: A Thoeretical Examination of the Concept Policy Network and its Problems', *Administration and Society*, vol. 28: 90–119.

Laffont, J.-J. and Tirole, J. (1993) *A Theory of Incentives in Public Procurement and Regulation*. Cambridge, MA: MIT Press.

Lane, J-E and Ersson, S. (1997) *Comparative Political Economy* (2nd edn). London: Pinter.

Lane, J-E and Maeland, R. (1998) 'Welfare States or Welfare Societies?', *Statsvetenskaplig Tidskrift*, vol. 101: 145–165.

Lane, J.-E., McKay, D. and Newton, K. (1996) *Political Data Handbook* (2nd edition). Oxford: Oxford University Press.

Ledyard, J.O. (1989) 'Incentive Compatibility', in Eatwell, J., Milgate, M. and Newman, P. (eds) *Allocation, Information and Markets*. London: Macmillan, pp. 141–151.

Leibenstein, H. (1966) 'Allocative Efficiency versus "X-Efficiency"', *American Economic Review*, 56: 392–415.

—— (1978) *General X-Efficiency Theory and Economic Development*. New York: Oxford University Press.

Lijphart, Arend (1999) *Patterns of Democracy. Government Forms and Performance in Thirty-Six Countries*. New Haven: Yale University Press.

Lindblom, C.E. (1959) 'The Science of "Muddling-Through"', *Public Administration Review*, vol. 19: 79–88.

—— (1965) *The Intelligence of Democracy*. New York: Free Press.

Lipsey, R.C. and Lancaster, K. (1956) 'The General Theory of Second Best', *Review of Economic Studies*, vol. 24: 11–32.

LIS (1999) *Luxembourg Income Study: LIS Inequality Indices* <http://lissy.ceps.lu/ineq.htm>

Loughlin, M. (1992) *Public Law and Political Theory*. Oxford: Clarendon.

Lowi, T.J. (1964) 'American Business, Public Policy, Case-Studies and Political Theory', *World Politics*, vol. 16: 677–715.

—— (1979) *The End of Liberalism*. New York: W.W. Norton.

—— (1985) 'The State in Politics', in Noll, R. (ed.) *Regulatory Policy and the Social Sciences*. Berkeley: University of California Press.

Lucas, R.E. (1987) *Models of Business Cycles*. Oxford: Blackwell.

Lybeck, J.A. and Henreksson, M. (1988) (eds) *Explaining the Growth of Government*. Amsterdam: North-Holland.

Macho-Stadler, I. and Perez-Castillo, D. (1997) *An Introduction to the Economics of Information*. Oxford: Oxford University Press.

Majone, G. (1996) *Regulating Europe*. London: Routledge.

—— (1999) 'The Regulatory State and Its Legitimacy Problem', *West European Politics*, vol. 22: 1–24.

Manley, J.F. (1975) *The Politics of Finance*. Boston, MA: Little, Brown & Co.

Maor, M. (1999) 'The Paradox of Managerialism', *Public Administration Review*, vol. 59(1): 5–18.

March, J.G. and Olsen, J.P. (1976) (eds) *Ambiguity and Choice in Organizations*. Oslo: Universitetsforlaget.

March, J.G. and Simon, H.A. (1958) *Organizations*. New York: John Wiley.

Marini, F. (1971) (ed.) *Toward a New Public Administration: The Minnowbrook Perspective*. Scrawton, PA: Chandler.

Marsh, D. and Rhodes, R.A.W. (1992) (eds) *Policy Networks in British Government*. Oxford: Clarendon Press.

May, J.V. and Wildavsky, A. (1978) (eds) *The Policy Cycle*. Beverly Hills, CA: Sage.

McLoughlin, P. and Rendell, C. (1992) *Law of Trusts*. London: Macmillan.

Mèny, Y., Muller, P. and Quermonne, J.L. (eds) (1996) *Adjusting to Europe: The Impact of the European Union on National Institutions and Policies*. London: Routledge.

Merton, R.K. (1957) *Social Theory and Social Structure*. New York: Free Press.

Meyerson, R.B. (1989) 'Mechanism Design', in Eatwell, J., Milgate, M. and Newman, P. (eds) *Allocation, Information and Markets*. London: Macmillan, pp. 191–206.

Milgrom, P. and Roberts, J. (1992) *Economics, Organization and Management*. Englewood Cliffs: Prentice-Hall.

Miller, D. (1976) *Social Justice*. Oxford: Clarendon Press.

—— (1997) *On Nationality*. Oxford: Oxford University Press.

Miller, D. and Moe, T.M. (1983) 'Bureaucrats, Legislators and the Size of Government', *American Political Review*, vol. 77: 297–322.

Minogue, M., Polidano, C. and Hulme, D. (1999) (eds) *Beyond the New Public Management: Changing Ideas and Practices in Governance*. Cheltenham: Edward Elgar Publications.

Mintzberg, H. (1983) *Structures in Five*. Englewood Cliffs, NJ: Prentice-Hall.

Mishan, E. (1981) *Introduction to Normative Economics*. Oxford: Oxford University Press.

Molho, I. (1997) *The Economics of Information*. Oxford: Blackwell.

Montin, S. (1998), 'Nytt offentligt lederskap och politikerrollen', in Klausen, K.-K. and Ståhlberg, K. (eds) *New Public Management i Norden. Nye organisations- og ledelseformer i den decentrala velfaerdsstat*. Odense: Odense Universitetsforlag, pp. 91–110.

Montin, S. and Persson, G. (1996), 'Local Institutional Change in Sweden – A Case Study', in Bogason, P. (ed.) *New Modes of Local Political Organizing*. Local Government Fragmentation in Scandinavia. New Jersey: NOVA Science Publishers.

Mueller, D. (1989) *Public Choice II*. Cambridge: Cambridge University Press.

Musgrave, R.A. (1959) *The Theory of Public Finance*. New York: McGraw-Hill.

Musgrave, R.A. and Jarrett, P. (1979) 'International Redistribution', *Kyklos*, vol. 32: 541–558.

Musgrave, R.A. and Musgrave, P.B. (1980) *Public Finance in Theory and Practice*. New York: McGraw-Hill.

—— (1989) *Public Finance in Theory and Practice*. New York: McGraw-Hill.

Nagel, T. (1991) *Equality and Partiality*. Oxford: Oxford University Press.

Naschold, F. *et al.* (1996) *New Frontiers in Public Sector Management*, trans. A. Watt. Berlin: De Gruyter.

Nathan, R.P. (1993) *Turning Promises into Performance: The Management Challenge of Implementing Workfare*. New York: Columbia University Press.

Niskanen, W.A. (1971) *Bureaucracy and Representative Government*. Chicago, IL: Aldine-Atherton.

—— (1976) 'The Peculiar Economics of Bureaucracy', in Amacher, R.C., Tollison, R.D. and Willett, T.D. (eds) *The Economic Approach to Public Policy*. Ithaca, NY: Cornell University Press.

Obinger, H. (1998) *Politische Institutionen und Sozialpolitik in der Schweiz*. Frankfurt am Main: Peter Lang.

OECD (1998) *The Structure of National Accounts, Main Economic Indicators*. Paris.

—— (1999) *Public Sector Statistics: A Statistical Window on the OECD Member Countries' Government Sectors*. <http://www.oecd.org/puma/stats/window/index.htm>

Okun, A.M. (1975) *Equality and Efficiency*. Washington, DC: Brookings.

Olson, M. (1982) *The Rise and Decline of Nations*. New Haven: Yale University Press.

Osborne, D. and Gaebler, T. (1993) *Reinventing Government*. New York: Plume Book.

Osborne, S. and Waterson, P. (1994) 'Defining Contracts Between the State and Charitable Organisations in National Accounts'. *Voluntas*, vol 5: 291–300.

Ostrom, E. (1990) *Governing the Commons*. Cambridge, MA: Cambridge University Press.

Ostrom, V. (1989) *The Intellectual Crisis in American Public Administration*. Tuscaloosa: University of Alabama Press.

Peltzman, Sam (1988) 'Toward a More General Theory of Regulation', in Stigler, George J. (ed.) *Chicago Studies in Political Economy*. Chicago: The University of Chicago Press.

Peters, G. (1997) 'Shouln't Row, Can't Steer': What's a Government to Do?' *Public Policy and Administration*, vol. 12: 51–61.

Pollitt, C. (1993) *Managerialism and Public Services: Cult or Cultural Change in the 1990s?* Oxford: Blackwell.

Pommerehne, W.W. and Schneider, F. (1978) 'Fiscal Illusion, Political Institutions and Local Public Spending', in *Kyklos*, vol. 31: 381–408.

Posner, R.A. (1992) *Economic Analysis of Law*. Boston: Little, Brown & Co.

Pressman, J. and Wildavsky, A. (1973, 1984) *Implementation*. Berkeley: University of California Press.

Raadschelders, C.N. (1998) *Handbook of Administrative History*. New Brunswick: Transaction Publishers.

Rao, C.P. (1998) *Globalization, Privatization and Free Market Economy*. Westport: Quorum Books.

Rasmusen, E. (1994) *Games and Information*. Oxford: Blackwell.

Rhodes, R.A.W. (1990) 'Policy Networks', *Journal of Theoretical Politics*, vol. 3: 291–318.

—— (1994) 'The Hollowing Out of the State', *Political Quarterly*, vol. 65: 138–151.

—— (1998) *Beyond Westminster and Whitehall: The Sub-Central Governments of Britain*. London: Unwin Hyman.

Rhodes, R.A.W. and Dunleavy, P. (1995) (eds) *Prime Minister, Cabinet and Core Executive*. London: Macmillan.

Ricketts, M. (1987) *The Economics of Business Enterprise*. Hemel Hempstead: Harvester Wheatsheaf.

Riker, W. and Ordeshook, P. (1973) *An Introduction to Formal Political Theory*. Englewood Cliffs, NJ: Prentice-Hall.

Rose, N.E. (1995) *Workfare or Fair Work: Women, Welfare and Government Work Programs*. Rutgers: Rutgers University Press.

Rosen, H.S. (1988) *Public Finance*. Homewood, IL: Irwin.

Rouban, L. (1999) (ed) *Citizens and the New Governance – Beyond New Public Management*. Amsterdam: IOS Press.

Sabatier, P. (1986) 'Top-Down and Bottom-Up Approaches to Implementation Research', *Journal of Public Policy*, vol. 6: 21–48.

Sabatier P. and Jenkins-Smith, H. (1993) (eds) *Policy Change and Learning: An Advocacy Coalition Approach*. Boulder, CO: Westview Press.

Scanlon, T.M. (1982) 'Contractualism and Utilitarianism', in Sen, A. and Williams, B. (eds) *Utilitarianism and Beyond*. Cambridge: Cambridge University Press, pp. 103–128.

Scharpf, F. (1997) *Games Real People Play*. Boulder, CO: Westview Press.

Schmidt, M.G. (1997) 'Determinants of Social Expenditure in Liberal Democracies: The Post World War II Experience', *Acta Politica*, vol. 32: 153–173.

Scott, W.R. (1984) *Organizations: Rational, Natural, and Open Systems*. Englewood Cliffs, NJ: Prentice-Hall.

—— (1995) *Institutions and Organizations*. Beverly Hills: Sage.

Self, P. (1985) *Political Theories of Modern Government, its Role and Reform*. London: Allen & Unwin.

Selznick, P. (1957) *Leadership in Administration*. Evanston, IL: Row & Peters.

Sharkansky, I. (1978) *Public Administration*. Chicago, IL: Rand McNally.

Shavall, S. (1998) 'Contracts', in P. Newman (ed.) *The New Palgrave Dictionary of Economics and the Law*. London: Macmillan.

Sherman, R. (1989) *The Regulation of Monopoly*. Cambridge: Cambridge University Press.

Shragge, E. (ed.) *Workfare. Ideology for a New Under-Class*. Toronto: Garamond Press.

Simon, H.A. (1957) *Models of Man*. New York: John Wiley & Sons, Inc.

—— (1965) *Administrative Behavior*. New York: Free Press.

Simon, H.A., Smithburg, D.W. and Thompson, V.A. (1950) *Public Administration*. New York: Alfred A. Knopf.

Smith, M.J. (1999) *The Core Executive in Britain*. London: Macmillan.

Smith, V.L. (1989) 'Auctions', in Eatwell, J., Milgate, M. and Newman, P. (eds) *Allocation, Information and Markets*. London: Macmillan, pp. 39–53.

Solow, R. (1988) *Growth Theory*. Oxford: Oxford University Press.

—— (1998) 'Work and Welfare Lectures I and II', in Gutmann, A. (ed.) *Work and Welfare*. Princeton: Princeton University Press.

Spulber, D.F. (1989) *Regulation and Markets*. Cambridge: MIT Press.

Spulber, N. (1997) *Redefining the State. Privatization and Welfare Reform in Industrial and Transitional Economies*. Cambridge: Cambridge University Press.

Statistisches Jahrbuch der Schweiz, 1960–1998. Zurich: Verlag Neue Zürcher Zeitung.

Stevens, J.B. (1993) *The Economics of Collective Choice*. Boulder, CO: Westview Press.

Stigler, G.J. (1970) 'Director's Law of Public Income Redistribution', *Journal of Law and Economics*, vol. 13: 1–10.

—— (1975) *The Citizen and the State*. Chicago: Chicago University Press.

—— (1976) 'The X-istence of X-efficiency', *American Economic Review*, vol. 66: 213–216.

—— (1988) (ed.) *Chicago Studies in Political Economy*. Chicago: University of Chicago Press.

Stiglitz, J. (1989) 'Principal and Agent', in Eatwell, J., Milgate, M. and Newman, P. (eds) *Allocation, Information and Markets*. London: Macmillan, pp. 241–253.

Streeck, W. and Schmitter P.C. (1996) 'Organized Interests in The European Union', in Kourvetaris G.A. and Moschonas, A. (eds) *The Impact of European Integration*. Westport, CT: Praeger Publishers.

Tarschys, D. (1975) 'The Growth of Public Expenditure: Nine Modes of Explanation', *Scandinavian Political Studies*, vol. 10: 9–31.

Thatcher, M. (1998) 'Institutions, Regulation, and Change: Regulatory Agencies in British Privatised Utilities', *West European Politics*, vol. 21: 120–147.

Thompson, J.D. (1967) *Organizations in Action*. New York: McGraw-Hill.

Thynne, I. (1994) 'The Incorporated Company as an Instrument of Government: A Quest for a Comparative Understanding', *Governance*, vol. 7: 59–80.

Tirole, J. (1993) *The Theory of Industrial Organization*. Cambridge, MA: The MIT Press.

Tollison, R.D. (1982) 'Rent-Seeking: A Survey', *Kyklos*, vol. 35: 575–592.

Tolstoy, L. (1994) *War and Peace*. Harmondsworth: Penguin.

UNDP (1998) *Human Development Report 1998*. New York: Oxford University Press.

Varian, H.R. (1987) *Microeconomic Analysis*. New York: Norton.

Verheijen, T. and Coombes, D.L. (1998) (eds) *Innovations in Public Management: Perspectives from East and West Europe*. Cheltenham: Edward Elgar Publications.

Vickers, J. and Wright, V. (1988) (eds) 'The Politics of Privatization in Western Europe', *West European Politics*, vol. 11.

Vickers, J. and Yarrow, G. (1989) *Privatization: An Economic Analysis*. Cambridge, MA: MIT Press.

Viscusi, W.K., Vernon, J.M. and Harrington, J.E. (1992) *Economics of Regulation and Antitrust*. Lexington: D.C. Heath and Company.

Wagner, A. (1877–1901) *Finanzwissenschaft*. 4 volumes. Leipzig and Heidelberg: Winter.

Waldo, D. (1984) *The Administrative State*. New York: Holmes and Meier.

Walsh, K. (1995) *Public Services and Market Mechanisms*. London: Macmillan.

Walzer, M. (1983) *Spheres of Justice*. New York: Basic Books.

Weber, M. (1978) *Economy and Society*, Vols I–II. Berkeley: University of California Press (original German edition 1922).

Wicksell, K. (1967) 'A New Principle of Just Taxation', in Musgrave, R.A. and Peacock, A.T. (eds) *Classics in the Theory of Public Finance*. New York: St Martin's Press.

Wildavsky, A. (1972) *The Revolt Against the Masses and Other Essays on Politics and Public Policy*. New York: Basic Books.

—— (1979) *Speaking Truth to Power: The Art and Craft of Policy Analysis*. Boston, MA: Little, Brown & Co.

—— (1984) *The Politics of the Budgetary Process*. Boston, MA: Little, Brown & Co. (original edition 1964).

—— (1986) *Budgeting: A Comparative Theory of the Budgetary Process*. Boston, MA: Little, Brown & Co. (original edition 1975).

—— (1988a) *The New Politics of the Budgetary Process*. Boston: Little, Brown & Co.

—— (1988b) *Searching For Safety*. Brunswick: Transaction.

Wilensky, H. (1975) *The Welfare State and Equality*. Berkeley: University of California Press.

—— (1976) *The 'New Corporation', Centralization and the Welfare State*. London: Sage.

Williamson, O. (1975) *Markets and Hierarchies*. New York: Free Press.

—— (1985) *The Economic Institutions of Capitalism*. New York: Free Press.

—— (1986) *Economic Organization*. Hemel Hempstead: Harvester Wheatsheaf.

Wilson, J.Q. (1989) *Bureaucracy*. New York: Basic Books.

World Bank (1983) *World Tables* (3rd edn). Baltimore: Johns Hopkins University Press.

—— (1997) *World Development Indicators*. Washington, DC: World Bank.

—— (1998a) *World Development Indicators*. Washington, DC: World Bank.

—— (1998b) *World Bank Atlas*. Washington, DC: World Bank.

Wright, V. (1994) (ed.) *Privatization in Western Europe*. London: Pinter.

Index